# FAILING OUR KIDS

*Television and Society: An Investigative Approach*
(with E. Krieger, 1985)

# FAILING OUR KIDS

## How We Are Ruining Our Public Schools

# CHARLES UNGERLEIDER

M&S

**National Library of Canada Cataloguing in Publication**

Ungerleider, Charles S.
Failing our kids: how we are ruining our public schools /
Charles Ungerleider.

Includes index.
ISBN 0-7710-8681-4 (bound).—ISBN 0-7710-8682-2 (pbk.)

1. Public schools – Canada. 2. Education – Aims and objectives – Canada.
I. Title.

LA412.U53 2003     370'.971     C2002-906021-4

We acknowledge the financial support of the Government of Canada
through the Book Publishing Industry Development Program and that of
the Government of Ontario through the Ontario Media Development
Corporation's Ontario Book Initiative. We further acknowledge the
support of the Canada Council for the Arts and the Ontario Arts Council
for our publishing program.

Typeset in Bembo by M&S, Toronto
Printed and bound in Canada

McClelland & Stewart Ltd.
*The Canadian Publishers*
481 University Avenue
Toronto, Ontario
M5G 2E9
www.mcclelland.com

1  2  3  4  5     08  07  06  05  04

*To my wife, Mary Ungerleider,*
*without whom there would be no book.*

# CONTENTS

# ACKNOWLEDGEMENTS

I HAVE BEEN FORTUNATE to have had opportunities that have enabled me to view public schools from a variety of perspectives. My primary and secondary education took place in public schools. I attended publicly supported colleges and universities. My brief attendance at a private university was made possible through public support.

Early in my career, I taught high school students whose life chances would have been markedly different if it were not for public schooling. Most of the students I have taught at the University of British Columbia (UBC) were also beneficiaries of public schooling and publicly supported post-secondary education. Like me, they might not have had the opportunities they did without a strong, healthy public school system.

For thirteen years of my tenure at UBC, I shared responsibility for a field-based teacher education program. In other words, the program of study for the student teachers was conducted in public schools rather than on the UBC campus and combined coursework and teaching experience throughout the school year. I was a daily participant in the lives of the schools in which we taught, observing the benefits and beneficiaries of public schooling.

Public institutions and issues have been the focus of my research and writing. Educational governance, student assessment, inter-group relations and multiculturalism, Canadian public issues, policing, and the impact of media on Canadian society are among the topics that have held my interest and attention for more than thirty years.

Like their mother and me, our children attended public schools. During that time, we were actively involved in parent committees in various capacities. I was a member of the Vancouver District Parents' Advisory Committee, working directly with other parents concerned about the public schools serving the wider community. Along the way, I was persuaded to seek office as a school trustee. After one unsuccessful attempt, I was elected to the Board of School Trustees for Vancouver.

For ten years, I combined administration and research at UBC. For the first five years, I was the person responsible for organizing and overseeing the field experiences – student teaching – of those preparing as elementary and secondary teachers. For the last five years, I was associate dean for teacher education for the faculty. During that time, I worked closely with teachers and administrators as well as the representatives of the various provincial organizations concerned about and involved in education.

In November 1998, I was appointed deputy minister of education by the cabinet of Premier Glen Clark. I would not have been able to undertake the responsibilities of the position without having been immersed in the issues affecting public schooling throughout my career. Impressions formed over thirty years in education crystallized during my term as deputy minister and have found expression in this book.

When my term ended in June 2001, I began to develop a working outline and to conduct interviews for this book. I travelled to eastern and central Canada to talk with people who were broadly knowledgeable about public education and public policy. Officials in the various provincial and Canadian organizations concerned with public schooling, as well as many colleagues, responded generously to my request for time to probe their thinking. The themes and issues across Canada are remarkably similar.

While there are differences, they are usually differences in degree not kind. As a consequence, to illustrate more general points I have selected examples from particular jurisdictions – often from British Columbia, the province with which I am most familiar.

McClelland & Stewart reacted quickly to the proposal for a book about public schooling that a friend had sent on my behalf. I appreciate the support and advice Doug Gibson and Jonathan Webb offered about the manuscript and my desire to see it reach a wide audience. I am indebted to my editor Alex Schultz and copy editor Heather Sangster for their sensitive consideration of the manuscript and thoughtful suggestions.

The Rockefeller Foundation extended an offer to be a resident scholar at its centre in Bellagio, Italy. Residency at Bellagio Centre facilitated my work by shielding me from the distractions that one normally encounters in one's community. Having a place to work, meals on a regular schedule, equipment and materials on hand, and others around me who were equally focused are just a few of the ways that residency assisted my work. I am grateful to the Rockefeller Foundation for its invitation.

I am also grateful to Kit Krieger for nearly thirty years of debate about education and public schooling. Our friendship is undiminished by his scorekeeping at bridge. Nancy Sheehan has provided valuable criticism and advice at crucial times in the development and execution of this project. Kit and Nancy are among a long list of people who contributed in important ways. That list also includes Barry Anderson, Joe Atkinson, Frank Barteaux, David Beers, Margaret Bell, Mike Benson, Tracey Burns, Julius Buski, Paul Cappon, Jim Carter, Ruby Chow, Debra Clarke, Dennis Cochrane, David and Diane Coulter, Susan Crompton, Raymond Daigle, Bonnie Davidson, Emery Dosdall, Jim Dysart, Jennifer Echols, Ivan Fellegi, Rob Gage, Victor Glickman, Dean Goodman, Britta Gundersen-Bryden, Judy Halbert, Don Haney, Wendy Harris, Shell Harvey, Suzanne Herbert, Alex Himmelfarb, Douglas Hodgkinson, Winston

Hunter, Vonnie Hutchingson, Shelly Hymel, Reva Joshee, Linda Kaser, Heather Kelleher, Chris Kelly, Deirdre Kelly, Jacquie Kendall, Veronica Lacey, Stewart Ladyman, Susan Langley, John and Katherine Lawrence, John Leonard, Ben Levin, David Levine, Gene Lewis, Ray Lortie, John Lundy, Dante Lupini, Jim MacKay, Joy MacPhail, Roxanne Madryga, Karen Mann, Lyndon Martin, Becky Matthews, Al Maxwell, Bruce McAskill, Shirley McBride, Erin McCall, Barry McFadden, Eulala Mills-Diment, Penny Milton, Heather Morin, Claire Morris, Norman Naimark, Betty Notar, Peter Owen, Paul Pallan, Lavinia Parrish-Zwicker, Charles Pascal, Tony Penikett, Marie Pierce, Greg Pollock, Penny Priddy, Paul Ramsey, Helen Raptis, David Robitaille, Claudia Roch, Anne Rodrique, Liz Sandals, Debbie Sanderson, Susan Scotti, Alan Sears, Bev Shaw, Jim Sherrill, Linda Siegel, Doug Smart, Peggy Speidel, Bill Standeven, Greg Stephens, Sue and Tom Stephens, Margaret Stewart, Teresa Sullivan, Shauna Sullivan-Curley, Leonard Taal, Hesh Troper, Tom Vincent, Jean-Pierre Voyer, Heather Walker, Nancy Walt, Harvey Weiner, Nancy Wells, Doug Willard, Lorna Williams, Doug Willms, Doug Wilson, Ian Wright, and Judith Wright.

I apologize for any omission from this lengthy roster of helpful colleagues. Please accept my gratitude for your time and effort. Despite your contribution, I alone take full responsibility for the ideas expressed in this book.

Charles Ungerleider
Vancouver, British Columbia

# INTRODUCTION

On the eve of school opening late last August, I was reading the *Globe and Mail* on-line. Journalist Margaret Wente had devoted an entire column to a parent who had decided to move her child from a Toronto public school to a private school. Wente quoted the parent as saying, "I truly believe in public education, but everyone's brought their politics into the school. They're turning my kid's education into a three-ring circus."

Wente catalogued a series of events that, cumulatively, forced the parent's decision. One was that her son would be in a class of thirty-six students. Another was that a group of parents had taken a kindergarten class to the office of their member of the provincial assembly to protest the recent funding cuts in Toronto. Third was that her son had allegedly spent three afternoons drawing a picture of an unmarried couple living together. The column also listed other events that contributed to the parent's decision to leave the public system, including a two-month social studies unit devoted to "children's rights" and conflict resolution training.

The opinion piece ridiculed Diverse Families Month, a month-long topical focus on tolerance that, Wente said, was an example of how fads and ideologies can take over public education and alienate even liberal-minded parents. According to Wente, Diverse Families Month had followed Black History Month and Global Harvest Festivals Month.

Wente recounted alleged features of Diverse Families Month. Students in grade four were learning about artificial insemination and sperm donors. The grade five class was studying transgendered people. Students in the second grade were learning about same-sex relationships. According to the column, the disaffected parent said, "They're giving my kid a college-level course in family sociology, but they can't teach him to spell 'family.'"

The parent had asked the school principal why parents hadn't been consulted and voiced the opinion that teaching such material was a waste of time. "They thought I was homophobic," Wente quoted the parent as saying. Wente said the principal admitted that the grade two teacher was teaching inappropriate material about diversity, but said she could do nothing about it. Curricula of the sort described in her column reflected, according to Wente, "a set of beliefs that many people in Ontario's education industry – teachers, trustees, consultants, parental activists and Queen's Park bureaucrats – hold dear."

Wente made it clear that the parent disagreed with much of the report prepared by the auditor assigned to review the Toronto School Board's budget and was dismayed by the government's funding cuts. However, she quoted that parent as saying, "But he [the auditor] also said something like, 'The trustees think they can solve every social ill through education.' And he's right. That's a big part of the public education system's problem."

Wente's column tapped into a vein of anxiety about public schooling not just in Toronto, but across Canada. That vein is fed from many sources.

Canadian media are like media almost everywhere. They thrive on a diet of bad news stories on a variety of subjects, including public schooling. And if the news about public schools is not exactly bad, the media use the image of a glass half empty to create the conflict that builds their audience. Improving graduation rates and test results become stories about "not improving enough" or "not doing as well as" (pick one) the district, province, or country next door, or all of the above.

Throughout the past decade of funding freezes and reductions, the media have featured a steady stream of articles and columns implying, like Wente's, that the system has sufficient resources that, if not devoted to frivolous activities, might be sufficient to do the job. They have suggested that the problem is not so much one of adequate resources as the need for accountability, fiscal and educational. And, if audits and testing will not by themselves improve public schools, increased competition and choice will.

But, as I said earlier, the media have been simply tapping into a vein of anxiety and giving it a little additional juice of their own. Our elected representatives are also feeding that vein of anxiety for political and ideological advantage. Some misrepresent data that indicate public education is actually doing quite well and gradually improving. Some feed the media's voracious appetite for invidious comparisons. These anxieties and misrepresentations fuel the growth of home and private schooling.

Some politicians appear eager to abandon public schooling in favour of a market-driven private system. They seem ready to discard long-standing Canadian values and practices without any public consultation. They seek to rid the public purse of the burden of preparing the next generation of Canadians. They do so by strangling the public system with reduced funding. They want to offer tax credits and other incentives to facilitate an exodus to the private system.

Teachers' unions also contribute to the anxiety of parents like the one in Wente's column. They seem to be constantly engaged in combat. Every initiative – from accountability to technology – is met with "shock and dismay." Concerned for their own welfare and for the consequences of funding reductions for students, they overdramatize the impact of such reductions.

Canadian parents cling firmly to competing ideas about what they want from public schools. Some want just the basics: reading, writing, and mathematics. Others want fine arts and modern languages. Their neighbours want preparation for work. The guy down the street wants more history and politics so that students will become good citizens.

Schools try to respond to each and every demand. Wente is mistaken to attribute Diverse Families Month, Black History Month, and Global Harvest Festivals Month to what she demeaningly refers to as the "education industry." Each of these initiatives has a Canadian constituency advocating for its inclusion. Wente should see what does *not* get incorporated into the public school curriculum.

I have been intimately involved with public schools for most of my life, as a student, teacher, parent, parent representative to a local school board, professor in a faculty of education responsible for the preparation of teachers, school trustee, and deputy minister of education for British Columbia. Each position has provided me with a different vantage point from which to view the considerable strengths of our public schools, their weaknesses, and their serious shortcomings.

This book explores some of the changes that have occurred in Canadian society and in Canadian public schools during the past century with an emphasis on the last thirty years. It questions the elasticity and the future of public schooling in the face of what appear to be irreconcilable tensions and demands that affect it.

Chapter One contains the central argument of the book, in which I contend that Canadians are guilty of *malign* neglect of public schooling. We make impossible demands upon our public schools, strangle them financially, make trivial changes for the sake of ideology, and avoid making more necessary ones for lack of fortitude. Ignoring the evidence, we say public school graduates don't measure up. We make simple-minded comparisons of one public school with another, diminish their accomplishments, or just plain overlook them.

Chapters Two, Three, and Four address some of the changes I think have significantly affected Canadian society and public schooling. Chapter Two focuses on the demographic and structural changes to the family and the impact of those changes on children and their schooling. I am not among those who want to go back to the good old days. As someone once said, "Things aren't what they used to be and never were."

Chapter Three addresses an issue some people would rather avoid: child poverty. I agree with those who think the evidence shows a growing income gap in Canadian society. That gap has a particularly devastating impact on children. The problems created and sustained by poverty are overcome by some, but not by the majority. Canada suffers the consequences. As a comparatively wealthy nation, we can afford to do better. I suggest how Canadian social policy can provide better support to families and communities to enable them to send children to school with a stronger foundation for success.

The media, peers, and morals are the subjects of Chapter Four. Popular culture and friends exert enormous influence, affecting the values, beliefs, and behaviour of children and youth. For many, the influences are benign, but for some the consequences are negative. Some of the things we can do to mitigate the negative influences are addressed in this chapter.

Many people wonder why schools teach as they do. Chapter Five outlines competing visions of education and illustrates their influence on public schooling. That sets the stage for the proposals in Chapter Six, in which I outline what I think schools should and should not teach. Admittedly, this is *my* vision of public schooling. It will likely differ from the vision of many readers, but I hope it stimulates discussion of what it is we really want from our public schools. If we don't have that discussion, we will remain mired in competing and conflicting expectations, philosophies, and methodologies.

Chapter Seven tackles a critical issue in Canadian education, the education of students with special needs. I talk about the strengths and the significant weaknesses of the present system. I discuss what is perhaps the most shameful failure of public schools, the miseducation of aboriginal Canadians. The basic argument of the chapter is that, in addition to aboriginal Canadians, most students with special needs are not getting the full benefit of their public schooling. Those concerned about improving public schooling and increasing success rates should be particularly attentive to what is and is not happening with students with special educational needs.

Teachers' work, unions, and professionalism are the focus of Chapter Eight. Many Canadians are perplexed by accounts in the media about teachers. Few appreciate the nature of their work and the impact of their working conditions on them and on students. In this chapter, I talk about what can be done to improve the status of teachers in the eyes of the wider community. I hope that the union leadership inclined to react with "shock and dismay" will withhold judgment on my suggestions until they have considered them dispassionately.

Chapter Nine takes on the issues of school choice and competition. Perhaps more than any other, this is an arena in which rhetoric prevails over reason. I try to reveal the complexity of the issues, discuss why they arise, and suggest what might be done about them.

Public school finance and governance have changed dramatically and are continuing to change. Chapter Ten addresses those changes, their implications, and makes recommendations for their improvement. Chapter Eleven tackles the related topic of leadership, talking frankly about its failure at every level. I examine the complexity of public schooling and make some suggestions for improving leadership.

Chapter Twelve is concerned with another of the central and difficult issues in public schooling: accountability. I talk about the different forms that accountability takes and might take. I also set out some conditions that need to be satisfied in order to realize the benefits of the large-scale student assessments currently in use as mechanisms of accountability.

Educational change, why it does and doesn't happen, is the focus of Chapter Thirteen. I've called the chapter "How to Change Public Schools," but I could have as easily called it "How Not to Change Public Schools." Here, I set out some of what is known about change and apply it to public schools. I also suggest what I think are some productive avenues for change.

In the conclusion, I draw together what I have said throughout the book and address some of the recommendations I've made about each of the topics. I remind readers why it is important to keep public schooling at the forefront of public consciousness. I recall once hearing Bob Dylan say, "You don't create a revolution by writin' a folk song." I don't want to create a revolution in public schooling. I will be pleased if this book stimulates debate among Canadians about the state of our public schools and about their future.

# chapter one

# YOU DON'T KNOW WHAT YOU HAVE TILL IT'S GONE

anadians might as well begin teaching their grand-children how to sing the "Star-Spangled Banner" and pledge allegiance to the American flag if they continue treating Canada's public schools the way they have been recently. Our public schools, and what they teach our children, help define Canada as a unique nation. But we are neglecting our public schools in a perversely malicious way: making impossible demands upon them, strangling them financially, creating trivial changes for the sake of ideology, avoiding necessary changes for lack of fortitude, saying their graduates don't measure up, making fatuous comparisons between one public school and another, decrying their accomplishments, and just plain ignoring them. It's true what they say, "You don't know what you have till it's gone." Our public schools are collapsing from *malign* neglect.

Canadians exhibit the wrong inclinations toward public schooling; they are miserly, ideological, cowardly, dishonest, and indifferent. When they get involved, they are often meddlesome rather than helpful. If Canadians do not change their approach to public schooling, we may lose the benefits that public schools provide and miss opportunities to make necessary improvements to a successful system.

Canadians forget the central part that public schools play in defining what it means to be Canadian and in sustaining Canada. They ignore the evidence that, if public schooling fails, Canada will lose its distinctive identity in a generation or two.

The paradox is that Canadian public schooling has never been healthier nor at greater risk. Canadians can take pride in the strengths of the system of public education they have created. At the same time, they should be worried about its vulnerabilities.

Despite unstable families, problems of poverty, and exposure to violent and tawdry media, Canadian youngsters are well served by public schools. Public schools face conflicting expectations, a crowded curriculum, clashes about philosophy and teaching methodologies, questionable leadership, growing numbers of students with special needs, high parental expectations and comparatively little parental support, attacks by the news media, and cash-starved governments. But the education they provide is better than ever.

Over the last half-century, the educational attainment of Canadians has risen steadily. The proportion of people with less than a grade nine education declined from 51.9 per cent in 1951 to 14.3 per cent in 1991. During the same period, the proportion of persons who earned university degrees increased fivefold.

During the past decade, education levels continued to improve substantially, with more young people graduating from high school and more high school graduates continuing on to post-secondary education. In 1990, 20 per cent of Canadians between the ages of twenty-five and twenty-nine had less than a grade twelve education. By 1998, the proportion had declined to 13 per cent. During the same period, the proportion of Canadians in this age group who had earned university degrees rose from 17 per cent to 26 per cent. When the member nations of the Organization for Economic Co-operation and Development (OECD) were surveyed in 1995, Canada had the highest percentage of the population (48 per cent) with some post-secondary education, compared with an average for the member countries of 23 per cent.

Canadian students perform well in reading, mathematics, and science, according to an OECD study that assessed the performance of fifteen-year-olds in these subjects. Canadian students ranked second in reading, fifth in science, and sixth in mathematics among the thirty-two countries that participated in the OECD's Programme for International Student Assessment (PISA). Only students in Finland performed significantly better than Canadian students in reading. Japanese and Korean students performed significantly better than Canadian students in mathematics. And only students in Korea, Japan, and Finland performed significantly better than Canadian students in science.

I must confess to some ambivalence about citing Canada's strong performance on international assessments. What gives me pause is that I know that some nations' schools are not as inclusive as Canada's. Some nations exclude from school, or from the samples drawn for international assessments, students who are routinely included in Canadian schools and in the international assessments. I also know that, for some nations, performing well on international assessments is a matter of national pride. In these countries, there is considerable pressure placed on the schools and students. Canadian students are more apt to ask the teacher administering the assessment, "Will this count for my mark?" Given the different emphases that nations place on these tests, Canadian students can take pride in their high scores.

## EDUCATION AND THE FUTURE

SOME AMONG US act as if the future is knowable in the way that we can know the past. They see schooling as preparation for a predictable life path. They would encourage education to focus on the acquisition of the procedural knowledge considered necessary for employment.

The difficulty is that individuals have different futures. My children's future will be different from that of your children. We cannot prepare individuals for their unique futures, but we can prepare them for their common future as citizens.

While we cannot know the future as we know the past, we can anticipate conditions that might prevail. We can make a forecast based upon an intelligent analysis of what has occurred in the past and is now occurring. Fortunately, we can influence the future by the choices we make.

People are less fettered by their social, political, and economic location now than at any time in the past. We enjoy more autonomy. We have rights, and they are better protected. These are good things.

Decisions today are more likely to be made on the basis of reason. This, too, is a good thing; tradition and authority too often dictated decisions. Now we take evidence into account in making decisions. People are more attentive to the reasons given for decisions.

Increasing autonomy and reason have brought with them perils as well. We have become narcissistic and individualistic in our pursuits. The individual has come to be the measure of all things, and satisfaction of individual needs and wants has come to be a dominant consideration. We are less concerned with *us* than we are with *you* and especially *me*. Canadians' growing emphasis on individual, rather than collective, well-being is reflected in our schools.

We have learned that our talents, abilities, and efforts enable us to transcend our social and economic locations. We are less confined by our social and economic origins than in the past. But the value of talents, abilities, and efforts has become largely market-driven. Economic considerations have come to dominate decision-making to the exclusion of other standards.

### THE FRAGILE NATION

PUBLIC SCHOOLS play a unique and pivotal role for Canada, countering the many threats to the unity of our young and fragile nation. Canadian society is becoming increasingly fragmented and Canadians increasingly alienated from one another. As a nation, we are becoming unglued. The centrifugal forces of regional alienation, Quebec nationalism, and ethnocentrism pull Canadians apart from one another, while economic globalization and American media weaken individual Canadians' identification with their country.

Michael Adams, president of the polling firm Environics, says, "Today in Canada there is consensus on the major political goals: fiscal rectitude, an efficient social welfare state, a sustainable environment and more choices for the people. But the consensus on social values is breaking down, as Canada adopts a 'pull' culture focused on personal autonomy and self-fulfillment."

People develop a sense of who they are and of what they are capable from the institutions, symbols, and myths that reflect their dreams, aspirations, and images. Canada's sense of self is relatively weak in comparison with nations such as the United States, Japan, and France. As a consequence, Canada is a fragile nation.

Canada is sparsely populated for its size. Our 32 million people live primarily in cities along a narrow corridor in close proximity to the border with the United States. So many Canadians live in Los Angeles, it is, as someone quipped, Canada's second-largest city. Our travel patterns seem to follow a geography that has us moving from north to south rather than east or west.

The dependency ratio is one of the vital signs used by demographers and economists to ascertain a country's health. It is the number of people younger than fifteen and older than sixty-five divided by the number of people of working age (fifteen to sixty-four). A rapidly aging population and no or slow population growth puts production, pension, health, and other systems at risk. While Canada is healthier than some developed nations, it needs to maintain population in order to support those people no longer active in the workforce.

We are unable to sustain our numbers through childbirth alone, as the number of children born to Canadian women is well below the replacement rate. To maintain our numbers, and a standard of living that depends on maintaining a workforce sufficiently large to support our social services, we rely on immigration. The number of immigrants is typically about 15 per cent. The constant influx of newcomers is a necessary and desirable feature of Canada. Ensuring their integration into Canadian society is a continuing task.

Fragmentation is the most apparent characteristic of the Canadian electoral landscape. Five official parties are represented in the House of Commons, each with a more or less regional base. The Canadian Alliance's strength is in the West, the Liberal strength is in Ontario and Quebec, the Bloc Québécois is exclusive to Quebec, the Progressive Conservatives are strongest in the East, and the New Democratic Party is supported here and there outside of central Canada. The regional differences and party differentiation account for the fact that the Liberals formed a majority government in 2000 even though they earned only 40 per cent of the popular vote.

Our symbols are not evocative. Where our neighbours have the bald eagle, a commanding presence, we have the beaver – a furry creature with dental structure that is easily caricatured. Our flag is less than forty years old. Our anthem is typically sung in both official languages, each version conveying subtle and not-so-subtle differences in meaning.

Canadian media are as fragmented as Canadian politics. At mid-century, the Canadian Broadcasting Corporation and the National Film Board of Canada provided a clear exposition of the values, experiences, and stories that Canadians shared. Today, Canadians have greater access to cable televisions than any other country in the world, providing a multiplicity of messages –

many originating outside of Canada's borders. Michael Adams says, "New communications and information technologies – cable TV, satellite TV, VCRs, the Internet – are allowing Canadians to watch, read, and listen to what they want, when they want, resulting in more individualistic and idiosyncratic worldviews."

We have systematically fettered our national broadcasting service to the point that its audiences are small, demographically isolated, and linguistically fragmented. Despite contentions to the contrary, we have no national newspaper and no national news magazine to convey to Canadians a sense of ourselves as a nation.

Our indigenous film industry is insignificant in comparison to that of our southern neighbour. And when a Canadian film *is* made, there is usually no money left for publicity. Canadian films do not draw the audiences that films from the United States do. We have no Canadian content quotas that would ensure that Canadian films are guaranteed screen time or distribution. Canada dares not even dream of invoking preferential measures for its film industry. If it did, representatives of American producers would fly north to threaten Canadian policy-makers and theatre owners with the retribution that would ensue if such measures were adopted.

From its beginning, Canada has been a confederation of provinces and territories that have fought to maintain their identities and sought to retain their powers in the face of the general welfare of all Canadians. Today, few Canadian politicians seem capable of seeing beyond the horizon of their local and regional interests. As a consequence, Canada's central institutions do not exert the national influence they should.

On the rare occasions when federal politicians exercise the prerogatives of their jurisdictions, they do so timidly. They are constantly on the defensive, wary of attacks by regional and provincial interests. The annual Premiers' Conference is a ritual reaffirmation of solidarity among provincial premiers in opposition to their own federal government.

In style and substance, Canadians seem more connected to people in the United States than to their neighbours in other provinces. In a recent survey, 2,505 Americans and 3,022 Canadians were asked about their acceptance of a common North American currency. Respondents were asked to consider three options: (1) that Canada should give up the Canadian dollar and adopt the U.S. dollar as its currency; (2) that Canada and Mexico should both give up their currencies and adopt the U.S. dollar; and (3) that Canada, the United States, and Mexico should give up their currencies and adopt a totally new one as a common North American currency.

A third of the Canadians polled (32 per cent) said that they would consider adopting the U.S. dollar. A third (34 per cent) indicated that they would be open to a new common currency for North America. And half of the Canadians said they were prepared to accept at least one of the three options. Only 43 per cent of the Canadian respondents said they were unprepared to accept any of the three proposals. Interestingly, Québécois were more supportive (44 per cent) of Canada adopting the U.S. dollar, and British Columbians least supportive (27 per cent).

This contrasts sharply with Americans, who were overwhelmingly opposed (84 per cent) to a common currency with Canada or Mexico, even if the common currency was the U.S. dollar.

The poll, conducted in March and April 2002, also asked Canadians and Americans if Canada should become part of the United States. Most people in both countries opposed the idea. However, nearly one in five Canadians (19 per cent) was in favour of the idea. One in four Québécois was in favour, a level of support that was the highest of all provinces.

In 2001, Frank Graves, president of EKOS Research Associates, addressed the Canadian Club in Ottawa. Referring to Canada's relations with the United States as the most important globalization issue for Canadians, Graves said that over time there has been a growing conviction among Canadians that "we are becoming more American." Although, for most Canadians, increasing Americanization was undesirable, "the incidence of those approving of increasing Americanization had grown from eight to fourteen per cent" during the preceding three years. In particular, he noted a gap between the general preference of Canadians (14 per cent) and private sector leaders (37 per cent). He also observed what I think is a worrisome trend. He said, "Young Canadians are also alarmingly uninterested in core Canadian institutions, much more connected to North America than other Canadians, and they remain largely disconnected from political institutions."

EKOS research indicates that a number of the differences between Canada and the United States are "more imagined than real." According to EKOS, "Compared with Americans, Canadians appear no more compassionate [arguably less so], reveal similar levels of trust in government as an institution and endorse the same broad policy choices and tradeoffs. Moreover, Canadian value orientations, while still distinguishable, are blurring under common forces of technology, globalization and post-modernism."

Ken Osborne, at the University of Manitoba, points out in his recent book *Education: A Guide to the Canadian School Debate* that Canada differs from countries such as France, Britain, and the United States in subtle but important ways. He attributes many of Canada's problems to our attempts to live as the citizens of those nations live. According to Osborne, Canada's citizens require "special qualities," including "acceptance of diversity, a willingness to live with ambiguity, an understanding of the nature of the country and a familiarity with its history, and, not least, the ability to enter into the continuing debate that characterizes Canadian public life." He laments the fact that, although "these qualities can and should be nurtured in the schools, most ministries of education in Canada these days seem willing to cast them aside."

## ANXIETY ABOUT PUBLIC SCHOOLING

THE ONE INSTITUTION capable of preserving Canada's fragile sense of self is the public school. It is a potentially powerful force for integrating Canadians and countering some of the forces fragmenting our society by communicating core Canadian values, teaching about our history and institutions, providing experience with democratic processes, and inculcating respect for people. But it, too, is increasingly limited.

Our public schools need our thoughtful attention. They are struggling to address rapid and unprecedented social and technological changes. At the same time, they are at risk of collapsing under the weight of competing and often conflicting expectations. Public schooling depends on a foundation of public confidence and support. But Canadians are losing confidence in public schooling.

Canadians are anxious about the state of the country's economy and the security of their own employment. The September 2001 terrorist attacks on the World Trade Center and the Pentagon appeared to stall economic recovery following a long period of economic recession. The elimination of barriers to trade and the movement of manufacturing to regions of the world in which labour is cheap have some Canadians worried about what will happen to their jobs. They have read newspaper and magazine articles stating that the next generation of workers will have as many as seven jobs during the course of their career, if they have a career at all. But as they worry, Canadians seem to have forgotten the link between a strong public education system and a sound economy. Canada's economy depends on our having a workforce that is literate, able to think clearly and creatively, has a facility with numbers and measurement, and is able to work co-operatively with others – core skills acquired in public schools.

During the late 1950s and 1960s, Canadian policy-makers and the public were told that schooling was an investment in the

development of human capital. Like an investment in manufacturing plants and equipment, investing in human capital paid off
for the economy. Politicians and parents said that a better life
could be had by acquiring more education. Students stayed in
school and the Canadian economy grew. The connection
between schooling and employment and earnings seemed clear.

Since the late 1950s, students who stayed in school improved
their chances of getting a good job. High school completion rates
improved dramatically. The numbers of students going on to
post-secondary study soared. Incomes increased for those who
graduated from high school and for those who went on to further
study after high school.

By the mid-1980s, the pace of economic growth had slowed
to a crawl, finally stalled, and eventually headed "south" into
recession in the early 1990s. At the same time as the Canadian
economy was in free fall, the economies of Germany and Japan
were buoyant and rapidly expanding.

Business leaders and politicians who knew better – or should
have known better – began to criticize public schools for the
failings of the economy. They said that Canadian workers were less
productive than their counterparts in other countries. They also
said that Canadian workers lacked the skills and knowledge that
German and Japanese workers possessed. The faltering economy
was blamed on poor preparation for work and on illiteracy instead
of poor economic management, low levels of research and development, and the failure to provide sufficient workplace training.

Political and business leaders made visits to schools in Germany
and Japan. They returned with ideas they thought would improve
public schooling and Canada's economy. They were sure these
two economic powerhouses had much to teach Canada.

By the mid-1990s, the German economy had slowed and the
Japanese economy bordered on collapse. Both were experiencing the vagaries of a market economy. In addition, Japan was
suffering the consequences of fiscal mismanagement so large that,

for a while at least, it threatened economies around the world.

Canadian politicians and business leaders no longer talk about applying the lessons learned from Germany's and Japan's educational systems to Canada's public schools. But the doubts about Canada's public schools raised in the 1990s continue to fuel our anxieties about the system. Canadians doubt whether public schools are preparing their children for a competitive economy. "Doubt" is the key word, because most Canadians aren't really sure. It is interesting that we are quick to condemn our schools when the economy performs poorly, and we are slow to assert their merits during periods of economic growth.

Lack of clear information is another factor contributing to Canadian anxiety about public schooling. The public, including parents, complains about having too little information about how well students are doing. We can track the progress of our hockey team in the rankings published in the morning newspaper. We measure financial progress by asking whether the "loonie" is up or down in relation to the U.S. dollar. And we try to apply the same "box score" mentality to our thinking about public schools. We are given to making snap judgments when we read about international comparisons or school rankings. Hungry for information about how well our children are doing, we jump to conclusions.

### WHAT *IS* THE PROBLEM WITH SCHOOLS?

WE ARE APT TO BELIEVE that the performance of Canadian students is mediocre in comparison with that of students in other countries. We don't know much about the tests used in international assessments. We don't know about the conditions affecting the administration of those tests. Simplistic rankings of provincial schools by the Fraser Institute and the media mislead us. We start to believe that the schools our children attend are not up to snuff. When asked by pollsters, we are apt to say that our children aren't getting as good an education as we did. But we really aren't sure. Maybe it *was* a bit better when we were in school, but maybe not.

Canadians who are asked if they have given serious thought to public schooling will admit they have not. Unless they have children. And often, even when they have children, most Canadians say they have not been in a public school since they themselves graduated. Parents and others who do give serious thought to public schooling say that it takes work to understand public schools. It takes time to visit and effort to understand school jargon.

Many parents say they are not comfortable visiting their child's school and do not feel especially welcome when they do visit. They are told they are supposed to be partners in the education of their children, but when they ask questions about their child's progress or make suggestions, the teachers can look uncomfortable, use jargon parents do not understand, and act defensively. Government attempts to legislate the access and influence of parents fuel conflict among parents, teachers, and school administrators as long-established relationships are altered.

Parents complain that they sometimes feel they and their children are being blamed for teacher inadequacies or school failure. Teachers retort that they are being held responsible for things over which they have no control. They are tired of being under attack in the media and by opportunistic politicians. They say they have spent considerable effort acquiring specialized professional knowledge, but that good teaching cannot overcome the consequences of poor parenting, poverty, discrimination, and abuse.

Many teachers say that each parent seems to think his or her child is the only one that counts. Some parents want to make all the educational decisions about what is best for their children. Teachers say they are obliged to use their knowledge for the benefit of the entire class. They think it is impossible to accommodate the idiosyncratic preferences of each parent.

Many people, especially those outside the teaching profession, think that public schools need to change. They think schools have not accommodated the changes in Canadian society that have occurred over the past fifty years. They also think that public schools are part of a vast, monolithic bureaucracy that is out of touch with reality and unwilling to change. On the other hand, some say that things appear to change too frequently in education. They complain that schools seem attracted to every passing fad or fashion. They ask why public schools don't do things the way they did in the good old days. We expect the impossible of our schools: that they preserve valued traditions while preparing children for an unknowable future.

Support for public schooling is being undermined by individual self-interest. Michael Adams of Environics says that following the terrorist attacks of September 11, 2001, Canadians "long to slow things down and escape from the constant onslaught of bad news." He has seen "a decline in Canadians' interest in others and a willingness to entertain different points of view." It is not a healthy sign that, "whether it is Canada's poor, Native Canadians on remote reserves, or Afghans who end up as 'collateral damage' in the war against terrorism, we are less willing to listen, imagine, and empathize."

Adams's observations are consistent with the evidence from other quarters. For example, in a recently published essay excerpted from his book *End Poverty by Ending Welfare as We Know It*, Fred McMahon of the Fraser Institute argues, "Poverty is largely a voluntary choice." McMahon contends that the poor, the unskilled, and teenage mothers are autonomous moral agents. These individuals are responsible for the consequences of their own decisions. Canadians appear increasingly accepting of this view of inequality. Canadians are putting greater emphasis on the individual's own resources and resourcefulness rather than other environmental and social factors.

Support for public schooling is being eroded by those who are tired of paying for public schools. They question why they should foot the bill, especially if they don't have children in public school. Canada's population is aging rapidly, and its school-age population is stable or declining. Governments are under enormous pressure to concentrate scarce resources on health care rather than public schooling.

Every Canadian who cares about the values that make Canada different from other societies, that make Canadians a distinctive people, should be concerned about preserving our public schools. They need to see how good public schools mean a better life for all of us.

### WHAT'S *PUBLIC* ABOUT PUBLIC SCHOOLS?

A NATION DEVELOPS "MEMORY" from the experiences it communicates from generation to generation. Memory provides a reference point for action. In an address in April 2000, author and philosopher John Ralston Saul reminded his audience that "the past – memory – is one of the most powerful, practical tools available to a civilized democracy." He used the familiar metaphor about history being an unbroken line from the past through the present into the future.

Saul said that history "reminds us of our successes and failures, of their context; it warns us, encourages us. Without memory we are a society suffering from advanced Alzheimer's, tackling each day like a baby with its finger stuck out before the flames." Historical memory teaches us how to behave in various situations. It shapes our identities. Canada is composed of persons from diverse backgrounds with a variety of "historical memories." Canada needs strong public schools to communicate the values that are the glue holding the country together.

Saul's comments and writing make frequent reference to the establishment of the Province of Canada as a result of the union of Lower Canada (Quebec) and Upper Canada (Ontario) under the leadership of Sir Louis-Hippolyte LaFontaine (1807–1864) and Robert Baldwin (1804–1858). With representatives from both Lower and Upper Canada, LaFontaine and Baldwin established progressive directions that have shaped Canada and made her unique among nations.

Saul refers to LaFontaine's "Address to the Electors of Terrebonne" in 1840 as "the cornerstone document of modern Canada." In it, LaFontaine said, "The only way in which the authorities can prevent us from succeeding is by destroying the social equality which is the distinctive characteristic of much of the populations of Upper Canada as of Lower Canada. This social equality must necessarily bring our political liberty. . . . No privileged caste can exist in Canada beyond and above the mass of its inhabitants." Saul notes, "Of course LaFontaine knew there would always be richer and poorer. But he – they – were inventing the idea of a profoundly middle class society, in which that middle class would be as inclusive as possible."

In the period before Confederation, Egerton Ryerson was a Methodist minister in Upper Canada. Ryerson campaigned for and established government-supported, tuition-free "common schools." Students typically attended such schools for six years. They acquired rudimentary knowledge of language, mathematics, science, and history as well as instruction in Christian moral values. Students learned by means of recitation and demonstrated what they had learned in oral examinations. Teachers threatened students who misbehaved and used physical punishment when those threats failed.

The common school of the late 1800s was roughly equivalent to today's elementary school. Only a very small, largely male, proportion of the students continued their education beyond the "common school." People with more education became ministers or teachers, or worked in other professions.

Over the course of its history, Canadian public schooling has evolved in accordance with a number of widely held principles. Most Canadians today would agree with Ryerson, who became Ontario's first superintendent of education, that education should be "as common as water, and as free as air." The principle that public schooling (which now, of course, includes secondary school) should be universally accessible and publicly funded is well accepted by Canadians. Another well-established principle is that all students should be able to complete an educational program that will provide a foundation for further study. Unless the students are not intellectually capable, the program should lead to productive employment and active citizenship.

These principles are reflected across Canada in provincial statutes and other documents devoted to public schooling. New Brunswick, for example, strives to ensure that students will become personally fulfilled lifelong learners. They should be capable of contributing to a "productive, just and democratic society." Quebec refers to helping "students develop qualifications and to promote equality of opportunity, access to education, student success and excellence." The preamble to Manitoba's Public Schools Act asserts that a strong public school system is "a fundamental element of a democratic society." Public school should "serve the best educational interests of students" and contribute to "the development of students' talents and abilities" and "a fair, compassionate, healthy and prosperous society." In British Columbia, the purpose of the school system is to "enable learners to develop their individual potential and to acquire the knowledge, skills, and attitudes needed to contribute to a healthy society and a prosperous and sustainable economy."

The concept of an inclusive society dedicated to elimination of social inequalities distinguishes Canada from other nations, states our goal, and proclaims who we are. Equality is an important value to Canadians, so much so that equality rights figure prominently in our constitution. Although we do not always live up to the ideal, we have the right to the equal protection and equal benefit of the law. That protection should be without discrimination based on race, national or ethnic origin, colour, religion, sex, age, mental or physical disability, or sexual orientation.

## CHANGING SOCIETY

CANADIANS HAVE TRIED to achieve a balance between the rights of the individual and the rights of the group. We enjoy protection of our fundamental freedoms – of speech, association, and religion – and recognize group rights. Minority language education rights of French and English speakers are protected. Also protected are denominational, separate, and dissentient rights and privileges. We value our multicultural heritage and mention it explicitly in our constitution. We seek to preserve and enhance our links to our ancestral origins by ensuring that our Charter rights are interpreted in a manner consistent with that heritage. Treaty rights of aboriginal peoples, their rights and freedoms enshrined in the Royal Proclamation of 1763, and the rights they have obtained or may obtain by means of land claims settlements are guaranteed.

The Canadian landscape is broad, and the regions of this vast country impose different conditions upon us. We have committed ourselves to addressing disparities by promoting equal opportunities for all Canadians no matter where they live. The Canadian government encourages economic development so that disparities in opportunities are reduced or eliminated. Essential public services such as health care and education are provided to all Canadians.

But these values we once considered distinct and took pains to express in our constitution no longer seem to provide direction for Canada. The institutions that once nurtured Canada have been weakened by changes to their structure and by our diminished confidence. Some say they have seen these symptoms before and that Canada will get over whatever it is that ails her. But conditions today are different.

Having endured the Depression and survived the Second World War, Canada emerged into the 1950s an increasingly prosperous and physically secure nation. Perhaps Canada was not as well off or as secure as our neighbour to the south, but we were nearly so.

Analysts such as University of Toronto political scientist Neil Nevitte have been studying the value changes that characterize nations such as Canada. Nevitte thinks that one consequence of our prosperity and security is that over the past twenty-five years we have changed our basic orientations to the political, social, and economic spheres of activity.

Nevitte bases his observations on data from a survey of values in post-industrial nations. He has analyzed information from nations in which more than half the population works in government or services of one kind or another. He chose as the title for his analysis *The Decline of Deference* to indicate that Canadians, like the citizens of other advanced industrialized countries, are less respectful of authority than they have been in the past.

As in every other country studied, Nevitte found Canadians have become less likely to agree with the statement that "greater respect for authority in the future would be a good thing." Our decreasing respect for authority is paralleled by lack of confidence in governmental and non-governmental institutions and decreasing national pride. This is not surprising. Many of our politicians rule by playing up our internal divisions and belittling our national institutions. They advocate the need for "continental" rather than national policies.

Canadian television and newspapers, largely controlled by a few wealthy business people, are particularly critical of publicly funded institutions. They tend to support a short-term, results-oriented, bottom-line approach to public services. This approach often ignores the underlying principle of providing government services for the common good.

According to Nevitte, "Canadians have become more assertive, less compliant, and . . . less confident in their governmental institutions, more interested in politics, and more willing than before to pursue their goals through unconventional forms of political action." We are more interested in politics, but our interests are not confined to familiar party structures. During the 1980s and 1990s, our political party allegiances and party structures changed dramatically. The Progressive Conservative party collapsed. Canada became more fragmented when two new regional parties were formed, the Reform/Alliance and Bloc Québécois.

As anyone who has watched the nightly news will recognize, we are more willing to protest now than at any time in our history. Nevitte's analysis shows that, from 1980 to 1990, fewer Canadians said they would *never* join in boycotts (-6.2 per cent), attend unlawful demonstrations (-3.5 per cent), join unofficial strikes (-12.6 per cent), or occupy buildings or factories (-2.8 per cent). These patterns are not unique to Canada. Similar patterns, to which the protests at meetings of the Asia–Pacific Economic Co-operation Conference (APEC) and the World Trade Organization (WTO) attest, are mirrored in other advanced industrial states.

According to Nevitte, a new work ethic is emerging in Canada and elsewhere, which "gives increasing prominence to such work values as responsibility, achievement, engagement, and initiative." Nevitte found that the importance of work and financial satisfaction had declined since 1980. At the same time, Canadians – especially younger, better educated ones – are increasingly likely to believe that people who are more productive should be paid more than those who are less productive. They also feel that poverty should be attributed to internal factors such as laziness rather than to external factors such as injustice.

Civil and moral permissiveness has increased. According to Nevitte, people are becoming less likely to regard as wrong: claiming government benefits to which they are not entitled; avoiding paying the fare for public transportation; cheating on taxes if they have the opportunity; keeping money they found that belongs to someone else; and lying in their own interest. Canadians are also becoming less religious. Church attendance rates, Nevitte observes, are "falling, personal beliefs in God are on the decline, and the moral authority of churches is waning." In just ten years, Canadians showed increasing acceptance of homosexuality (+11.1 per cent), euthanasia (+12.1 per cent), and divorce (+13.8 per cent).

As our respect for authority declines, so, too, does our confidence in institutions, including education. Neil Guppy, at the University of British Columbia, and Scott Davies, at McMaster University, examined Canadians' confidence in public institutions. They wanted to provide context for their analysis of Canadians' confidence in public education. They found that between 1974 and 1995, there was widespread erosion of confidence in modern institutions.

Guppy and Davies observed that, while there was a decline in school confidence, "compared with other institutions, schools fared quite well." Schools ranked behind the Church and the Supreme Court and ahead of the House of Commons, newspapers, labour unions, large corporations, and political parties. Some critics of public schooling attribute the decline in confidence to poor system performance. Guppy and Davies disagree, attributing it instead to a gap between the performance of the educational system in relation to heightened public expectations.

Guppy and Davies argue that the gap between reality and expectation is what underlies declining confidence. Like Nevitte, they see a changing cultural context. "Greater uncertainty in society coupled with a more knowledgeable public has generated a 'malaise of modernity,' seen most directly, perhaps, in greater public cynicism about core institutions." Cynicism seems to be "coupled with higher expectations for institutions, particularly education which . . . is increasingly criticized because the public deems it increasingly crucial for individual and societal well-being."

Consistent with Nevitte and Guppy and Davies, Darrell Bricker and Edward Greenspon's book *Searching for Certainty* describes a new "mindset" about education. They point out that, when asked by Angus Reid polling staff to volunteer "top-of-mind" priority issues in the past, education was typically mentioned by 5 per cent of the respondents in all polls prior to 2000. But suddenly, in March 2000, education was mentioned by 29 per cent of Canadians polled. Bricker and Greenspon describe the new mindset on education as one that "demanded tougher standards, greater discipline, and heightened accountability."

That mantra – standards, discipline, and accountability – is largely a spillover from the rhetoric of our southern neighbours. Since the Soviets beat them in the first round of the space race, many Americans have been convinced that their schools have failed and are beyond repair. Living as close to the "elephant" as we do, it is understandable that when it trumpets its message it is heard from Vancouver to St. Johns and as far north as Iqaluit.

### THE PURPOSE OF SCHOOL

DIVISION IS ONE OF THE MOST OBVIOUS features of the Canadian political landscape today. So it isn't surprising that voters of various parties assign importance to different dimensions of public schooling.

Members of four of the five main political parties rank "training youth for the work world" as the most important task of schools. Only the New Democrats (NDP) – left-of-centre social democrats – rank "creating good citizens" and "creating inquiring minds" as more important. Members of the Bloc Québécois – a left-of-centre separatist party – are disproportionately inclined to see education as a means of preparing youth for work. The task of "creating good citizens" was only supported by 11 per cent of Bloc Québécois members.

The low support for "creating citizens" among Bloc Québécois voters is understandable: they are a party that seeks Quebec independence from the rest of Canada. To the Bloc Québécois, "creating citizens" sounds like code words for creating citizens of Canada. Alliance voters tend to agree. Like the Bloc, Alliance is a regionally based party with relatively weaker ties to Canada as a whole. Alliance voters are thought to express feelings of alienation from the traditionally strong control that Central Canadian voters – primarily Liberals – seem to exert on Canada's political processes. They see the political strength of Central Canada as being detrimental to the Alliance's regionally focused supporters in Western Canada. Alliance voters express low levels of support for "creating citizens" as a goal of public education.

The primary contribution of schooling is to the society as a whole rather than to the individual. Education is not so much about you or me as it is about *us*. That is the reason societies establish schools in the first place. They want to make sure that the society survives and improves from generation to generation.

There is no question that individuals benefit greatly from schooling in many ways. But individuals are not the primary beneficiaries of what public schools do. Society benefits directly and indirectly from public schooling. There are dramatic differences between the lives of those who complete secondary school and those who do not. And there are dramatic cost differences to society in general.

Having a well-educated population provides tangible economic benefits to all Canadians – even those without children or grandchildren. High school graduates have more and better knowledge of the behaviours that contribute to a healthy lifestyle. Indeed, their health status is about 13 per cent better than those who have not completed high school. As a consequence, they make fewer visits to physicians. In other words, the effort that has been expended in ensuring that students stay in school longer produces both direct benefits for the individual and indirect, but no less tangible, benefits for the society as a whole in reduced costs for health care.

**Educational Purpose by Political Party Affiliation**

*Question: "Which of the following eight purposes of education is most important or valuable in your judgment?"*

PER CENT

| Educational Purpose | Overall | Liberal | Alliance | PC | NDP | Bloc | Other |
|---|---|---|---|---|---|---|---|
| | | Voters | Voters | Voters | Voters | Voters | Voters |
| Training youth for the work world | 32 | 36 | 35 | 26 | 19 | 41 | 16 |
| Creating good citizens | 23 | 23 | 15 | 31 | 38 | 11 | 35 |
| Creating inquiring minds | 17 | 16 | 15 | 25 | 33 | 8 | 14 |
| Creating happy people | 7 | 5 | 7 | 3 | 4 | 22 | 6 |
| Teaching ethics | 7 | 6 | 15 | 6 | 4 | 14 | 6 |
| Teaching religious values | 4 | 5 | 5 | 2 | 0 | 0 | 4 |
| Producing good parents | 3 | 3 | 3 | 3 | 0 | 3 | 4 |
| Encouraging people to question authority | 2 | 4 | 0 | 0 | 0 | 3 | 4 |
| None of the above (unprompted) | 1 | 1 | 2 | 2 | 0 | 0 | 4 |
| Don't know (unprompted) | 5 | 3 | 3 | 3 | 2 | 0 | 6 |

*Source: COMPAS/National Post, 2001: Table 19*

A similar pattern holds with respect to the justice system. About 66 per cent of the Canadian population has completed high school. Non-graduates account for 34 per cent of the population. But 75 per cent of the prison inmate population did not complete secondary school!

Several years ago, British Columbia tracked 84,000 students to study patterns of incarceration. In the study population, 61 per cent of all the students graduated from high school and 39 per cent did not. Those who graduated accounted for 34,800 days in custody. Those who did not graduate accounted for 503,600 days in custody, about 94 per cent of the days in custody to which students in the study were sentenced! Again, the payoff for the larger community of students completing secondary school is clear. Graduates are far less likely to be involved in criminal activity and to require expensive custody. For every child at risk who is prevented from spending a year in prison, Canada "saves" between $40,000 and $55,000.

Education also reduces dependence on social assistance. Less than 7 per cent of those who graduate from high school receive income assistance. However, nearly one-third of those who do not graduate from high school are recipients of income assistance. In fact, 85 per cent of income assistance is spent on persons who have not completed high school.

The current economy rewards young people for their educational achievement. Statistics Canada reports that recent university graduates are already earning more than twice that of high school dropouts of the same age. This difference grows over time.

Another payoff from education is a stronger commitment to Canada and its communities. Generally speaking, the more education a person has, the more likely that person is to vote. People with more education identify better with the larger community, and are more willing and able to contribute to it – for example, by volunteering – than do people with less education.

To flourish, democratic societies such as Canada must develop an educated citizenry capable of exercising the responsibilities of adult citizenship. Public schooling is an important process for overcoming the limits of our prior experiences, no matter how extensive or limited that prior experience may be.

I like to say that school is where we send our children to overcome the limitations of their families. As a parent, I wanted my children to learn values that would guide them long after they left home. But I recognized that I would do a disservice to my children if they were simply exposed to the values of my family. While those values have served us well, our children couldn't navigate their way as adults if that was all they were exposed to.

Education recognizes that people see things differently based upon their previous knowledge and experience. People with different perspectives may not easily agree about issues. There will be controversy. Students bump up against ideas that challenge their beliefs and values and cause them to reconsider their initial positions. The process is noisy and messy. Tolerance for ambiguity and respect for others are essential to the process.

According to John Ralston Saul, the founders of Canada's universal, publicly funded school system understood that such a system "was – and this remains – the key to our functioning democracy." Public schools help to transcend our differences to see what we have in common. They free us from the encapsulation of our own experience by exposing us to others. They cultivate our individual strengths and dispose us to treat others as we would like to be treated.

Public schools are remarkable among institutions for their enduring success. They are the only institutions capable of communicating the shared history, symbols, and values that distinguish Canada from other nations. Schools instill in the next generation a sense of belonging to Canada. They develop the knowledge base that Canada needs to survive and thrive.

But, like Canada itself, our public schools are at risk. Conflicting and competing demands upon public schools limit their capacity to nourish, unite, and guide us. Hobbled by a swollen curriculum, public schools are attempting to do too much with too few resources. If the competing demands are not reconciled, the curriculum reduced, and adequate resources found, our public schools may be permanently crippled.

# chapter two

# CHANGED LIVES OF CANADIAN CHILDREN

anadians have never placed a higher value on education. Parents want and expect more from schools today than in the past. This is largely because of changes in Canadian society and the Canadian family. They recognize that becoming an adult and the demands of adulthood are more difficult now. The volume of information and rapid pace of events make work more complex and demanding. Making ends meet often demands multiple incomes. As a result, today's children have less family and community support than in the past, placing greater pressure on public schools to compensate for the failure of other social systems.

## CHANGED FAMILIES

TODAY'S CHILDREN GROW UP in a world vastly different than the one in which their parents and, especially, their grandparents grew up, because of the rate and nature of the changes that have occurred during the last half-century. Families, which once exerted enormous – sometimes stifling – influence on the identities, beliefs, and behaviours of the young, have seen their influence decline. In the past, a child's moral framework was developed and nurtured primarily by the family and the church. Today, the child is subject to other influences, many as powerful as the family and more potent than religion.

Religion used to be a strong force in defining the values that Canadians held, but that is no longer the case. Over the last fifty years, the lives of Canadians have become increasingly secularized. Today, only about 20 per cent of adults say they attend church, mosque, temple, or synagogue regularly. By comparison, in the United States approximately 40 per cent of the adult population claims regular attendance in a place of worship.

For our grandparents, information and entertainment were separate spheres. Today, the distinction between them is blurred. Popular culture exerts an influence unparalleled in previous generations. The influence is seen in the identities, beliefs, and behaviours of the young – and in their responses to education. The importance of the peer group in the lives of young people has also increased. These complexities make the assumption of the responsibilities of adulthood more difficult than they were for our grandparents.

The family of the twenty-first century is a loosely organized social group compared with its predecessors. Once a unit that very often worked together as well as spent leisure time together, families now rarely engage in collective activities. Families today have more physical space and fewer shared possessions or activities than families in the past. Both parents commonly work outside the home with no clear responsibility assigned for child-rearing. The separation of work from their place of residence has also diminished the parents' influence on the lives of children.

The family is simply less important to one's physical and economic survival than it was a hundred years ago. The services provided by the state – health care, old age pensions, income assistance, education, and so on – compensate for what families tried, but were unable, to do.

The decline in the family's importance and in the influence of organized religion has increased the demands on the remaining community agencies responsible for the young. This is especially true for the public school, upon which Canadian society has become more dependent for the moral instruction of children.

Increased mobility and suburbanization have also affected families. There are fewer parents at home today than at any previous time. Two-thirds of all women aged twenty-five to sixty-four now have jobs outside the home. Twenty years ago, this rate was about 50 per cent. Families often move long distances for work. Children are less likely to live close to their grandparents and other relatives. The opportunities for extended family members to participate in child-rearing have been diminished.

There was a time when public schools assumed that children would come to school eager to learn, properly fed and clothed, appropriately behaved, and deferential to adult authority. Children who did not meet these expectations were treated as odd cases. Even during the Depression, when hunger was a painful fact for some, schools believed they could count on the other conditions being fulfilled. While these assumptions were violated more often in the past than most people remember, schools today can no longer routinely hold such expectations.

Every day, Vancouver teacher George Thomas cycles east across town to the "inner-city" elementary school where he has taught a split-grade class for eleven years. The "inner-city" designation reflects the fact that about 65 per cent of the students attending the school come from families struggling to make ends meet. The other 35 per cent come from middle- and upper-income families. Regardless of their economic situation, about 80 per cent of the students are immigrants or the offspring of immigrants. Parents of students in the school speak more than fifty different languages. George, who has travelled to China, has taken lessons in Mandarin to be able to greet some of the parents in the community.

George's school faces a number of challenges. It is located across the street from a theatre that shows xxx-rated movies beginning at 2:00 P.M. Prostitutes often hang out on a nearby corner. The teachers and administrators have been working to make the tone of the school a positive one. George is the school's liaison with the district anti-bullying initiative, and has led workshops for his peers on classroom management.

One of George's grade seven students recently told him a disturbing story. One of the boys in his class and that boy's older brother were going to pay a grade six girl to have sex with one of the older boy's friends. "I informed the principal, and she called the police liaison officer immediately," recounts George. "It took some digging, but the story was true. In fact, it turned out that two of the grade six girls had been approached. Nothing had happened to the girls, yet. The school counsellor and a social worker are working with them." The grade seven boy was suspended from school. His older brother is under police investigation.

George arrives at school at 7:45 A.M. and changes from his cycling gear to slacks and a sports shirt. He picks up the mail and announcements from his mailbox and makes his way to the staff room. On his way, he greets two of the students in his class who come to school as soon as the doors are opened at 8:00. They fall in step with George and enter the staff room with him. George scans his mail, makes a mental note of the workshop on child abuse scheduled for 3:15, and gathers three bowls, cereal, and milk. He pours the cereal and milk and hands a bowl to each of the students. It is a routine George has been following since the school year began. Later he explains, "They are just two of the hungry kids in my class. The others get fed as part of the hot meals program."

I ask how many children receive lunch as part of the meals program. "Half of the class gets a meal at reduced or no cost as part of the program," he replies. George explains that no student knows if, or how much, another child's parents pay for the hot meal. Every student gets an envelope each month. They are all the same. The student writes his or her name on the envelope and returns it either empty or with some money inside. Just before lunch, George gives a ticket to each child receiving a hot meal. He also takes one for himself. "I used to bring my own lunch, but since the meals program I don't. I pay for one myself and eat with the kids. It is a good time to get to know more about them, and it helps keep a lid on things in the lunchroom."

George doesn't dwell on the problems that the school routinely faces. Perennially upbeat in a streetwise way, an optimist, and a hard worker, George is more inclined to talk about the science fair winners, the choir, and the other facets of school life. He has seen many of the students in this school succeed. His flair for teaching mathematics and language arts ensures that his students have a good grounding for the work they will do in high school.

The problems faced by the staff in George Thomas's school are not typical of most Canadian schools. However, they are representative of some of the more extreme problems that schools must routinely address. These problems couldn't have been imagined when the public school system began in the latter half of the 1800s.

## THE "GOOD" OLD DAYS

CANADA, AT ITS FOUNDING, was an agricultural society. Eighty per cent of the population lived in small, closely knit rural communities. Even when farm families were spread out from one another by geography, people in rural communities knew one another and went to church together. Their children attended the same school.

Stewart and Louise Ecker moved to Manitoba from Ontario in 1910 with their five children. Mary was twelve, Franklin was ten, William eight, Rose six, and Mabel two. The Eckers had bought a house and a square mile of land they would farm.

In addition to the furnishings they brought from Ontario, Stewart and Louise had six large draught horses, two dozen cattle, some pigs, numerous chickens, and a dog. Their farmhouse had two storeys. The upper floor had three bedrooms: one for the girls, one for the boys, and one for Stewart and Louise. The lower floor had a kitchen, sitting room, and a dining room used only on special occasions. Lacking insulation, the rooms were cold in the winter and hot in summer.

Work began early each morning – milking the cows, feeding the chickens, and collecting the eggs. From the time he was old enough, the oldest boy, Frank, helped his father and Henry Bose, the hired man who lived in an outbuilding adjacent to the barn. After breakfast each day, Henry and Stewart would start work on the farm. They ploughed and planted in the spring, harvested in the fall, repaired the buildings, equipment, and fences the rest of the year. They hauled water from a well daily for livestock and family.

Mary, the oldest child, stayed home, helped Louise prepare breakfast, lunch, and dinner, and got the other children ready for school. When the weather was cold, Stewart would take the younger children to school in a wagon pulled by the horses. In warmer weather they would walk the three kilometres. Each child carried a lunch.

The children attended a one-room school that enrolled twenty-nine children from grades one to nine. At one point, all of Louise and Stewart's children except Mary were in the school together. The boys played baseball in the schoolyard, the girls played hopscotch and red-light green-light, and both took buckets of water into the fields to drown gophers.

It would be a mistake to romanticize Canada's rural past. Few, if any, would want to return to the difficult conditions farm life imposed. The hardships required resilience, interdependence, and practical intelligence. Families worked together, and neighbours helped one another out of necessity.

Families were large. Poor nutrition, crude health care, and high accident rates meant fewer children survived. Childhood, at least the childhood familiar to us today, was almost non-existent. There were relatively few differences between children and adults. Family members, including children, were expected to share in the work.

By today's standards, there was comparatively little leisure time on the small family farm. Vast distances and limited mobility meant that families spent much of their time together. The interdependence of family members and the significant amount of time spent working together contributed to the family's enormous influence on the young. Community values were quite similar. Some people – especially those who were a bit different – found them oppressive.

In the early twentieth century, each passing census noted the change in the relationship between Canada's rural and urban populations. By 1921, the two were equal in size. A decade later, Canada's population was more urban than rural. Even so, Canadians who endured the hardships of the Depression and survived the Second World War were largely unprepared for the economic and social changes they would face.

### POSTWAR CANADA

PROPELLED BY INDUSTRIALIZATION and urbanization, Canada emerged from the postwar period an urban, advanced industrial society. Despite the spectre of the Cold War, Canadians had good reason to be optimistic. Incomes were rising, capital investment was increasing, and there was a boom in home building. Technologies developed during wartime were being adapted for domestic purposes. With higher incomes and the restrictions of wartime production lifted, Canadians had unprecedented access to consumer goods. Television brought new images to Canadians – largely from their neighbours to the south, where it had developed and spread more rapidly.

The impact on the family of this transformation has been profound. Industrialization brought changes to the nature of work, increased concentration of population in cities, and decreased family size. Children were no longer needed to share in the family's work. Average family size steadily decreased from its high in 1881, when the average was 5.3 persons. By 1969, despite the surge in births between 1945 and 1965, the average family size was 3.9. In 1996, the average number of children born to Canadian women (the replacement rate) was 1.59, bringing the average family size to 3.59. But the replacement rate needed to offset the Canadian death rate is 2.1 children per woman.

Low replacement rates are, in part, a result of fewer people marrying, marrying later in life, and having fewer children. My wife and I were both twenty years old when we married in 1964. This was not unusual. Our first child was born three years later, and our second two years after that. By the time my younger child entered school in the mid-1970s, the average age of women having their first child was 23.4 years of age; twenty years later, it was 26.6 years of age.

In 1976, 62 per cent of first-time mothers were under the age of twenty-five. By 1996, the percentage had declined to 36 per cent. In that same twenty years, the first births to women over thirty tripled, accounting for three out of every ten first births. According to Dr. Berna Skrypnek, a professor of human ecology at the University of Alberta, "Increasingly, we've become so materialistic, our wants and desires are so high, we're postponing childbearing until we have some of those material kinds of things in place. And because we're postponing childbearing, we're post-poning marriage."

Bryan and Karen are examples of people who married later – after living together for a number of years – and delayed having children until their careers were well established. They are both attorneys. She specializes in taxation, and he is an expert in avi-ation law. They met in their early thirties and lived together until they were married a few years later. Jennie was born when Karen was thirty-five.

Karen returned to work a year after Jennie was born. Because their combined incomes put them among Canada's most advan-taged families, they were able to hire a nanny, who, in addition to caring for Jennie, also taught her to speak French. Jennie is now seven years old and in grade two. She attends a public school, but not one in her neighbourhood. Believing that they should build on the capacity that their nanny cultivated, Bryan and Karen have had Jennie in early French immersion since kindergarten.

Jennie's nanny picks her up after school in a car provided by Karen and Bryan. Two afternoons per week, Jennie attends an after-school arts program, where she learns ballet. On the afternoons when she is not dancing, she often has "play dates" with other children or helps her nanny prepare dinner.

Karen is home by dinnertime most days. Bryan arrives in time for dinner four out of five nights. Both Karen and Bryan spend the period between dinner and Jennie's bedtime with their daughter, reading, talking about school, and planning the many excursions they take on weekends together. Since Jennie began school, Karen and Bryan have never missed a parent-teacher interview or a Christmas concert. The family has travelled every summer, and last year went to France.

Jennie is an intelligent, happy, well-adjusted child. She is confident and polite. She does well in school and has many friends. Her parents have the resources to provide her with opportunities unavailable to many other children.

Karen and Bryan come from similar backgrounds, but this is not always the case in marriage today. A common background is now considered less important in determining what makes for a successful marriage. Instead, mutual respect, appreciation, tolerance, and understanding are seen as very important.

There are more types of families and relationships than in the past. More and more young people choose to live together before forming a long-term common-law relationship or getting married. In fact, the first conjugal relationship for most Canadians is living common law. According to Statistics Canada, between 1990 and 1995, more than 50 per cent of the people who entered their first conjugal relationship chose to live together rather than get married.

Family and marital history influence the type of conjugal relationship people choose. Women whose parents had separated or divorced were 75 per cent more likely to have a common-law relationship as their first union. The chance that a single mother would form a common-law relationship was twice as great as it was for women without children. French-speaking women living in Quebec were more likely to live common law than were Quebec residents who did not speak French, or French-speakers living outside of Quebec.

Separation is about twice as likely in first-time common-law relationships than in first-time marriages. About 60 per cent of common-law first relationships for couples in their thirties and forties do not last. The separation rate among first-marriage couples is 30 per cent. For those who do separate, subsequent living arrangements are more likely to be common law, a bond that seems less strong than formal marriage.

It is undeniable that high rates of separation and divorce, more stepfamilies and blended families, and an increase in single parenthood have brought about changes to the Canadian family. University of Toronto political scientist Neil Nevitte studied the value changes in Canada and in other developed nations from 1980 to 1990 using data from the World Values Survey. What is surprising, says Nevitte, is the "huge and increasing majority of people [who] still cleave to the idea that a child needs a conventional family environment to 'grow up happily.'"

Just as with rural family life, we should resist any temptation to romanticize the past or "conventional" family life. While there is much of value in the traditional, two-parent, long-term family, there has always been a dark side. Child and spousal abuse within families is not new, although today it is much more widely discussed than ever before. For much of Canada's history, abuse was a family secret.

*Family Violence in Canada* is a recent Statistics Canada report examining child abuse, children at risk, and spousal violence and homicides. The report, the fourth in a series, analyzes data from the National Longitudinal Survey of Children and Youth. Consistent with similar studies, the report finds that "children who are exposed to physical violence in the home tend to exhibit higher rates of depression, worry and frustration." Children who have seen or heard physical fights between adults or teens in their home are more than twice as likely to be physically aggressive, display emotional disorders, and to commit delinquent acts against property than those who have neither seen nor heard such fights.

Sadly, children are also victims of abuse and violence leading to death. Homicide rates for children and youth fluctuate from year to year, but over the twenty-six-year period covered by the study, family members were responsible for more than 60 per cent of the solved children and youth homicides.

Although the stresses and social problems affecting Canadian children and youth occur largely outside of school, Canadians increasingly look to their public schools to address them. Over the last two decades, public schools have adopted policies and practices to address a variety of social problems once the concern of the family and other institutions. For example, many public schools, like the inner-city school where George Thomas teaches, routinely provide hungry students with snacks or meals, and cognizant that family distress sometimes involves physical and sexual abuse, many school jurisdictions mount programs to teach children how to avoid abuse and how to disclose abuse if it occurs.

### WORK, WOMEN, AND CHILDREN

THE DEMANDS OF EMPLOYMENT stress the family and, in turn, schools. The shorter workweek promised by the postwar boom has not materialized for most Canadians. In fact, people are working longer hours, partly due to the shift in employment trends toward managerial and professional jobs that demand long hours. Today, almost one in five people works some over-time in any given week. Among those who aren't putting in extra hours at their day job, the trend toward moonlighting is particularly strong.

Over the past fifty years, more and more jobs were directly or indirectly tied to government services. Now, many governments are reducing health, education, and social services and eliminat-ing jobs. The transition from a resource to a service economy, uncertainty in employment as a consequence of economic reces-sion and globalization, cutbacks in government services, and increasing privatization have changed the nature of work. Canadians can no longer count on long-term employment.

A recent report by Statistics Canada proclaimed that "the entry of women into the paid workforce has been one of the dominant social trends in Canada over the last half century." In 1976, approximately 42 per cent of women fifteen years of age and older worked outside of the home. Today, the proportion is 56 per cent. In 1976, they comprised 37 per cent of the paid workforce. Women make up almost half the workforce today, but they often hold low-wage, part-time jobs. Currently, 10 per cent of men with paid employment work fewer than thirty hours per week. For women, the proportion is nearly 30 per cent.

How a society treats women and children is one indicator of its health. The single most important strategy to improve social and economic conditions is the education of women. By edu-cating women, a society improves the health of families and its economic and social vitality. And, in Canada, most families rely either substantially or solely on the earnings of women to main-tain their standard of living.

The Canadian situation is a good news, bad news story. The good news for Canada is that women have made significant achievements in education and employment over the past fifty years. The bad news is the persistence of barriers to full equality and the impact of inequalities on women, their children, and society.

According to Statistics Canada, between 1971 and 1996 the proportion of women with a university degree increased four times. A small gap remains between the number of university-educated women and men, but the difference is likely to decline further, because currently more than half of full-time students in universities are women. That's good news. The bad news is that women are still discouraged from taking courses in mathematics, science, and computer science, disciplines that tend to lead to higher paying jobs. And even if women do enter these fields, they often meet with a chilly reception.

The probability of women being employed increases with education. Only 38 per cent of women who attended, but did not complete, high school are employed. The proportion increases to approximately 60 per cent for those who have completed high school and/or taken some additional post-secondary education. Sixty-eight per cent of women who have earned a certificate or diploma from a community college are employed. And the employment rate climbs to 76 per cent of the women who have earned a university degree.

The economic value of getting a good education is clear from the Statistics Canada data reported above. What is even more striking is what happens to young men and women who have less than a grade nine education. Only 31 per cent of young men with less than grade nine are employed, and for women the percentage drops to 14 per cent.

Women continue to work in what some call occupational ghettos. Nearly 70 per cent of all women work in the traditional female spheres of teaching, health-related occupations, in clerical and administrative positions, and in sales or other service jobs. There has been some modest improvement over the past few years. In 1987, that proportion was 74 per cent.

Canadian women have been crossing occupational boundaries and breaking through glass ceilings. Today they make up about half of business and financial professionals, nearly half of all doctors and dentists, and approximately one-third of those in managerial positions. As I mentioned earlier, the picture in engineering, mathematics, and the sciences is not so rosy. In those fields, women make up only about 20 per cent of the workforce – and the proportion hasn't changed much over the past fifteen years.

The earnings gap between women and men is diminishing, but the gap remains significant, and the improvement has been small over the past twenty years. In most jobs, women today make about seventy-three cents for every dollar earned by a man performing the same work. Women also far outnumber men among low-income earners. Approximately half of the unattached senior women and more than half of all families headed by single mothers had incomes considered to be poverty level.

One of the striking income patterns in the post–Second World War period is the sharp increase in the employment rate for women with children. In the last twenty-five years, the rate has increased very sharply, especially for women with preschool-aged children. Today, approximately 60 per cent of women with children under age three are employed, about twice the rate in 1976. For single mothers with children under sixteen years of age, the employment rate is about 63 per cent, while 71 per cent of the mothers in two-parent families work outside the home.

There is little doubt that women have made significant gains in education and employment, though full equality has not been achieved. According to Neil Nevitte, even spousal relations among Canadians are becoming increasingly equal. This sounds like good news, but the reality is that women still do a disproportionate share of the unpaid work involved in caring for family and home. According to Statistics Canada, married women who are employed full-time and have at least one child under the age of nineteen spend an additional five hours per day in unpaid work. That's about an hour and a half more than their partners.

There are plenty of exceptions to this, of course. My friend Dave is a writer whose wife works outside of their home. Dave writes at home and is responsible for most of the child-rearing and homemaking. But he is a statistical oddity. In the vast majority of Canadian families, child-rearing remains primarily the responsibility of women. This is true even though the number of two-parent families with women working outside the home has increased dramatically.

Canada is a better society for having achieved greater equality in the workplace and the home for women, but the playing field is still uneven. Women still earn less than men, and even though there is strong evidence of greater equality between the sexes in conjugal relationships, significant inequalities remain. Women still provide most of the intellectual and emotional support for school-aged children in the home and at school.

The sharing of work within families usually does at least improve over time, the amount of time spent by fathers and mothers on childcare becoming more equal as children age. Equality is achieved by the time offspring are in their teens. Single mothers, of course, do not usually have the support of another adult in the home.

## CHANGING FAMILY CIRCUMSTANCES

PARENTAL INCOME AND EDUCATION exert strong influences on child-rearing and education, and couples beginning families later in life tend to have more formal education and higher incomes. Children in advantaged families are growing in number, but the number of children living in much more difficult circumstances is also increasing dramatically.

The Canadian Council on Social Development is an independent, national non-profit organization focusing on issues of social and economic security. The council considered the relationship of income to the well-being of children. Its report, authored by David Ross and Paul Roberts, found that in 1973 there was very little equality of income in Canada. But they discovered that it is worse today. In 1973, the poorest 40 per cent of Canadian families with children earned only 18.8 per cent of all income. About twenty-five years later, the poorest 40 per cent earned 13.6 per cent of all income. At the same time, the wealthiest 40 per cent of Canadian families with children saw their share of income rise from 62.6 per cent to 68.2 per cent. Put another way, in 1973 the most advantaged families had about three times the market income of low-income families. A quarter-century later, the gap between top and bottom was fivefold!

The presence of two parents contributes to the well-being of children. Children living in families with two parents are better adjusted and do better at school than children living in single-parent families or stepfamilies. This is true even when socio-economic conditions are controlled. Unfortunately, more than 30 per cent of all Canadian marriages and more than 60 per cent of common-law relationships end in divorce or separation.

The breakup of families can have a long-term effect on the lives of children. Children of families that have experienced divorce or separation are more likely to leave home at an earlier age because of family conflict. They are also less likely to return home after they have left. Teens whose parents divorce are more likely to remain unmarried. If they do marry, they are more likely to marry later and have their own marriages end in divorce or separation.

In 1968, Canada liberalized its divorce laws, freeing men and women from abusive and unfulfilling relationships. The divorce rate soared. Today, approximately one million Canadian families are headed by a single parent, typically a young woman between the ages of twenty-five and forty-four. Slightly more than half of female single parents work outside the home. As we have seen, single-parent families – especially those headed by women – are more likely to live in poverty.

Georgia confronts some of the challenges faced by single parents. She and her husband were first-year students at Concordia University in Montreal when Jeremy – now seven years old – was born. When Jeremy was less than a year old, Georgia discovered that her husband was having an affair with one of his classmates. When their attempts to address the problem were unsuccessful, they agreed to a divorce, with Georgia having custody for Jeremy. Jeremy's father moved to the United States and provides no child support.

Georgia left school to find work and establish a home for her and Jeremy. It was difficult to find a job in a depressed economy, but her few years of studying business enabled her to find a job as a bookkeeper. The small machinery company that hired Georgia started her at $9.00 an hour. Impressed by her work ethic and intelligence, they raised her salary six months later to $11.50 per hour. She now makes about $23,000 per year including benefits.

The neighbourhood in which Georgia found an apartment is not the best, but living there keeps the rent affordable. The apartment is located on a bus line that takes Georgia directly to work. The apartment is also near a park, where Georgia takes Jeremy on weekends. During the day, the park is pleasant enough, but in the evenings people, including teenagers from the community, use it as a place to buy drugs and drink.

Georgia is lucky that, despite the problems in the neighbourhood, there is an elementary school nearby with a childcare facility in the basement. Each weekday morning, Georgia takes Jeremy to the childcare centre. After school, Jeremy returns to the centre, where he plays until Georgia picks him up. But

Georgia worries that she may not be able to afford the centre's fees next year. Strapped for cash, the school board has threatened to raise the rent it charges the childcare centre.

Jeremy enjoys school, and is well liked by his teacher and peers. He is an average student but has problems with math concepts. When Georgia raised the matter with Jeremy's teacher, the teacher noted that Jeremy is one of the younger children in the class. She remarked that his difficulty with arithmetic is probably developmental – something he would "grow out of." Georgia asked Jeremy's teacher if Jeremy should be tested for a learning disability, but the teacher said there were many children with more serious problems. She suggested that Georgia work with Jeremy at home, and she provided some ideas about the sort of things they could do together.

Georgia is more fortunate than many single parents. Her income is above Statistics Canada's low-income cut-off, and Jeremy has before- and after-school care, which lets her work a normal schedule. Unlike many of the neighbourhood children, Jeremy participates in an organized activity outside of school, a Saturday-morning class in karate. He enjoys the class, and Georgia thinks it will build his self-confidence. Nevertheless, the demands on Georgia are significant. She has to do all the parenting plus working, preparing meals, and worrying about finances. She is particularly concerned about Jeremy's problems with arithmetic and about the influence of the social environment. Georgia has heard rumours of bullying in the neighbourhood.

Georgia and Jeremy would be in dire straits if it were not for social supports such as working-condition and wage legislation, health care, and the existence of daycare and community centres. But I've noticed that, as they age, baby boomers are complaining increasingly about "big government" and the taxes they pay to support government services and regulation. It's a topic that comes up frequently in conversation, fuelled in part by an increasingly pervasive ideology of individualism.

The complaints are aimed at a broad range of policies and services. Labour legislation is a frequent target, especially minimum-wage laws, regulations limiting hours of work and requiring payment for overtime, and maternity-leave provisions. People also complain about government-supported health care, social assistance, employment insurance premiums, and pension regulations.

What some critics of government do not recognize, or wilfully ignore, is that these regulations and policies provide essential support for families and communities. Without this support, families and communities cannot do their job of raising the young and preparing them for school. Without support – and sometimes even *with* support – children have a more difficult time in school, are more susceptible to negative peer and media influences, more likely to quit school before graduation, and run a greater risk of winding up unemployed or in jail.

Investing in families and communities pays permanent societal dividends. We should be *improving* the support we provide. But in some Canadian provinces, labour legislation is being amended to provide fewer protections and benefits for workers. Benefits, such as minimum wages and income assistance, are being reduced, and the range of services covered by health care is being pared down. These cutbacks create further stresses, especially among those who need the services most. It's no wonder that people are nostalgic for the (largely fictional) "good old days."

chapter three

# CHILDREN AND POVERTY

hen one of the body's organs is impaired, greater demands are placed on the body's other systems. Similarly, additional strain on the Canadian family, and on the resources it has for nurturing the young, places greater demands on Canada's other systems. If the other systems are healthy, they can help compensate for the impairment. If they are stressed, the help they provide is limited and the burden on other systems increases. Canada's failure to address child poverty contributes to its malaise. Child poverty stresses the other systems of support for Canadian families, including the public school.

In 1980, Rennie came from the Philippines to work in Canada as a nanny. She was eighteen. She cared for the children of a couple on Vancouver's west side who worked in the financial industry. In 1992, when the youngest child began secondary school, the couple helped Rennie find work cleaning the homes of their friends to supplement the income they paid her. They also wanted to help Rennie make the transition to other employment.

Rennie wanted to remain in Canada and bring her husband, Jorge, here as well. Jorge and Rennie had married in the mid-1980s, when Rennie went home to visit her family and friends. In 1993, Rennie's employers helped find a job for Jorge with a clothing manufacturing firm, enabling him to immigrate to

Canada. In 1995, Rennie gave birth to Lucia, and two years later to Miguel.

The Philippine community in Vancouver is very close and supportive of its members. This enabled Rennie to return to work soon after each baby was born. Other nannies took care of Lucia and Miguel when Rennie was either cleaning or stocking shelves at a department store.

By the time Lucia began school, in 2000, things were going well for Rennie and Jorge. They lived in a two-bedroom basement apartment in the home of friends of Rennie's first employer. Both were earning a steady income, and were even able to save a modest amount. But in 2001, the clothing manufacturer that Jorge worked for announced that in a few months it would be moving its manufacturing out of the country. Jorge began looking for work, hoping to find a job before the company moved.

Things have not worked out as Rennie and Jorge hoped. Jorge has been unable to find permanent employment. He looks for work regularly and takes whatever opportunities come his way. He gardens, works in construction, and helps Rennie clean the homes of her clients. They barely get by. There are times when there isn't enough money for food and Jorge and Rennie have to reduce the variety of food in their diet and eat more rice. They have skipped meals from time to time to feed the children. If things become much worse, they will probably look to their friends in the Philippine community for help rather than the food bank or social services.

Rennie and Jorge worry about their children's future. They see teenagers from immigrant communities being recruited to gangs and do not like the materialism that attracts these kids to gang membership. They see the power that television and other media have to promote the material goods their children ask for. However, despite their social and economic concerns, Rennie and Jorge are willing to do whatever it takes to remain in Canada.

## GROWING INEQUALITIES

DESPITE CANADA'S WEALTH, a growing number of Canadian families are poor. According to Canada's submission to the United Nations in September 2001, "The average Canadian family requires 75.4 weeks per year on the job at an average wage to cover basic annual expenses." In other words, Canadian families need more than one full-time wage to meet annual expenditures and stay out of poverty.

About one-fifth of all Canadian children live in poverty. But for children living in single-parent families, the situation is considerably worse. More than half of them live below the poverty level. Among young families – those in which the eldest person is thirty years old or younger – the rate of poverty has doubled over the past ten years. On the other hand, smaller families and delayed first births reduce the likelihood of child poverty for older parents.

The growing inequalities between the older parents and younger parents and between two-parent and single-parent families have consequences for the success of children. Jeremy and his single mom, Georgia, whom we met in the previous chapter, have a good relationship. Jeremy is well fed and clothed. Georgia has strong parenting skills. She is trying to help Jeremy overcome his difficulty with arithmetic, and provides a positive environment for Jeremy. The situation for other children living in low-income families is sometimes less positive. According to the Canadian Council on Social Development report authored by Roberts and Ross, low-income families are about twice as likely as high-income families to function poorly.

Georgia and Jeremy are representative of the one-quarter of low-income families living in neighbourhoods where there is drug use, excessive public drinking, or youth unrest. Happily, Jeremy seems to have formed good relations with other children and developed self-discipline and positive values – through karate and the example that Georgia sets for him. But, Jeremy is still young. The situation could change as he grows older. Ross and Roberts found that children in low-income families are much more likely to exhibit delinquent behaviours than are children in high-income families. They are also much more apt to have health problems and delayed vocabulary development and less likely to participate in organized sports or be employed in their teens.

The accident rate among poor children is ten times what it is for children not classified as poor, and the disability rate is twice as high. Young people from poor families are more likely to smoke, use drugs, and have problems with alcohol. Low birth weight is 1.4 times more likely, and the infant death rate is twice as high in poor families than in families that are not poor. With advanced medical techniques, the survival rate of low-birth-weight babies resulting from alcohol or drug abuse has increased dramatically. This has led to a parallel increase in the number of children entering schools with impaired physical and intellectual abilities.

Hunger is common for children from low-income households. Some schools – like the one where George Thomas teaches – provide breakfast and lunch programs to ensure that poor students have sufficient nourishment to attend to their studies. It is very difficult to think clearly on an empty stomach. Sadly, the problem of child hunger is simply too widespread and resources to meagre to meet the need fully.

According to a study conducted by Human Resources Development Canada (HRDC), the children who come to school hungry are six times as likely to live in one-parent families as in two-parent families. Hungry children are also more than eight times as likely to live in a family receiving social assistance than not. It is a mistake, however, to attribute hunger to lack of employment, since more than half the households that experience hunger receive their main income from employment. Their earnings are simply insufficient to meet their needs.

Families where a child is hungry have caregivers who are in poorer health, are more often affected by asthma, and smoke twice the number of cigarettes as caregivers in households that are not hungry. The HRDC study, using data from the National Longitudinal Survey of Children and Youth, found that hunger among children is also associated with the absence of two bio-logical parents, larger families, a mother who has not completed high school, and/or an aboriginal background.

Aboriginal families are overrepresented among Canada's poor. The average income gap between aboriginal and non-aboriginal Canadians remains large, despite the fact that it has narrowed somewhat over the past fifteen years. The consequences of poverty for aboriginal children are devastating. According to Canada's report to the United Nations, the rates of Fetal Alcohol Syndrome and Fetal Alcohol Effects among aboriginal peoples were between 10 and 30 per cent higher than the world inci-dence. Suicide rates for aboriginals are three times higher than for non-aboriginals in Canada. Aboriginal children are five times more likely to be in the care of family and social service agen-cies than non-aboriginal children.

The challenge of poverty is huge. Fortunately, we know what should be done. The disparity between the wages of women and men must be eliminated. Canada must ensure equal pay for work of equal value. The gap between the wages of women and men makes it much more likely that women who are lone parents will live with their children in poverty.

As I said before, women earn 30 per cent less than men performing the same work, predominate in seven of the ten lowest-paid occupations, and hold the majority of non-standard, part-time, and casual work. While two-thirds of men's work is paid, two-thirds of women's work is unpaid. Today, one family in five is headed by a lone parent, and more than 80 per cent of the time the parent is a woman. Children living with two parents have only about one chance in ten of living in poverty. But, for children living with lone parents, the chances are two out of three that they are poor.

Disadvantaged children often have developmental difficulties that impede their progress in school. Resources at home, such as books and computers, are fewer. Low-income parents often have less time to spend with their children.

## CHILDCARE

CHANGES IN CANADIAN SOCIETY, including a changing labour force, have increased the demand for childcare in Canada. The growing number of women in the labour force has helped drive the demand for childcare. According to Statistics Canada, between 1979 and 1999 the proportion of working mothers with children under the age of sixteen doubled to a record 69 per cent. Women who were employed during pregnancy typically return to work after giving birth, many within six months of childbirth and most within a year.

While childcare is beneficial, many Canadians cannot afford it. It makes intuitive sense, however, that quality childcare can alleviate some of the worst consequences of poverty for children. Dr. Ercilla Palacio-Quintin, a professor (now retired) in the department of psychology at Université du Québec à Trois-Rivières, compiled what is known about the impact of childcare on child development. The findings have implications for all children, but are especially important for children from less advantaged backgrounds.

Palacio-Quintin points out that it is important to differentiate among the different types of non-parental childcare services. She uses the term "day care" to refer to childcare centres, crèches, or day nurseries employing trained staff; family daycare centres; and individual daycare provided by a relative or babysitter. Daycare is beneficial for children whose cognitive and language abilities are not stimulated at home. According to Palacio-Quintin, a child's intellectual development, knowledge, and language are positively influenced by attending daycare. Greater benefits are achieved from facilities where staff have had training and have developed positive relationships with the children. The longer the child attends, the greater are the benefits. Children who have attended daycare perform better when they arrive at school and continue to perform better in language and mathematics as they progress through school.

The benefits of daycare for children are not confined to language and cognitive abilities. The moral development of attendees is greater than the moral development of non-attendees. "They are better able to assess the intent behind actions and to distinguish between moral and social transgressions," says Palacio-Quintin. When they are observed at play, children attending daycare are more social, more affectionate, more co-operative, and demonstrate more pro-social and less negative behaviour than children who do not attend.

Children with special needs also benefit from daycare centres. "Abused children who attend quality day-care centres," writes Palacio-Quintin, "have more [social] contact and more appropriate contact with teachers, express their affection to children and adults more often, seek emotional support from adults more often, and use positive means to attract attention" than abused children who do not attend daycare.

Few people dispute the benefits of early childhood education and its complement childcare. In a report published by the Childcare Resource and Research Unit of the University of Toronto's Centre for Urban and Community Studies, Gillian Doherty produced a review of studies comparing children who had non-parental childcare with those who didn't. She found that children who had non-parental childcare were better prepared for school than the children who had not had such experiences.

Doherty's report indicated that, by the time they entered school and in later elementary grades, children in non-parental childcare get along better with other children. Their teachers report that they make an easier transition to school. They have better cognitive and classroom skills, such as better developed vocabularies, and better ability to follow direction and resist distraction. These benefits seem to continue through the elementary years.

In a recent article, University of Toronto economist Michael Krashinsky reported that, in a study with his colleague Gordon Cleveland, they found a 2:1 payoff for public expenditures for childcare. "We measured two dollars of benefits for every dollar the government spent to enhance childcare." Krashinsky said that half of the benefit of the investment in daycare was realized in increased labour-force participation of mothers. The remaining benefits were derived from higher quality, early educational experiences that the children had, regardless of whether their parents worked.

Unfortunately, despite a number of promises, there is no Canadian policy to provide quality daycare for children. Politicians have teased nearly three generations of Canadian parents with promises of a national strategy on children that includes daycare. During Pierre Trudeau's tenure as prime minister, a task force on children looked promising. The Special Committee on Child Care established during Brian Mulroney's tenure also offered hope. And, in the election year of 1993, Jean Chrétien's Liberals made similar promises in its Red Book.

Jocelyne Tougas, a consultant on Quebec's childcare policy, says that the rest of Canada can learn much from Quebec. In a recent speech she explained why Quebec, despite an obsession with deficit reduction, decided to adopt a costly policy that other jurisdictions in Canada have avoided.

According to Tougas, the Quebec childcare strategy is one element in its policy of support for families. The policy includes a child benefit for low-income families, an improved maternity and parental insurance plan, and an education strategy for young children. She said, "By simultaneously promoting both full-time kindergarten for five-year-olds and multi-faceted early childhood and childcare agencies for children four years and under, the government gave credence to the central role it sees for childcare in children's healthy development, their success in school and their social integration."

The Quebec policy is based on the idea of universality. According to Tougas, "The idea is that all children, rich or poor, should be allowed to grow up in a stimulating and caring environment, whether their parents spend the day at home, at work or studying." Since the policy was implemented in 1997, the number of daycare centres in Quebec has doubled, and appears to be growing. Stable funding has enabled the agencies responsible to provide daycare on weekends and at hours outside of the eight-to-six pattern of most daycare facilities. Rural areas are being served, offering parents a choice between centre-based daycare and family daycare.

The fact that 98 per cent of the five-year-olds in Quebec are enrolled in full-day kindergarten indicates that its complementary policy is also working well. As Quebec's policies take hold, there has also been growth in school-related daycare enrolment.

Studies are unanimous, says Palacio-Quintin, that children do better in daycare centres with the following characteristics: "a qualified and stable staff, a good educational program, good teacher-child and parent-daycare relationships, groups that are not too big, a reasonable amount of safe space, and safe hygiene practices."

The bad news is that there aren't sufficient daycare facilities in Canada, and that it is more likely that advantaged children will attend them than disadvantaged children.

In 1998, the Childcare Resource and Research Unit at the University of Toronto counted the number of centre-based full-day and part-day childcare spaces in Canada. They found 329,950 spaces. In addition, there were 155,163 school-aged daycare spaces and 70,270 regulated in-home family daycare spaces. The total, slightly more than a half-million spaces, is far from enough for the children up to twelve years of age in Canada who need such care.

## PROVIDING CHILDCARE IN SCHOOLS

SEVERAL YEARS AGO, I was invited to address a branch of the Women's Canadian Club about the issues facing education. I told them I thought Canadians were fortunate in having forged a strong system of education that, despite many challenges, was serving us well. However, I said I was concerned about the young men and women of high school age. They seemed to me to be desperately looking for a connection with the larger community. Like me, the young people I knew could see that the opportunities for them to assume adult responsibilities were becoming more limited. Jobs for young people were relatively scarce. More and more of their older siblings were returning home to live while they tried to find work or while they gathered resources to start a family of their own. The period of adolescent dependence seemed to be increasing.

I told the women of the Canadian Club that I felt these young people were looking for the opportunity to connect with the community and make a meaningful contribution. They asked what might be done to foster such a connection, and I said we should make secondary schools the centre for universal daycare and have the secondary students help the primary caregivers and teachers working in those centres.

Notwithstanding my concerns about an increasingly crowded school curriculum, I suggested that all secondary school students should have the opportunity to enrol in a year-long child development class during grades eight or nine. In the class they would learn about the needs of infants and young children and about the complexity of caring for those needs. Those who successfully completed the course would be permitted to work as a teacher's assistant in the daycare centre and earn credit toward graduation.

I thought the proposal had a number of important features to recommend it. First, and perhaps most important, young people would learn about their responsibilities to the young and develop capacities that should enable them to become better parents. Second, the provision of daycare by secondary school students would provide them with demonstrably meaningful work that should develop their self-esteem in a way that flipping hamburgers at a fast-food restaurant cannot. Third, in addition to the social and educational benefits, daycare would be less costly to society. The proposal also makes secondary schools less age-segregated by including the children attending daycare and their parents.

## CANADA LAGS BEHIND

ACCORDING TO A REPORT by the Canadian Policy Research Networks, Canada lags behind many European countries in the policies it has made to support young children and families. The report, authored by Sharon Stroick and Jane Jenson, attributes the gap between Canada and the European countries to value differences. In Canada, the United States, and Britain, children are seen primarily as a responsibility of the family. In countries such as Norway, France, the Netherlands, Germany, and Sweden, children are seen as a responsibility of both the family and the larger society.

The value differences are evident in the maternity benefits of different countries. According to Stroick and Jenson, the differences are ones of degree rather than kind. For example, although the period of support for maternity leave in the European countries and Canada is about the same, the European countries provide for between 80 and 100 per cent of earnings. Canada's maternity benefit is about 55 per cent of earnings.

The value differences are also evident in the number of children aged three to six in publicly funded daycare or school. For Canada, the proportion is approximately 45 per cent. In Europe, 45 per cent is the low end of the scale, which ranges from 45 per cent (in Norway) to 99 per cent (in France). Even countries that place primary emphasis for the care of children on families do better than Canada. In Italy, 91 per cent of children between the ages of three and six are in publicly funded childcare. In Spain, the figure is 84 per cent. In the Federal Republic of Germany, it is 78 per cent.

Our public schools are struggling to address the problems caused by Canada's failure to provide better support for families. We need more family-friendly policies. As I mentioned earlier, Canada must eliminate the wage gap between women and men. Canada also needs a policy of universal quality daycare. The policy should be integrated with other measures, such as generous maternity and parental leaves and full-day kindergarten for all children. Parents should be able to visit schools to talk with teachers about their child's progress without being penalized by loss of pay or worse. These initiatives should be free or heavily subsidized by government. The long-term benefits will more than offset the investment.

Without strong, healthy communities, advantaged Canadians may soon be doing what their counterparts in other countries have already done: erecting compounds surrounded by razor wire to defend their privileges from the disadvantaged. All levels of government are cutting programs in the name of fiscal responsibility. They are reacting to public and media campaigns to cut the deficit. They forget that it is sometimes necessary to borrow money (like a mortgage) in order to put our social house in order.

There are disturbing signs that the improvements made between 1960 and the mid-1980s have been eroded. The campaign to lower public debt has developed into a frenzied attack against the use of taxation to reduce income inequality. Also under attack are health and social programs developed to shield Canadians from the most negative consequences of poverty.

One of the lessons learned in the marketplace is that "you get what you pay for." That is no less true with public schooling. Governmental stinginess has its consequences.

We seem to be going in the wrong direction. We should be enhancing health, social, and educational programs. It makes economic and social sense to provide affordable daycare for children and ensure they have access to full-day kindergarten. Society benefits when both parents do not have to work outside the home during the most crucial period of the children's development – the first few years of life – and when parents are able to visit their children's school without losing pay.

Succumbing to deficit mania may reduce government expenditures in the short run, but it won't do much to address Canada's main problem: the disintegration of community. Governments should be pursuing social policies that increase the connections between children and their parents.

With increasing independence and individualism, Canada must seek ways of recreating community. Our efforts will be well spent if we can start the next generation off on a firm foundation by providing them and their families with the support they need to take advantage of the opportunities that public schooling provides. We owe at least this much to them and to ourselves. In fact, Canada's survival as a healthy, productive nation depends upon it.

# chapter four

# MEDIA, PEERS, AND MORALS

More Canadian children today have less adult supervision than at any previous time. Only the most affluent parents can afford daycare, and even they may be unable to make satisfactory arrangements. Initial socialization was once provided directly by family members. Now, it is provided by a combination of parents, caregivers, peers, and the media. Sometimes referred to as "the other parent," television has exposed young children to values and experiences that children fifty years ago would not have acquired until they had attended school for some time, if ever. Though still eager to learn when they come to school, today's youngsters are equally eager to be entertained.

## THE "OTHER" PARENTS

TODAY, CANADIAN CHILDREN spend more time with their friends, television, the Internet, DVDs, electronic games, films, and magazines than they do in school or with adult family members. They are more sophisticated and better informed about politics, social problems, and cultural trends than previous generations of children. At the same time, they are subjected to a steady diet of aggression, violence, sexually explicit content, and Cinderella fantasies. They have access to images and information that affect their attitudes toward school, their capacity for learning, and their behaviour toward one another in and outside of school.

While washing my car in the driveway one day, I overhear two kids from the neighbourhood bragging about having just made a "big score." Jagwant and Randy, twelve-year-old video-game aficionados, have found where Randy's older brother, Keenan, keeps his video-game collection. And, despite repeated warnings from Randy's mother, they have just played Keenan's most recent acquisition, GTA III, or Grand Theft Auto III to the uninitiated like me.

Jagwant and Randy are hanging out with friends, boasting about their find. From what I gather, GTA III is a game in which the player is a criminal working his way up the ladder through car theft, murder, and, obviously, evading the police. I infer from what they are telling their friends that the graphics are incredible and the choices afforded the player (or players, since I can't tell from what they have said) are numerous. A player who is caught by the police must begin again at the bottom.

Randy and Jagwant know this game is not intended for kids their age. Like many such games, violence is a main theme. Players use machine guns, assault rifles, and hand grenades. There are "penalties" for killing, but a player can amass six penalty points before he has to start again at the beginning. Automobiles crash and, apparently, at some point during the game a prostitute also propositions the player. If the player kills her, he gets back the money he and others have paid her.

I do not think that Randy and Jagwant or their friends confuse game violence with real violence. These are good kids. They play hockey and help with chores when their parents ask them (or issue mild threats, like most of us do). While they haven't offered to help me polish the car, they speak when spoken to and are typically polite. I say "typically" because when they were into the WWE (World Wresting Entertainment) on television a few years back, they often acted out what they saw on TV, complete with verbal pyrotechnics and headlocks.

## MEDIA AND VIOLENCE

IN THE AFTERMATH of the 1999 shooting at Columbine High School in Littleton, Colorado, during which thirteen students were killed by two fellow students, United States President Bill Clinton asked the U.S. Federal Trade Commission (FTC) and the Department of Justice to study the way that the movie, music recording, and computer and video-game industries "market and advertise products with violent content to youngsters." Clinton asked two questions: "Do the industries promote products they themselves acknowledge warrant parental caution in venues where children make up a substantial percentage of the audience? And are these advertisements intended to attract children and teenagers?" When the FTC released its report in September 2000, it said the answer to both questions was "yes" for each of the sectors in the entertainment industry it had been asked to study.

The commission selected for study 118 video games rated "Mature" because of their violent content. Eighty-three games were marketed to children under seventeen. In fact, the marketing plans for sixty of the games expressly included children under seventeen in the target audience. The marketing plans for another twenty-three games indicated they would be advertised in magazines or on television shows where a majority or substantial proportion of the audience was less than seventeen years of age.

The commission also studied musical recordings labelled as having explicitly violent content, and the results were much the same.

The results for the movie industry were even more dramatic. The commission studied the marketing plans for forty-four movies rated R for violent content. It found that advertising for thirty-five movies was aimed at children under seventeen. The marketing plans for twenty-eight movies said directly that the movie's intended audience included children under seventeen. The plans for the remaining movies detailed strategies directed toward the under-seventeen audience such as promoting them in high schools or publications with a substantial under-seventeen audience.

The commission also studied children's ability to buy or view violent entertainment material. It found that "most retailers make little effort to restrict children's access to products with violent content." Slightly less than half of the movie theatres studied allowed unaccompanied children ages thirteen to sixteen to see R-rated films. It found that children ages thirteen to sixteen without adult supervision were able to buy explicit recordings as well as Mature-rated video games a staggering 85 per cent of the time.

I don't think playing GTA III or watching WWE is making Randy and Jagwant more aggressive, but I am not certain. Research by Craig Anderson and Karen Dill appearing in the April 2000 issue of the *Journal of Personality and Social Psychology* provides evidence that should prompt concern about video games and aggressive thoughts, feelings, and behaviour. Most studies linking violent video games with aggression do so by correlating one with the other. Showing a correlation between two things is not the same as demonstrating cause and effect.

Anderson and Dill's laboratory experiment was able to show a causal connection between playing violent video games and aggression. They recruited university students for a laboratory experiment. In the experiment the students who played a violent video game behaved more aggressively toward an opponent in a subsequent assessment than did students who had played a non-violent video game.

Anderson and Dill caution that a direct connection between playing violent video games and aggression cannot be established with a single study. Nonetheless, they expressed the view that their results "confirm that parents, educators, and society in general should be concerned about the prevalence of violent video games in modern society, especially given recent advances in the realism of video game violence."

Anderson and Dill argue that some "characteristics of violent video games suggests that their dangers may well be greater than the dangers of violent television or violent movies." By assuming the identity of the hero in a violent video game, controlling the player's actions, and seeing the action "through the eyes of that character," the impact of a video game is potentially greater than other media.

A second reason for concern, according to Anderson and Dill, is that the active role of the video-game player may lead to a more aggressive behavioural pattern than that of a passive viewer identifying with a hero in a violent movie or television drama. Another difference is that violent video-game players are immersed in a complete environment in which aggression is modelled, rehearsed, and rewarded. These conditions are not as powerful when watching movies or television.

Anderson and Dill's research isn't conclusive by any means. But it does make me uneasy about Jagwant and Randy's exposure to violent games like GTA III. Much more research is needed on the effects of violent video games. If the effects of playing such games turn out to be detrimental and affect behaviour in other settings, we need to decide how to address one of the more pervasive influences on young men and women.

All in all, Randy and Jagwant seem typical of kids their age. They get "hyped" by what they see or the games they play, but it doesn't appear to affect their behaviour in the long term. The consequences for children who live in families in distress, or who are physically abused, emotionally disturbed, or have learning disabilities may be different.

## YOUTH AGGRESSION

RANDY AND JAGWANT come from families that supervise their behaviour. The boys have learned to use means other than physical aggression to solve problems. But for children who do not learn such lessons early in life the situation is much different. Those children are at greater risk of having a variety of problems.

According to Richard Tremblay, Canada research chair of child development at the University of Montreal, children who do not learn alternatives to physical aggression early in life are more likely to be hyperactive and inattentive. They are less likely to respond when others need help. They are often rejected or isolated by their classmates. They are more disruptive in school. Their grades are lower. Substance abuse and sexual intercourse occur earlier and more frequently than for children who have learned to solve conflicts peacefully. They are more likely to leave school before graduation, to have serious accidents, to engage in violent behaviour, and to be charged under Canada's Young Offenders Act.

Schools suffer the consequences of failed parenting and pre-school socialization. Although violence and aggression are relatively uncommon, their increasing occurrence has become an issue that schools cannot ignore. Over the course of the last two decades, many school districts adopted policies of zero tolerance for, and programs to address, violence and aggression. Most school jurisdictions have implemented a variety of child-abuse prevention, bully-proofing, and "effective discipline" programs. They are attempting to address problems that have their origin in failed pre-school socialization.

According to Tremblay, studies following aggressive children into their adult years have shown that there are extremely negative consequences for aggressive individuals, for their mates, their children, and for the communities in which they live. These consequences include early parenthood, unemployment, family violence, and poverty. "From this perspective," says Tremblay, "failure to teach children to regulate violent behaviour during the early years leads to poverty much more clearly than poverty leads to violence."

Aggression between young people is creating stress in schools. Although they are reputed to underreport, about 15 per cent of Canadian students say their peers abuse them. This figure is consistent with reports from other countries. In 1997, the National Crime Prevention Council of Canada interviewed six thousand Canadian students from grade one to eight. Six per cent of the students admitted to bullying other children more than once or twice in the previous six weeks. Twenty per cent admitted to being involved as either a bully or victim more than once or twice during the school term.

The death of fourteen-year-old Reena Virk in November 1997 is an indication that bullying is a serious problem for children and youth, including girls and young women. Virk, described by the media as an overweight Indo-Canadian teenager who did not fit in, was beaten and drowned in a suburban community outside of Victoria, B.C. Six young women and one young man between the ages of fourteen and sixteen were sentenced for their respective roles in the beating.

Eighteen months after the Virk death, a fourteen-year-old student in a high school in Taber, Alberta, shot three students, killing one. He said that he had been teased and beaten by other students throughout his school career. In Surrey, B.C., less than a year later, Hamed Nastoh jumped to his death from a bridge. He left a lengthy note about how he had been called names and teased at school. These incidents attracted considerable media attention and prompted speculation about the factors that contribute to deviant behaviour.

Scholars from the University of Guelph and University of Toronto analyzed data from the National Longitudinal Survey of Children and Youth. While their findings may not apply to the Virk, Taber, and Nastoh incidents, they shed light on what they call problem behaviour and delinquency. They found a number of interesting connections between self-reported involvement in aggressive behaviours and perceived academic ability and aspirations. Although they caution against imputing a causal connection to any of the factors, they found that "children who were less committed to schools were more likely to be involved in aggressive behaviour."

Their research found that children who report disliking school are three times more likely to say they have been involved in aggressive acts than are children who say they like school a lot. In general, "children who do not like school, think they are not doing well, think grades are not important, and do not want to go far in school are more likely to be involved in aggressive acts." They also found that the social relationships that students had in school were related to their involvement in aggressive acts. According to their study, published by Statistics Canada, children are more likely to be involved in aggressive behaviours when they "feel unsafe at school, that they are being bullied, that other children say mean things to them, and that they feel like an outsider."

Youth involved in delinquent acts involving property are, similarly, more likely to have low educational aspirations. In general, "children who do not like school, whose school progress is poor and think that grades are not important are more likely to be involved in delinquent acts involving property." Low educational aspirations, the belief that teachers do not like them and do not treat them fairly, and skipping classes are also associated with delinquent acts involving property.

School academic and social factors are not the only things leading to delinquent and aggressive behaviour. Risk factors in the family and environment are also associated with such behaviours. Basically, the more risk factors children and youth face, the more likely they are to say they are engaged in aggressive and delinquent behaviours.

## YOUNG WOMEN AND MEDIA

JACQUIE AND HER FRIEND CAITLIN, two of the many kids in my neighbourhood, are as different from Jagwant and Randy as night from day. Although they are about the same age as Randy and Jag, they have very different interests. As soon as they return from school, they go to Jacquie's house, where the family room has a television and a home computer. Jacquie's parents both work outside of the home, but Jacquie's mother, a secretary at a local high school, gets home most afternoons between 4:45 and 5:00.

Jacquie and Caitlin use instant messaging to communicate with friends from whom they have just parted at school and with whom they will talk on the telephone at some point over the next few hours. They multitask, sending messages to their friends, visiting on-line chat rooms, and watching television simultaneously. They also consume a steady diet of CDs, fashion magazines, and music videos.

Jacquie's mother, Lynne, and her father, Tom, are attentive parents, concerned about Jacquie's welfare. "I thought I was raising a feminist," Lynne remarks. We had been talking about the challenges of raising children. "We tried to avoid reinforcing stereotypes by not buying games and toys that are targeted to girls. I don't wear much makeup or buy those fashion or diet magazines that you find at the checkout counter. Tom shares the housework, when he can."

"What gets me are those magazines and the TV," adds Lynne. "I mean, where does she get her interest in them?" Like many of their friends, Caitlin and Jacquie are conscious of their appearance. It isn't surprising that weight, fashion, and relationships figure prominently in their conversations. Jacquie and Caitlin are heavy media consumers. In addition to fashion magazines, Jacquie and Caitlin see advertisements about weight loss regimes advertised on the Internet. And though they don't watch as much television as some of their friends, they do watch.

The Canadian average for kids their age is about sixteen hours of TV per week, but Jacquie's parents limit her amount of TV time to ten hours per week, which Lynne monitors. "I get home early enough after school that I can put some limits on the amount of television they watch. I know that Cait's folks put limits too. But it's the content that just boggles my mind. I think of myself as pretty liberated, but the images those kids see wouldn't have even occurred to us when we were kids." Like many other girls their age, Caitlin and Jacquie are fans of Britney Spears and Christina Aquilera. They read *Seventeen*, a magazine whose cover recently asked, "IS THAT MY BUTT?"

We feed young women stories in the media that tell them a man will rescue them from their social situation. It is an insidious fairy tale. One of the problems with the "Cinderella myth" is that it misleads and debilitates young women and it teaches young men the wrong attitudes toward the opposite sex. Economic independence of women is essential for a democratic society. Canada is moving in the right direction, but it has a long way to go.

## MEDIA CONSUMPTION TRENDS

TELEVISION VIEWING among all Canadians has been declining in recent years. According to Statistics Canada, the amount of time that Canadians spend watching television has declined approximately 6 per cent, from 23.1 hours per week in 1990 to 21.6 hours in 1999. The change for children between the ages of two and eleven and for teens twelve to seventeen is more dramatic. Television viewing among children has dropped more than 19 per cent, from 19.2 hours per week to 15.5 hours. Among teens, the drop was more than 8 per cent, from 16.9 hours per week to 15.5 hours.

There is considerable variation among Canadian children and teens in their television viewing patterns. Children in British Columbia and teens in Prince Edward Island watch less television than their peers, about 13 hours per week. New Brunswick teens, children in Newfoundland, and French-speaking children in Quebec watch the most television of all, about 17.5 hours per week for New Brunswick teens and 19 hours per week for the children in Quebec and Newfoundland.

One probable reason for the decline in television viewing is the rapid growth in use of video games, the Internet, and the convergence of Internet and television technologies. High-speed Internet connections make it possible for kids like Jacquie and Caitlin to watch videos on the computer and listen to music on the radio while they e-mail their friends. Images and music can be saved on their home computers and seen or heard repeatedly. Another factor is that Canadians are going to the movies more than ever before. In 1998–99, Canadians made 112.8 million visits to the movies, a thirty-eight-year high.

## TITANIC MARKETING

TEENAGERS, ESPECIALLY GIRLS, are avid media consumers willing to spend money. According to Cynthia Fuchs, a film studies professor at George Mason University, the film *Titanic* was a key moment for corporations involved in the music, fashion, and fast-food industries. Industry marketing analysts noted that it was repeated visits by teenage girls that gave *Titanic* its huge box-office receipts.

When the *Titanic* video debuted in September 1998, Paramount Home Video mounted the largest marketing campaign it had ever conducted. The campaign included corporate partnerships with Sprint and Max Factor. Among them, the corporate sponsors spent $50 million.

Customers who signed up for Sprint long-distance services received a voucher they could use to purchase the video. Alternately, customers who purchased the video could redeem a coupon if they switched to Sprint. The Sprint promotion was supported with TV, print, on-line, and in-store advertising, and with

more than five thousand Sprint displays in Radio Shack outlets.
For Max Factor, the deal with Paramount was its largest
marketing campaign ever. Max Factor created a special line of
cosmetics supposedly inspired by the film. Customers who purchased the *Titanic* video and ten dollars' worth of Max Factor
products received a free copy of the book *James Cameron's Titanic*.
Max Factor promoted its *Titanic* line of cosmetics with sixty
thousand in-store displays.

## MEDIA AND SEXUALITY

ALTHOUGH THEY ARE NOT YET TEENAGERS, I asked Jacquie and
Caitlin whom they would most like to be, if they could change
places with anyone for just one day. Without hesitation they both
said Britney Spears. "Why?" I asked. "Justin is so cute," giggled
Cait. She was referring to Britney's fellow former Mouseketeer,
Justin Timberlake of 'NSYNC, who was rumoured at the time
to be Britney's boyfriend.

Timberlake and Spears represent a long tradition of inaccessi-
ble teen idols that enable kids like Jacquie and Cait to explore their
growing sexuality. They can have, as Cait does, a foldout poster
of Timberlake in their bedrooms and watch him in music videos.
"I draw the line at the concerts," says Jacquie's mother. "Those
kids are just too young to go to concerts by themselves . . . and
they wouldn't be caught dead at one with a parent! So concerts
are out for now."

Lynne, Jacquie's mother, sees the girls' infatuation with Justin
Timberlake as harmless, much like her own infatuation with
David Cassidy from *The Partridge Family* in the early 1970s.

Jeffrey Epstein is a contributor to magazines such as *Teen
Movieline*, *Cosmo Girl*, and the *Advocate*, a gay and lesbian news-
magazine. He observes that "teen idols have long served as a
bridge between childhood and sexual maturity" for young girls
by providing "safe objects of first affection – training crushes, so

to speak. . . .What's been largely unspoken until recently," says Epstein, "is that these pop stars often serve a similar role for boys who are discovering their same-sex orientation."

A valuable source of entertainment and information for young and old alike, the Internet poses some hazards. "We keep the computer and the TV in the family room so that we can monitor what Jacquie sees," explains Lynne, "at least when we are home." "I get e-mails that I don't want to get, just from being connected," she says. "Pornography and Viagra, stock tips, and all sorts of products. If you think adults receive a lot of unwanted junk, you should see what the kids get when they browse the on-line music sites and fan magazines. All sorts of stuff pops up. That's why I like to keep an eye on things."

Culled from who-knows-where, e-mail addresses are used to broadcast e-mails to people who have never solicited the material, including messages advertising how cheaply one can send such mass e-mail messages to others. Children are exposed to images that, in times past, they would rarely see or see only with great difficulty. Annoying for adults, it can be disturbing for children.

Children are also approached on the Internet by predatory adults posing as children or teens in on-line chat rooms.

Parents who have the time and are media-aware, like Lynne, are relatively few. Schools increasingly fill the void left by parents strapped for time or who lack the knowledge or comfort level addressing such topics.

"In the school district where I work, they use a program about Internet safety called *Missing*," says Lynne. The program shows how children are recruited by predators and uses a game format to challenge them to find a child who has been persuaded to run away by a predator. "It is pretty realistic and frightening, but I guess it helps reinforce the message about being cautious on the Internet."

## MEDIA MESSAGES

MEDIA BOMBARD US with messages to consume endless goods and services. At the same time, Canada's poor have barely enough money to get by. The message is that those with money are worthy, and those without money are out of luck. If you don't measure up economically, it's your own fault. This is not a physically, emotionally, or socially healthy situation.

Canada has traditionally relied on the family, church, and community to provide the structure that young children need. That may have worked in small, rural communities, where families were units that worked together. But if it did work – and I think we have romanticized the past – it no longer does. Families are overburdened, communities are more fragmented, and religion is less influential than in the past.

Today, we leave too much of the early socialization of children to chance or the media. Young children need to be taught to be co-operative human beings, and we miss crucial opportunities by not doing so until children enter school. Schools cannot overcome the failure of pre-school socialization. We overburden schools by expecting them to make up in kindergarten or grade one for what children should have received in the first five years. Our society imposes many pressures on schools. Should schools, as a consequence, expand their scope of activities or should they, in turn, demand that other institutions do more to address these pressures?

Veteran teachers say they can see the consequences of exposure to television, film, video games, and popular music. They say although aggression and violence have increased, schools are, however, still the safest places for children in most communities. Teachers are much more attentive to bullying, aggression, and violence and better equipped to address them than in the past.

A more common consequence of media exposure is that students expect their teachers to entertain them and deliver fast-paced lessons. The problem is that much schoolwork demands systematic and sustained mental effort that many students find difficult or boring. It is a problem for which there are no easy solutions.

Limiting the exposure of students to popular media and balancing it with physical activity and social play is helpful. But parents whose work keeps them out of the home until after their children have returned from school find imposing reasonable limits on media and arranging and supervising physical activity and social play challenging, if not impossible.

It is also helpful if parents provide an example of selective use of media for their children, express support for education, provide their children with places to study that are free from competing distractions, and ensure that their children get sufficient sleep. Each of these practices contributes to the child's receptivity to education.

# chapter five

# CONFLICTING PHILOSOPHIES

A few years ago, the father of a student in West Vancouver, B.C., went to court because his son's teacher did not teach him about the Industrial Revolution. The father hired someone to tutor his son. The father then went to small claims court to recover the money he had paid, plus an additional amount for "disability" arising from the teacher's failure to instruct his son and his classmates on the topic.

The parent believed that teachers should be required to teach all of the material in the provincial curriculum guides and that he should be able to compare a teacher's course outline with the curriculum guidelines to determine if there was a gap. The school board's chairperson said that would be impractical, if not impossible. He pointed out that the guidelines contain much more material than can be addressed in the time allotted and that teachers should be free to tailor the curriculum to the needs and characteristics of the students in the class.

In dismissing the case, the judge noted that the curriculum is a broad framework within which teachers must have discretion. The boy's father considered it unacceptable that teachers can decide what content they include to address the goals of the curriculum, though he did agree that they should have discretion about teaching methodology.

Not all parents agree that teachers should be able to choose their teaching methods. Local news media often contain stories on the controversies about public schooling that erupt in communities from time to time, and debates about content and instructional methods in reading, mathematics, science, and social studies are often heated. They fuel conflicts in schools and in the community.

An example of such conflict arose not long ago in Richmond, B.C., where parents launched a proposal to establish a "traditional" school. The clash over this proposal illustrates many of the differences in educational philosophy affecting public schools and the tensions such differences create in communities.

## A "TRADITIONAL" SCHOOL DEBATE

IN 1995, A GROUP OF PARENTS in Richmond petitioned the local school board for a "traditional" school. The group was composed primarily of Chinese immigrants who had come to Canada seeking a better education for their children and better lives for themselves. They were at first unfamiliar, and later uncomfortable, with the informality of the elementary school education their children were receiving. The parents requested that the Board of School Trustees establish a school that focused on reading, writing, and arithmetic and required homework. They wanted an emphasis on "traditional" values, such as honesty, courtesy, and responsibility. They also wanted letter grades used to assess student work, "direct instruction," and school uniforms. They did not want multi-grade classes.

The parents who supported the program said, "Rather than expecting a single system to meet everyone's needs, public education should reflect our democratic society and provide choice." The parents argued that other school districts already made provision for a variety of alternative programs, such as French, Montessori, visual and fine arts, "fundamental," academic, as well as "traditional" schools. Their submission to the school board contained proposals addressing various facets of school life. These included the curriculum, the instructional methods used, the nature of the school's administration, and its facilities.

In December 1995, the Richmond School Board referred the parents' proposal to its District Management Committee for analysis and comment. From there, it was sent to the board's Education Committee. That committee made recommendations to the full board. The details of the parents' proposal, and the analysis and commentary by the District Management Committee, read much like the educational debates that have occurred for nearly a hundred years.

The parents proposed a curriculum consistent with requirements of the Ministry of Education, "though structured in a manner which is systematic, consistent, and sequential yet flexible enough to meet the needs and abilities of individual students." The proposed "traditional" school was to be available to all students in the district on a "first come, first served" basis. In proposing such a school, the parents wanted more than "opportunities to learn." They also wanted proof; they included a requirement that each student "demonstrate that he has learned."

In its response, the District Management Committee recounted the remark of a kindergarten teacher who said, "You can't yell 'bloom' at a rose," to illustrate that children learn at different rates. The parents' interest in ensuring that students learn was consistent with both board and ministry policy, the management committee said, but the "apparent expectation for the degree of control which can actually be gained over learning is not consistent with these policies or with educational research and experience."

Teachers, wrote the committee, "can and do provide a highly structured educational learning program," the purpose of which is to "support" rather than "control" student learning. The purpose of assessment is "not to provide quality control but to provide feedback."

The parents' proposal quoted extensively from Helen Raham, the executive director of Teachers for Excellence, in support of "direct instruction." Direct instruction is an approach to teaching basic skills that emphasizes sequential, small-step, teacher-led instruction. Teachers using this approach guide student activity to ensure a high-level of accuracy. They correct errors before students can "practise" their mistakes and develop habits that are difficult to change. When students have achieved a high level of mastery, the teacher provides independent practice to ensure they can respond fluently. At that point, students should not have to think through basic operations each time they encounter problems involving the same thought processes.

According to Raham, "The sequential learning instruction will be the constant that gives students the capabilities they need to become independent learners and problem solvers." The common-sense logic of direct instruction was very appealing to the Richmond parents. It related directly to their concerns. But the district committee said the ideas were "simplistic and do not reflect an achievable reality." The committee asserted, "The statement and the beliefs that underlie it are not consistent with the basic principles of the educational program in British Columbia." The committee asked, "What happens if a student is unable to master a particular skill at the time and in the way that it is presented due to personal stress, neurological differences or even lack of will?"

The committee saw a "building block" analogy implicit in Raham's "sequential learning structure" and rejected it. It argued that "even when students do experience success it was misleading to speak of 'mastery,'" because "learning does not consist of the sequential accumulation of discrete bits of knowledge or skill." The committee believed that although children can understand concepts such as "probability at some level, the concept itself is sufficiently complex that it continues to be re-examined right through to graduate level of university."

In her defence of direct instruction, Raham had tried to make clear that she was not advocating "rote learning or memoriza- tion without meaning" or "lock-step instruction." According to Raham, direct instruction involves "active learning" for which teachers will use "a whole range of grouping, activities, resources, and delivery techniques."

The "building block" analogy, the question about a stu- dent unable to master a particular skill, and the complexity of probability, were rhetorical devices that avoided the issue of the suitability of direct instruction as an appropriate approach. Nevertheless, in 1996, after months of study, the Richmond School Board rejected the request by a vote of six to one.

Two years later, in April 1998, the Traditional School Parents' Group (Richmond Division) submitted another proposal to develop a "traditional" elementary school. In support of their proposal, they submitted a petition signed by three thousand Richmond residents. This second proposal described its mission as "striving toward individual excellence in education by pro- viding a structured approach to learning whereby students acquire skills in a systematic way, by establishing a clearly defined standard of behaviour and by encouraging a partnership between home and school."

The proposal rekindled the controversy that had begun three years earlier. The proposal made clear that the school, in accor- dance with the School Act, would not teach any doctrinal beliefs. The proposal asserted that the school would operate with "stan- dards of behaviour which have traditionally been regarded as foundational to our Canadian society." Its statement of philoso- phy called for "respect for human and property rights of others, respect for roles of legitimate authority in home, community, and country, and respect for the contributions of those more or less capable than oneself in given areas." It also called for progressively greater responsibility for students as they demonstrated maturity and self-discipline.

The proposed philosophy also addressed "concern for others" and "a sense of one's own self-worth." The former was defined to include "helpfulness in school and community; co-operation and harmony between individuals and groups throughout the school; tolerance towards those with whose ideas one disagrees; politeness and kindness." "Violence, ridicule, and rude, profane or obscene language" would not be tolerated. A sense of one's self-worth was defined to include a "developing awareness in each student of the unique contribution he/she can make to his/her own well-being, and that of society, by fulfilling his/her capacity for clear, honest thinking, bodily fitness, and appreciation for non-materialistic concepts such as beauty, truth, and sensitivity to the needs of others."

Under the heading "purposefulness," the proposal called upon teachers to be responsible for setting worthwhile goals. It argued that goals should be consistent with a student's potential "to advance the highest possible intellectual, creative, physical, social and ethical development." It envisioned that teachers would assist students to understand the purposes of these goals, and to set worthwhile goals for themselves. The proposal called for phonics, direct instruction, an explicit homework policy, single grade classes, a school uniform, regular reporting of student academic performance and conduct, and support for teachers and parents to meet to exchange views.

Charges of elitism and racism swirled through the community. Newspaper accounts contained claims and counterclaims. A retired teacher sympathetic to the parent group seeking the "traditional" school claimed that Richmond's schools promoted illiteracy by forbidding teachers from teaching grammar and spelling. Teachers expressed concern that by accepting such a proposal, the school board would be limiting teachers' professional autonomy. Students with special needs would, some charged, be excluded from the "traditional" school.

On April 6, 1998, Chris Kelly, superintendent of schools for the Richmond School Board, wrote to trustees about their willingness to establish a "traditional" school. He sought a mandate from the board to open such a school by September of that year. In his memorandum, Kelly identified three issues of significance: (1) the advisability of establishing a "traditional" school as a separate program; (2) the educational merit of the proposal; and (3) the feasibility of establishing an alternative school if the board were to decide that it was desirable to do so.

The Richmond Board of School Trustees wanted more time to consider the issue. In June 1998, they passed a resolution calling for approval in principle of a "traditional" school program. They set up a special committee to consider the program and asked staff to recommend a process for community consultation. They set the second board meeting in February 1999 as the date for approval of a Richmond Traditional School Program. For the next seven months, vigorous and often heated debate ensued throughout the Richmond community and in the media.

The Traditional Program Planning Committee established by the board met ten times for lengthy sessions. It was composed of representatives of administration, teaching, support staff, and parents, and two representatives of the Traditional Program Parent Group. It was co-chaired by the board's chair and a retired Chinese-Canadian school principal. The meetings were described as being "intense, thoughtful, respectful, and orderly."

In its report to the board, the committee identified two dominant issues. The first was the need to enhance communication between parents and schools. The second was the need for a reasonable degree of consistency – "not uniformity" – in day-to-day school and classroom practices. The committee acknowledged that the attempts by the Richmond School Board to reach out to parents – especially recent immigrants – were not working as effectively as had been hoped. The committee recognized that the lack of "consistency and predictability from year to year and from school to school" was a cause of anxiety for parents. The report acknowledged that, for some parents, the lack of consistency and predictability resulted in "an unwarranted erosion of trust and confidence in the quality of education students are receiving."

In a fashion familiar to observers of Canadian politics, local elites brokered a compromise. The committee recommended that instead of establishing a single traditional school, elements of the traditional school proposal be incorporated into *all* Richmond elementary schools. These elements included adherence to the provincially mandated curriculum for public schools, the board's statement of philosophy, goals, and inclusion policy, its "image statement" of the educated person, as well as existing collective agreements.

The committee report proposed six areas of emphasis. It recommended establishing a code of student conduct and a program that emphasized: literacy (reading, oral, and written comprehension, phonics, grammar, composition, and handwriting); cognitive development; problem-solving; and studying mathematics, computer science, social sciences, fine arts, and physical education. The report also recommended: regular assessment and reporting as required in the School Act; the establishment of homework/home-study guidelines; agreement that parents, administration, staff, and students jointly develop acceptable guidelines for a dress code; and the offering of single-grade classes whenever numbers permit.

The board received the committee's report and approved its use as a framework for the development of a "foundations program." The program, to be implemented in all Richmond elementary schools, began to be phased in starting in September 2000.

The introduction of features of the "traditional" school proposal to all of the elementary schools in Richmond was a compromise. Although the changes introduced were less dramatic than the ones the parents sought, they have altered

Richmond elementary schools. Codes of conduct have been introduced. Teachers have responded to parental concerns about the development of basic skills. Schools are more attentive to keeping parents informed about their children's progress. The subtlety of the changes has prompted some of the more cynical observers to comment, quoting Alphonse Karr, that "the more things change, the more they remain the same." Some critics have said the Richmond board was typical of the educational establishment: monolithic, bureaucratic, and unwilling to change.

What was the conflict in Richmond really about? Was it about parents wanting their children to have schools like they had? Was it because parents thought rigour would inoculate their children against drugs, sex, and bullying? Was it because parents thought rigour would weed out students with special needs? I think it was about making public schools more like selective, elite private schools.

### PROGRESSIVES VERSUS TRADITIONALISTS

THE CONFLICT ABOUT CURRICULUM and teaching practices that erupted in Richmond has been repeated throughout Canada. The value differences at the heart of such conflicts are traceable to two main currents of educational thought that have influenced education throughout much of the past century. One side of the debate is commonly labelled "traditional" and the other "progressive." These simplistic labels are convenient referents for the differences between them. Among those differences are views about the purpose of public schooling, the nature of curriculum and instruction, assessment and reporting practices, and the roles of teachers and students.

On the traditional side are those who believe that schools should devote most of their resources to identifying and cultivating individuals who show ability. Opposing them are the progressives who believe that schools should fully develop all students. The difference is sometimes expressed as excellence versus equality. It is a major theme in the reading and mathematics "wars," the battles between subject-centred versus integrated programs, academic versus comprehensive schools, and values education versus secular schooling. These themes have occurred again and again over the past one hundred years.

During the first half of the last century, education beyond elementary school was selective. R. D. Gidney, at the University of Western Ontario, points out that before 1950, more than half of the children in Ontario left school by the time they were sixteen years old. Elementary and secondary public schooling was characterized by formality, an emphasis on management, and a focus on the acquisition of basic knowledge of reading, writing, and arithmetic. A relatively small number of students continued to high school. Those who did were normally preparing for university attendance and the professions, for teaching, and for the relatively few white-collar occupations that required a more advanced education. According to Gidney, the senior high school "was one of the key gatekeepers of the social system and, at the same time, a guardian of the cultural order. It identified those destined for leadership, broadly construed, and inculcated the values and knowledge that constituted the good and the true."

Progressives advocated for a variety of changes that eventually changed the character of the public school. They were very much influenced by the new discipline of psychology. Progressives believed that educational experiences are built upon prior experience and develop as a result of interaction among students, their teachers, and the wider community. The influence of industrialization can be seen in the progressives desire to expand the curriculum to include practical subjects such as industrial arts and accounting as well as academic subjects. And the influence of increasing democratization can be seen in the progressives' desire that students express their own ideas rather than passively accept the ideas of others.

The progressive movement in Canada has never been as strong as in the United States. Its influence is evident, however, in a number of changes in this country. These changes include approaches that are purportedly more child-centred than subject-centred, build upon the student's prior experience, encourage students to work actively with the ideas being taught, and help students to apply what they have learned outside of class.

The impact of progressive education, felt initially in the 1930s, was more evident at the elementary level than in the high school. According to Gidney, "The educational mandate for the first ten years of schooling was to ensure that the next generation achieved literacy and numeracy, acquired an elementary familiarity with their rights and duties as citizens, and were exposed to a modicum of the common culture." The small set of academic subjects that formerly dominated the high school curriculum was moved to the last years of high school.

Gidney points out that progressivism also provided an identity for elementary teachers that was different from their secondary counterparts. Secondary teachers derived their status from two things: their preparation as subject specialists, and the part they played in determining which students were suited to university education. Elementary teachers, in contrast, had a "child-centred" rather than "subject-centred" orientation. In language commonly heard in school staff rooms, they taught *students* whereas their secondary school counterparts taught *subjects*.

Progressives felt that schooling should be relevant to the lives of students and to their interests in areas beyond a narrow range of academic subjects. Citizenship education, vocationally oriented courses, courses in home economics, bookkeeping and accounting, technology studies, "applied academics," media studies, and courses in "guidance," or personal, educational, and career planning are legacies of that philosophy. Group and project work, active engagement with ideas and materials, debates, simulations, and case studies are evidence of the progressive belief that learning is both an individual and social activity requiring the active involvement of the learner.

The debate between traditionalists and progressives continues today. A study by Larry Kuehn, director of research and technology for the British Columbia Teachers' Federation, shows that these philosophical differences are still at play in public schools.

Kuehn administered a questionnaire to a sample of 735 B.C. teachers, asking them to respond to seventeen phrases. The phrases referred to "aspects of teaching" and were organized into "paradigms." "Paradigm A" contained aspects of teaching associated with the traditional view of schooling, while "Paradigm B" contained aspects associated with the progressive view.

Teachers were asked to indicate where they would *prefer* to be in their own teaching practice. Overall, they preferred to be on the progressive side of the continuum. On all seventeen items, the preference for progressive practices was stronger among elementary teachers than among secondary teachers.

Secondary teachers lean toward the acquisition of content in discrete disciplines that have a prescribed scope and sequence. Elementary teachers – especially teachers from kindergarten to grade three – tend to prefer a curriculum that integrates subjects to enable students to progress continuously in "learning how to learn."

Secondary teachers are more inclined than their elementary colleagues to favour "direct instruction" and "competition" rather than "active" and "co-operative" learning. Secondary teachers are more accepting of letter grades and norm-referenced, standardized tests than their colleagues at the elementary level. Elementary teachers, on the other hand, prefer to use checklists to assess performance for anecdotal reports to parents about a student's progress.

## Philosophical Preferences of British Columbia Teachers

| Paradigm A | Paradigm B |
|---|---|

### Curriculum

| Paradigm A | Paradigm B |
|---|---|
| Major focus on content | Major focus on process |
| Discrete discipline | Integration of subjects |
| Content acquisition | Learning to learn |
| Prescribed scope and sequence | Continuous progress |

### Instruction

| Paradigm A | Paradigm B |
|---|---|
| Teacher-centred instruction | Child-centred instruction |
| Single instructional style | Multiple instructional styles |
| Direct instruction | Active learning |

### School environment

| Paradigm A | Paradigm B |
|---|---|
| Single grade grouping | Multi-age grouping |
| Competition | Co-operative learning |
| Teacher role as supervisor of learners | Self-directed learners |
| Hierarchical administrative structures | Professional/collegial relationships |
| Teacher as independent professional | Collaborative inter-dependent relationships |
| School as a closed system | School within a community context |
| Little encouragement for community involvement | Community involvement actively sought |

### Assessment & Reporting

| Paradigm A | Paradigm B |
|---|---|
| Standard tests | Authentic (performance) assessment |
| Letter grades | Anecdotal reporting |
| Norm references exams | Reference sets of checklists |

*Source: Kuehn, L. (1993) "Changing Teaching Practice: Teachers' Aspirations Meet School Realities" BCTF Research Report 93-E1-05.*

## "SO LITTLE FOR THE MIND?"

IN 1953, HILDA NEATBY, professor and head of the department of history at the University of Saskatchewan, wrote *So Little for the Mind: An Indictment of Canadian Education*, an attack on progressivism in Canadian education. She charged that "intellectual leaders of the future literally cannot read, write, or think. They are good at word recognition, but ... too often they cannot construct a grammatical sentence. They can emit platitudes, but they can neither explain nor defend them. They are often as incapable of the use of logic as they are ignorant of its very name."

In a speech to the Canadian Association of School Superintendents and Inspectors in Saskatoon in 1959, Neatby complained about the changes that had occurred in Canadian education. "[W]e are throwing too many things out of the curriculum or reducing their importance because they are difficult: grammar, languages, pure science, mathematics. And we are distorting other good things in order to make them immediately useful, in order to convert knowledge to 'know-how.' Thus, history, geography, and old-fashioned 'civics' disappear into 'social studies' – a vague blend of material chosen to convey to all children as painlessly as possible a minimum of background knowledge and relevant facts about the society in which they live."

Neatby's critique finds currency and support among some education critics today. Many of the differences among parents and teachers and between teachers and parents are due to the progressive versus traditional point of view. Arguments flare up over various approaches to education: academic versus applied studies; disciplinary versus interdisciplinary or integrated studies; "constructivist teaching" versus "direct instruction"; whole language versus phonics; social studies versus the discrete disciplines of history and geography; integration versus segregation of students with special needs; and so on.

In her indictments of Canadian education, Neatby expressed concern that, in democratizing high schools, the value of intel-         ˙ lectual pursuit had been diminished, if not extinguished. She argued that the approach to students "must . . . be freed from the false notions of democracy which have made equality a first consideration." She called for streaming; that is, separating the more intellectually capable students from the rest. She argued that, in the absence of streaming, neither group would learn all that they might.

The call for streaming is a familiar argument and one that con-tinues to influence public schooling today. Whether officially sanctioned (as it is in Ontario), Canadian high schools are de facto streamed as a consequence of having parallel, but not equivalent, courses in mathematics and English at the same grade level. Given the way high school timetables are constructed, once stu-dents are streamed in mathematics or English, they are streamed in most of their remaining courses.

## THE DEBATE ABOUT READING
## AND MATHEMATICS

IT IS NOT SURPRISING that language arts — especially reading — and mathematics are the focus of controversies in education. Most people feel strongly about how well the next generation fares in areas as central to everyday life as reading and mathe-matics. Controversies concerning reading and mathematics reveal significant philosophical differences about education and its pur-poses and, not surprisingly, political differences as well.

The issue hit the editorial page of a recent edition of the *Globe and Mail* (April 5, 2002) when the Council of Ministers of Education Canada released results from the School Achievement Indicators Program. Under the headline "WHEN STUDENTS SLIDE," the *Globe* observed that "low expectations are a burden that does none of Canada's schoolchildren any good." The edi-torial castigated education ministers for what the *Globe* thought was either indifference or an inability to recognize that "Canada's students are not progressing at an acceptable level in mathematics." This the paper had concluded from the results from a national sample of Canadian students. Much more important than the results themselves, intoned the editorial, was "whether governments prefer to set the achievement bar low so they need not help the students leap high."

More often than not, reading gets more attention than mathematics because of the central part reading plays in life. Reading is the subject of what has been referred to as "the great debate." Writers use the language of combat to describe "the reading wars." There are enemies. Students are "victims." The implication is that society sustains "collateral damage."

The origins of the controversy can be traced to the ideas of philosopher Jean-Jacques Rousseau (1712–1778). He believed that children become adults by passing through different stages of development that required different educational forms. According to Rousseau, children differed even within stages, requiring that their education be tailored to their characteristics. He felt that people must learn to make sense of the world in their own ways rather than accept the authority of others, including teachers. However, Rousseau recognized the importance of teachers controlling the environment from which, and in which, children learned.

Regardless of its derivation, the controversy about reading instruction divides school staffs, parents, and communities. It erupts on the national stage when results such as those from the School Achievement Indicators Program are released. At issue are differences in what the proponents believe about how children learn to read and, as a consequence, how they should be taught.

Sticking with the combat metaphor, one camp believes that learning to read is a natural process much like learning to speak. By immersing children in what is described as a "print-rich" environment in which they see simple printed words and hear them spoken, children will begin to read what they see written on the page. The opposing camp sees reading as a matter of decoding the symbols that are combined to form words and express meaning. This is similar to a telegrapher decoding the dashes and dots that make up Morse code or musicians decoding the notes in a score.

Depending upon where and when you grew up, one or the other approach was probably dominant. When I grew up, my grade one teacher used books – now ridiculed – such as *Dick and Jane*. She taught us to read by recognizing whole words in simple sentences like "See Dick" and "See Dick run." When I was a teenager, my mother, a grade one teacher, taught phonics. The children in her class learned the alphabet and the forty-four sounds from which English words are formed. They decoded words using those tools. Today, whole language – learning to read whole words from simple stories such as those written by Dr. Seuss (much as I did with *Dick and Jane*) – is the dominant approach used in the many of the schools in Canada.

Teaching using a phonetic approach is an explicit, teacher-led, and sequential process. Students learn to sound out letters and combinations of letters. They are exposed to a tightly controlled initial vocabulary, and practise what they have learned until they are fluent. Whole language is no less explicit. It relies on teachers preparing the classroom environment by providing sufficient, attractive, and interesting print material at a level appropriate to the children. They read to the children frequently and plan activities such as listening centres and daily journal writing that will ensure the students' frequent exposure to, and use of, print material.

Whole language proponents believe that phonics is a "drill and kill" approach that stifles any thirst young children might develop for literature. Advocates of phonics argue that the whole language approach absolves teachers of their responsibility for ensuring that children learn to read. They concede that whole language might work with children who have well-developed vocabularies, parents who read newspapers, magazines, and books regularly, and who read frequently to their children. But such conditions, they point out, are not the norm. Many of the children who arrive at school have limited vocabularies and parents who do not read for pleasure or are too busy to read to their children.

Both approaches contribute in different ways to literacy. For simplicity's sake, phonics can be considered as a means of developing a foundation for reading. Whole language gives an appreciation for the richness of experience derived from reading. However, the warring factions often act as if there is no middle ground. Their followers are recruited like soldiers to a battle or, at least, voters in an election campaign. Evidence and reason might help to develop an informed appreciation of the contributions and limitations of each approach, but ideology, religion, and politics intrude.

Phonics has become a rallying point for the political and religious right. The Freedom Party of Ontario is a libertarian party that believes "freedom is having the right to choose, and it is our freedom of choice that is at the heart of every political issue." According to its Web site, "Because of the collectivist philosophies of the major Canadian political parties (both federal and provincial), freedom has come under severe attack in Canada." The Freedom Party was founded "to present a defence against these attacks, on both moral and intellectual grounds, by forcing a discussion of freedom's fundamental principles into the global political marketplace, and by offering the electorate in the province of Ontario an alternative to statist philosophy and government."

The Freedom Party's Web site contains a lengthy discussion of whole language. "If parents could choose how their children are taught to read and write," says Freedom Party Leader Robert Metz, "there would be no 'whole language' debate. Unfortunately, parents who find that their children have been handicapped by whole language also discover that they must pay twice to remedy the situation – once to a government monopoly system that is doing more harm than good, and once again to remedy the damage through alternate schooling or private tutoring."

## MATH WARS

A CONTROVERSY, similar to the one about reading, simmers in the debate about how mathematics should or shouldn't be taught. From time to time, the controversy boils over, as it did in 1999. On November 18 of that year, a large group of scientists, mathematicians, and educators signed an open letter published in the *Washington Post*. They called into question ten mathematics programs considered exemplary by the U.S. Department of Education. The letter was written in part because parents had beseeched its author, David Klein, to help them do something about the way mathematics was being taught.

In an article in the April 2000 issue of the *American School Board Journal*, Klein accused the U.S. Department of Education of promoting the mathematical equivalent of "whole language." Klein said that the program being advocated by the U.S. Department of Education was "watered-down" because it de-emphasized arithmetic and algebra. Klein compared mathematics to martial arts and music. "A novice cannot hope to achieve mastery in the martial arts without first learning basic katas or exercises in movement," argued Klein. "A violinist who has not mastered elementary bowing techniques and vibrato has no hope of evoking the emotions of an audience through sonorous tones and elegant phrasing. Arguably the most hierarchical of human endeavours, mathematics also depends on sequential mastery of basic skills."

A related criticism made by Klein – and other signatories of the 1999 letter – is that "the standard algorithms for arithmetic (that is, the standard procedures for addition, subtraction, multiplication, and division of numbers) are missing or abridged." Klein said that such omissions were at odds with the views of the mathematicians who signed the letter.

There are similar camps regarding the teaching of mathematics in Canada. David Robitaille, the Canadian study director for the Third International Mathematics and Science Study, a collaborative effort of forty-two nations, agrees with the critics who say students need to know the basics. "You can't be comfortable doing mathematics if you have to think about what seven times eight is. And you shouldn't need to use a calculator to estimate the cost of several purchases at a store." He argues that students need to develop good "number sense" and a high level of comfort with numbers and how they work. On the other hand, Robitaille says that students do not need to do worksheets of long division with multi-digit dividends and divisors.

When I served as deputy minister of education for British Columbia, I wanted to know whether the superior mathematics performance of students in Quebec might be explained by differences between the curricula and teaching methods used in the two jurisdictions. I asked Helen Raptis, at the time a graduate student from the University of Victoria working as a co-op student in the ministry, to appraise the situation.

Raptis did a comparative content analysis of the mathematics curricula of British Columbia and Quebec at grades four, eight, and eleven. She identified similarities and differences between the two programs of study. She compared the curricular objectives item by item and analyzed the philosophies and mission statements. Her analysis found that, although the two provincial curricula addressed similar topics, the quality, quantity, and arrangement of their objectives differed significantly, as did the philosophies and mission statements. The differences, wrote Raptis, indicated "two differing ideological orientations at the heart of each province's mathematics curricula."

Raptis found that Quebec's curricula for grades four, eight, and eleven were narrower and deeper than British Columbia's. In other words, the B.C. curriculum contained more topics and more objectives than Quebec's, and many of the B.C. topics and objectives were repeated from year to year. In Quebec, the range of skills and operations within a specific topic area was more focused. Emphasis was placed on moving back and forth between thinking about abstract concepts and learning concrete operations and rote processes. Raptis found the B.C. curriculum inconsistent in its treatment of abstract and concrete concepts.

According to her analysis, the overall layout, mandate, and philosophies of the two province's curricula differed. She found that, in Quebec, the curriculum was "subject-centred." All students were considered capable of learning mathematics through grade ten. On the other hand, she found that the mathematics curriculum in British Columbia was "learner-centred." It was focused on preparing students for a career and made allowances for differences among students by grouping and streaming. Quebec made provision for differentiation after grade ten by modifying how deeply students were to address the same subject matter. Learners in British Columbia were placed in different streams that addressed completely different subject matters.

In Quebec, the objectives and notes to the teacher in the curriculum emphasized the view that mathematics learning is interrelated and cumulative. Teachers were encouraged to link prior learning to current content. The purpose of such linking, according to Raptis, was to show students that "all of their prior learning is available for problem-solving in the real, physical world." Raptis did not find evidence in the B.C. mathematics curriculum of these conscious links. Instead, she found repetition of learning objectives from previous years.

### THE NEED FOR UNDERSTANDING

MANY PARENTS ARE LIKE the West Vancouver father who wants reassurance that schools will teach particular topics, or like the parents in Richmond who want teachers to use particular methods of instruction. As taxpayers, they see themselves as "clients" of the public school system. And they wonder why the system cannot deliver the services they want in the way that they want them. The changes that occur do so only slowly and with too much effort. They wonder why schools "can't just get on with it."

For many parents, public schooling is a means to an end no different than an automobile providing transportation to a destination or a washing machine supplying clean clothes. They can see the competing philosophies at work in the education system, but they don't like them. To many parents, such conflicts are just an obstacle to their children getting a good education.

Canadian public schools have not done a particularly good job of explaining to parents and the wider community how the system works. Citizens are rarely engaged in meaningful discussions of the purposes of public schooling.

Involving parents in such discussions is a tricky business. Once involved, they will soon discover that behind some, but not all, of the philosophical differences are competing views of the purposes of education, the way that students should be treated, and the nature of the learning process. Parents might not find such discussions comforting. They will have their own views and wish to see them taken into account.

As challenging as it might seem, I do not think there is any alternative to engaging parents in a discussion about whom public schools serve and how they should carry out their work. But such discussions cannot be confined to parents and the professionals involved in the education system. If our schools represent a delicate balance between serving the individual needs of students and the broader needs of the society as a whole, educational discussions must engage members of the wider community.

Such discussions will be particularly challenging to education professionals and school trustees who have been accustomed to going about their work with relatively little public interaction. They have evolved a vocabulary for talking about school matters that excludes those less familiar with the workings of the system.

They have become relatively comfortable working in an environment of low public visibility. That will have to change.

If people are not more fully involved in discussions about public schooling, they will rely on the impressions formed from informal conversations with neighbours, from reports about conflicts in the public media, and from politically motivated and misleading reports from groups like the Fraser Institute. Misinformed about the complexities, strengths, and weaknesses of the schools they think should serve them, their confidence in public schooling will continue to erode, and with it their support.

# chapter six

# WHAT PUBLIC SCHOOLS SHOULD TEACH

P arents wonder why the enthusiasm and anticipation that their children brought to kindergarten have eroded by the time they are in grade four and given way to boredom by grade eight. Too many see their sons and daughters in grade ten worn out and defeated by school. A number of parents have to exhort their children just to hang on until grade twelve to get their diploma. And many of those who do hang on until they graduate leave feeling alienated from learning, vowing that they will not continue their education.

The problem is the curriculum. The curriculum of the public school has become bloated, fragmented, mired in trivia, and short on ideas. It does not demand that students connect what they learn with anything else. It does not challenge them to reach beyond their limits. The curriculum stifles curiosity. Although it demands effort, it does not reward deep thought.

Part of the problem is that public schooling is seen as a step to something else – work or further schooling – rather than something of value for its own sake. Our public schools are capable of creating an experience that will challenge both the students who will complete their schooling with high school graduation and those who will go on to further study. But first, we need to clean house.

## THE CROWDED CURRICULUM

WE ARE AMBUSHED by "factoids" and assaulted with data. We wake up to a radio announcer reminding us about the birthdays of celebrities to whom we had no intention of sending greetings. Following the lead of the electronic media, our morning papers summarize the stories we don't have time to read. PalmPilots in hand, we check our schedules and read our e-mail as we travel to work.

A motorist on the 401 in Ontario was recently stopped for travelling too slowly in the fast lane. He told the police officer he was checking his stock portfolio in the newspaper. In the passing lane! On the 401!

We are drowning in a sea of information. Each day another tsunami heads our way. Most people mistakenly confuse information with knowledge and trivia with education. It is one of the reasons the curricula of our schools are overcrowded.

Our schools are well-placed institutions; too well placed. Public schools are suitably situated to ensure that all – or nearly all – persons of a given age are exposed to information thought worthy of their attention. Schools are society's last meeting place. Thus, when there are notable increases in teen suicide, deaths due to unsafe driving practices, or sexual abuse, the school is thought to be the place where these issues should be addressed.

There doesn't seem to be an issue or topic beyond the scope and expertise of the public school. We expect public schools to fix children who have gorged on a media diet of Cinderella myths, macho heroes, and fantasies. And when problems such as eating disorders, teen pregnancy, sexually transmitted diseases, and suicide reach unacceptable proportions, these topics spawn programs in public schools.

Most public schools implement a variety of bully-proofing and effective discipline programs in an attempt to address problems that have their origin in failed pre-school socialization. Career education, life skills, and media studies have earned a place among the more familiar subjects of language, literature, and history in the curriculum of the public school. The problem is that as topics are added, there has been little, if any, corresponding increase in the time devoted to public schooling. This makes it increasingly difficult to address in an intellectually honest and systematic manner the subjects, topics, and issues included in the school curriculum.

We need to evaluate the worth of programs that try to make up for the failures of other institutions. If we want our schools to be places where health and social problems are addressed, we should acknowledge those goals. We should provide space for the provision of those services, and we should hire medical and social workers to deliver the programs. We should not try to inject into an already overburdened teaching day material that is more appropriately addressed by other professionals. Let's allow our teachers to do what they were hired to do.

Schools can do something about this situation, but not if we persist in treating the school like a supermarket and schooling like a shopping cart. We should not confuse getting an education with amassing courses and credits. As a student might say, "Let's get real." We should acknowledge that some subjects and experiences are more important than others.

## WHAT SHOULD OUR PUBLIC SCHOOLS TEACH?

WE WILL NOT ACCOMPLISH anything of value if we do not agree on our priorities for public schooling. What shall we emphasize and what shall we leave for other institutions to address or for students to explore on their own? What principles should guide our decisions about what to include and what to exclude? What is it we want from our public schools?

Some people hold the mistaken view that public schooling is about *training* students for the future, rather than about *educating* for the future. Although there is some overlap between education and training, the difference between the two is important. Training involves the mastery of techniques and their application to circumstances similar to the ones for which the techniques were originally developed. Education involves the acquisition of knowledge and its application to issues and problems both familiar and unanticipated. Training is more limited and limiting than education.

Educating students for their economic roles is a legitimate function of public schooling. But not workplace training. Employers should provide workplace training in the workplace. It is perfectly legitimate for employers to want graduates who can read and write well, use numbers appropriately and intelligently, analyze a problem, and generate a creative approach to its solution. Graduates should be able to speak intelligently and work collaboratively with the person at the next desk. But it is not reasonable to ask that graduates be trained to perform work unique to a particular workplace.

Preparing students for employment is crowding out preparation for more broadly based active citizenship. Public schools do a good job of giving students basic skills they will need for further study and for productive work as adults. But too often students do not learn what they need to know to be socially responsible citizens. The disciplines that help people understand who they are, and how they are related to the larger human community, seem less important than they once were. But if we want a society in which people can think critically about the problems that the society must confront, that must change.

The curriculum of the public school should exhibit four attributes. (1) It should be meaningful, enabling students to connect what they learn in class with their lives outside of school. (2) Students should be challenged by the curriculum to reach beyond previous boundaries in knowledge and experience. (3) The curriculum should stimulate students' curiosity, prompting them to want to know more. And (4) the curriculum must require students to think deeply, to invest mental effort in their learning.

It is doubtful that, on the eve of the twentieth century, anyone could have predicted the events and developments that would unfold in just its first twenty years. Given her age, one might have anticipated the death of Queen Victoria, but who would have predicted the articulation of quantum theory, or the Russian Revolution? The development of the one-dollar Kodak Brownie camera might have been predicted as a natural step in the evolution of photography, but who knew that Picasso would introduce cubism or Einstein would develop his theory of relativity? It might have been inevitable that Robert Peary or someone like him would reach the North Pole in the first twenty years of the twentieth century, but it is doubtful that anyone could have predicted the invention of plastic, the Chinese Revolution, or the assassination of the Archduke Ferdinand and its aftermath.

We should not try to prepare the next generation for a specific set of circumstances, since we are unable to predict even with modest accuracy what the future will hold. We would serve our society well if our schools ensured that the next generation possessed a strong foundation in reading, writing, and numeracy; was disposed to treat others with respect; had the ability to work co-operatively with others; appreciated and acted upon the values and principles that make us human; understood Canada and could appraise its strengths and limitations; and could exercise a critical intelligence that was adaptable to circumstances unforeseen.

We must provide young people with the opportunity to make a meaningful contribution to their community. Many young Canadians are looking for opportunities to connect with the larger society. Working in fast-food restaurants and coffee chains provides them with income, but the work is neither permanent nor meaningful. Many want more. They want to give to others and be recognized for their contributions.

In an earlier chapter I talked about involving students in providing much needed childcare. We could give them many other opportunities – cleaning up the environment, caring for the aged, tutoring younger peers – if we used our imagination and thought about public schooling a bit differently than we do. Schooling is preparation for adult citizenship, but one's engagement with the larger society does not have to be deferred until one leaves school. It can and should begin in school, where it can be guided by skilled professionals and linked to one's intellectual development.

Schooling through grade ten should be divided into two components. Seventy per cent of the school week should be devoted to foundation studies, consisting of language, mathematics, science, and social studies. The remaining 30 per cent should be allocated for elective studies in areas such as art, music, athletics, and second-language studies. By grade eleven, students should have chosen a specialized studies program in such areas as language and literature; trades and technologies; social and behavioural science; mathematics and science; fine and performing arts; and business. No particular prerequisites should be required for the specialized studies program except successful completion of the foundation studies program through grade ten. Specialized studies programs might consist of more than two years of study, as is the case with Collège d'enseignement général et professionnel (CEGEP) in Quebec. Students would earn a diploma in their area of specialization.

This proposal should not be construed as support for politicians who, driven by parsimony or ideology, may wish to reduce public expenditures for education by ending public schooling at grade ten. Specialized studies such as I propose are as much a benefit to the society as to the individual. They provide a foundation for further study and preparation for productive employment. With such study, students would be better equipped to face the demands of society.

We must promote a more rigorous, engaging, and socially useful experience for all students. We should reorganize secondary schools into smaller, more manageable units of 120 to 160 students working with a team of six to eight teachers within the larger school. Aware of the outcomes expected of all secondary school students, the teachers would be responsible for the education of those students throughout their entire secondary school experience.

The anonymity of large and relatively impersonal secondary schools engenders feelings of alienation among too many students. The close working relationship between students and teachers in the mini-schools would help to create an environment in which students feel that who they are and what they do make a difference.

The closer relationship between teachers, students, and their parents would also promote better communications and authentic accountability. Many teachers are frustrated about working in isolation from their peers and the students for whom they are responsible. Allowing teachers to exercise their professional discretion about how best to achieve the outcomes of education for a particular group of students would reduce that frustration.

Proposals for changing secondary schools typically fail. One reason is the viselike grip university entrance requirements exert on secondary schools and on the parents of most students, even the parents of students unlikely to apply for university admission. Parents are fearful of changes to the secondary school curriculum that might jeopardize their children's chances for admission to university. As a consequence, proposals for changes to secondary schools typically afford students the opportunity to move seamlessly from one program option to another. This constrains the range of alternatives that schools offer. Another impediment to change is the size of schools. Secondary schools with small enrolments find it difficult, if not impossible, to provide many alternatives without incurring significantly higher per-student costs, a feature that already distinguishes small, remote secondary schools from their urban counterparts.

The first obstacle could be overcome if universities were open to rethinking secondary schooling and willing to reconsider their requirements for admission. For example, although it is not required for study in many fields, advanced mathematics is a prerequisite to university admission in many jurisdictions. I asked the head of UBC's mathematics department if he would recommend the more broadly useful applied mathematics as a requirement for admission to those fields that do not require calculus, but he declined. His main reason was the possibility that, if students later decided to switch to a field requiring calculus, "then we would be under great pressure to offer a course at the university level that is now offered at the high school level." To him, offering introductory calculus would amount to "watering down" the university curriculum.

Addressing the problem of offering alternatives in small, remote secondary schools would require extraordinary co-operation among educational institutions serving rural and remote regions. Such institutions working on a pan-Canadian basis could develop high-quality courseware and make it available on the Internet with instructional support provided at the local level. The initial cost of developing the courseware would be high, as would the development of the instructional support. In the long run, costs would diminish, bringing the per-student cost into line with classroom expenditure levels. The benefit would be the provision of a meaningful and challenging secondary programs for rural learners and for students unable to attend their local schools because they are hospital- or home-bound.

The co-operation that such proposals require may be beyond our grasp. Scarce resources have made institutions and provincial jurisdictions increasingly conscious and protective of their "turf" and less inclined to co-operate for mutual benefit. It might be helpful to overcome the inertia with leadership from the Council of Ministers of Education Canada and the Government of Canada. Although infrequent, co-operation among these levels of government has occurred in the past.

I am aware that my proposals for changing secondary schooling are not mutually compatible. I advance a variety of proposals to stimulate thought about what might be possible. Each has its advantages and limitations, but they deserve consideration along with others. For example, post-secondary institutions – including universities – should accredit secondary teachers to offer entry-level post-secondary courses.

Students, teachers, and the larger society want an education system in which everyone reaches beyond their previous boundaries in knowledge and experience. A key ingredient in ensuring such a system is trust and mutual obligation. They are the glue that holds democratic societies together.

## EQUALITY AND DIVERSITY IN EDUCATION

IN CANADA, we have developed a number of policies and practices to assist in achieving our vision of equality among citizens. The Official Languages Act is one such policy. Possession of one of Canada's official languages is central to success in school and beyond. Therefore, schools often provide additional assistance to students for whom English – or, in Quebec, French – is not their first language.

Over the years, we have also made better provision for including and educating students with special educational needs. Canadian public schools have begun to realize they have not fulfilled their promise for students of aboriginal origin, and have only recently begun to become attuned to students who are gay, lesbian, or transgendered. There is a long way to go in making sure that they are treated fairly. Canadians believe that socio-economic background should not prevent students from getting the benefit that public schools have to offer. Public schools are beginning to make a special effort to ensure that a student's educational success cannot be predicted by the social conditions in which the student lives.

The public school should help people be whom they choose to be and still achieve the full benefits of participation in society. Schools should promote the values expressed in the Charter of Rights and Freedoms, and the Citizenship, Official Languages, Multiculturalism, and Human Rights acts – values that all Canadians share. We have the responsibility to ensure that every student who calls Canada home is able to take a full and active part in the affairs of the community and the country, engage in active democratic citizenship.

Public schools should be the place where democratic citizenship is learned. They should be places in which cultural, religious, and linguistic differences can be both understood and appreciated. Public schools should foster healthy inter-group relations by eroding cultural stereotypes. Schools should try to imbue in all students an appreciation for Canada's values, traditions, and institutions through instruction in language, literature, art, history, music, and in other curricular areas. And teachers should work to overcome the barriers to success that some students face because of the characteristics they bring with them when they come to school.

Linguistic, cultural, and ethnic diversity have long been features of Canadian society, distinguishing Canada from other countries in which pluralism is less evident and less well regarded. However, the value of cultural pluralism requires cultivation.

## TEACHING ABOUT CANADA

MOST CANADIANS who have travelled abroad have felt the pleasure of recognizing other Canadians. The sense of kinship is recognition that we have some shared experience. Our schools have contributed to this very positive experience by teaching us about our history, institutions, and the values that distinguish Canadians from others. They also teach us how a civil society conducts itself.

A subjective feeling of kinship with fellow Canadians is a good thing in moderation. Too much of such a feeling can lead to ethnocentrism and too little can threaten our cohesion. We rely on our public schools to achieve the right balance. They are our cultural gyroscopes, maintaining our course and balance at the same time. If they don't work, neither can Canada.

Our public schools are responsible for building and preserving the community that is Canada. They also play an important part in helping Canada define its future by influencing the sort of society Canada will become. Our public schools are crucial to ensuring the expression of values that distinguish Canada from other nations and creating a civil society. This is why Canada's interest in its public school should be different from its interest in manufacturing or agriculture.

Canada has developed a unique response to a common question: How much and what kind of diversity can and should Canada accommodate and still preserve its identity and cohesion as a nation? Over the last sixty years, Canada has tried to become a society in which its citizens can retain the characteristics and values of the group or groups with which they identify. At the same time, they enjoy the full benefits of a citizenship founded on shared rights, freedoms, and obligations. In other words, Canadians should be able to retain the characteristics and values of their ancestors so long as that retention does not create inequality. These ideals are so important that they are spelled out in Canada's constitution.

There are some who do not share this national vision and do not think it should be communicated in our public schools. They think schooling is primarily about preparation for work. They argue that if public schools can't or won't prepare people for work, then private schools can and should. They do not value equality and they do not believe that governments should try to make it possible for people to participate in society on an equal footing. This group is relatively small, but their numbers and their influence are growing. I think most Canadians still believe, however, that people should be able to retain the characteristics of the groups to which they belong and still enjoy the full benefit of participating in Canadian society.

The school curriculum should give expression to Canada's ideals in both obvious and subtle ways. Students should develop an understanding of Canada's history and institutions. They should read and study literature with the themes and symbols that are distinctly Canadian, along with the literature of other nations.

Much of this could be provided under the ambit of social studies, once seen as central to the development of the knowledge and attitudes that Canadian students needed to take a full and active part in society. Today, social studies is an increasingly marginal subject.

Among the reasons for the decline in the importance of social studies (and in the humanities as well) is the ascendancy of mathematics, the sciences, and most recently computer sciences. Cognizant that today's students live in a society increasingly dependent upon technology, parents, administrators, and teachers are placing greater emphasis and value upon subjects that appear – on the surface – to equip students better for getting a job and earning a living in such a society. Social studies should be returned to a more central place in the classroom so that students are also well prepared to be citizens of a democratic society.

Educational leaders can do two things to promote active citizenship without incurring additional expenditures or forcing schools to reorganize. Canadian school boards should demand that social studies plays a more prominent part in the lives of students. They should require that those who teach social studies be properly prepared for this important responsibility. Social studies should not continue to be a timetable slot to be filled by teachers who lack prior preparation for instruction in this vital area.

## SALVATION WILL NOT COME FROM A
## MICROPROCESSOR – AT LEAST NOT YET

THERE HAS BEEN MUCH DEBATE about the role of information and communication technologies (ICT) in education, especially since the advent of the personal computer.

Before I talk further about technological change in public schooling, I need to point out that I am a frequent and avid computer user. I was using mainframe computers to analyze statistical data in the mid-1960s. I bought the first model of portable microcomputer in the late 1970s. And although that computer used 5½-inch floppy disks and had only 64K of memory, I wrote my first book on it. I am writing this book on a laptop that has more computing power than the mainframe I used nearly forty years ago. I have a high-speed connection to the Internet and use it all the time to obtain information and check facts. I hope you will keep that in mind as I talk about technology, change, and computers in education.

Most parents want their children to learn to use the new technologies. They want their children to have a competitive edge in the "knowledge economy." And what institution is better situated than the public school to ensure that the next generation is adept at information and communication technologies upon which Canada's future as a "knowledge-based" economy will depend?

Parents and educators in the late 1980s and early 1990s were subjected to hyperbole about educational benefits of information and communication technologies. Schools, school districts, parent organizations, corporate Canada, and governments were swept up in frenzied attempts to ensure that students would be prepared for a future in which technologies – especially information and communication technologies – would figure prominently.

Canada was faced with depleting natural resources and increasingly uncompetitive industries. An economy in which knowledge was the chief commodity presented seemingly limitless and environmentally clean promise. Some advocates looked forward to radical societal changes with the introduction of computers to the classroom.

The stock market soared on the strength of economic growth in the technology sector. Advocates of increased use of computers spouted formulas about the exponential growth in information. They talked about the continually changing education requirements for technical occupations. They promised that with computers teaching would be transformed. Teachers would become "the guide on the side" instead of "the sage on the stage."

Teachers and students are making increasing use of computers each year, though not perhaps in the ways that some envisioned. If you look closely at the changes that have occurred, they have not been as radical or "transformative" as implied by the rhetoric. The reason is simple to understand. People will adapt easily to new practices that they regard as equivalent alternatives to existing practices.

Most of the applications of new technologies have been in areas for which the computer is an equivalent substitute: typing, bookkeeping, drafting, graphics, record-keeping, writing, demonstrating, and simulating. The activities performed using the new technologies are similar, if not identical, to the ones performed by hand or with older technologies like typewriters and overhead projectors.

Because computers look like and behave like typewriters, typing teachers and students had little difficulty adapting. Teachers responsible for bookkeeping and accounting found that they were able to make effective use of the new technology in preparing balance sheets and maintaining accounts, much as they had when calculators replaced adding machines. Drafting and graphics teachers found that the computer software mimicked familiar processes, enabling students to do the same kind of work more quickly than they could by hand.

Once software manufacturers created record-keeping pro-grams that looked like the manual ones teachers had been using, teachers made the switch. As their comfort level improved, they started using computers to prepare their lessons and to find infor-mation on the Internet. Teachers who once made extensive use of the overhead projector are now beginning to use presentation software and large screens to present information. Some science teachers make use of software that simulates experiments that are too dangerous or costly to carry out in the classroom.

A gap once existed between students who were comfortable with the new technologies and their older, somewhat techno-phobic teachers. This has declined dramatically as younger people have entered teaching. With 40 per cent of the teaching population set to retire in the next eight years, the gap will soon disappear.

Students report extensive use of computers. The Internet makes it possible for them to acquire huge amounts of informa-tion about almost any topic. For example, students can find ample information about Canadian Confederation on the Internet. But without a skilful teacher, they are unlikely to be able to construct a coherent argument about the nature of the political compro-mise that Confederation represents and its recurring impact on Canadian civic life.

All of this change has occurred rather painlessly, unless you count the significant economic expenditure. But teaching has not been transformed. The predictions of the "guide on the side" believers have not been borne out. There has been relatively little use made of new technologies in areas requiring complex teacher explanation and classroom orchestration.

It took considerable expense and enormous effort to develop a computer that possessed sufficient strategic intelligence to play chess as well as one of the world's masters. Teachers already have a vast storehouse of strategic knowledge that enables them to select

examples, interpretations, and explanations geared to the particular characteristics of the students with whom they interact over
a vast range of subjects. Until someone can make a computer with
the strategic intelligence possessed by most teachers, teachers are
here to stay – along with computers.

At the invitation of the Canadian Education Statistics Council
and the Council of Ministers of Education Canada in 2001, my
colleague Tracey Burns and I undertook to review the available
evidence about the impact of information and communication
technology (ICT) on teaching and learning in elementary, secondary, or post-secondary education in Canada. We wanted to find
evidence behind the claims supporting ICT in schools. We hoped
such evidence would enable those responsible for the formation
or implementation of policy to make informed decisions about the
use of scarce resources. But few, if any, claims were sufficiently well
researched or well evidenced to provide direction for policy. Simply
put, none of us knows enough about the impact of the use of ICT
in elementary or secondary schooling to warrant diverting large
sums of public money to those technologies.

Public schools across the country have spent millions – perhaps
billions – of scarce resources on information and communication technologies. Libraries have insufficient print resources
because schools have purchased so much software. Schools find
it impossible to keep up with the demand to replace "obsolete"
computers, networks, and software purchased only a few years
before. Teachers have to allocate time to keeping up to date with
equipment and programs. Students spend valuable time using the
new technologies, but there is little evidence of the benefits and
little consideration of what has been sacrificed to make the hard-
ware and software available.

We need to reconsider the place of new technologies in public
schooling. While they have a place, it is likely to be much less
prominent than the one they presently occupy. We need a more

focused and well-evidenced approach to replace the "cyperbole" so prevalent today.

## AN ANTIDOTE FOR STUDENT BOREDOM AND ALIENATION

OUR PUBLIC SCHOOLS, especially our secondary schools, have not made allowances for the increasing maturity of students. Students today are more sophisticated than their parents were at the same age, and much more sophisticated than their grandparents. But secondary schools continue to treat students as students were treated fifty or sixty years ago.

One of the principal sources of student alienation from schooling is that school is bland and inoffensive. Censorship of texts, fear of controversy, and inexorable routine conspire to rob schooling of its excitement by removing its primary function: education. Education necessarily involves uncertainty and controversy.

Too many Canadian teachers are wary of controversy. They have become fearful of discussing topics and issues that might provoke debate for fear that such debates might erupt into controversies in the wider community. Human rights and environmental, consumer, technological, and other social issues in the curriculum raise the question: Will parents, the community, administrators, and trustees approve of these issues being raised in school? Too often the issues have not been addressed in the classroom because the answer has been "no!" We must support teachers who engage their students in grappling with important and controversial ideas. They must be free to discuss ideas that may challenge the beliefs of parents and the wider community.

Parents and community groups are often resistant to the introduction of controversial ideas and issues in schools. Not long ago, several groups in Nova Scotia requested the elimination of Harper Lee's anti-racism novel *To Kill a Mockingbird* on the grounds that it contained the epithet "nigger." They argued that the presence of the word in the book would encourage the use of that epithet toward Black Canadian students.

In a similar vein, parents in Saskatoon sought to have J. K. Rowling's Harry Potter books banned from the schools operated by the Roman Catholic School Board. The parents said the books and the movie glorified witchcraft, encouraging children to lie and cheat.

Neither request nor the reasoning supporting it was accepted. Although the books remain in the schools, the controversies remind teachers how easy it is to offend parents and other community members.

On average, students are more intellectually mature than their parents or grandparents were when they were teenagers, but schools have not made sufficient allowances for such student maturity. We need to foster a climate in schools that supports the examination of contemporary issues and their implications. The development of such a climate of inquiry depends to a great extent on the ability of teachers to address potentially contentious issues in an intellectually honest manner. Teachers must be inclined and formally prepared for the inclusion of such topics as income inequality, unfair labour practices, euthanasia, abortion, female infanticide and genital mutilation, human cloning, state-sponsored terrorism, religious intolerance, teenage prostitution, and pornography.

During their preparation, teachers must learn the danger of taking the position that "all opinions or view points are equal." It is true that there should be relatively few limits on expression, but the view that all opinions are equal suggests that it is impossible to make judgments about the claims of others. Such a view is antithetical to understanding how logic, evidence, and moral precepts inform our judgments.

There are concepts and standards of reasoning that students must learn in order to help them rationally address the decisions they must make as adult citizens. One of them is the ability to distinguish between facts and values, and to know the standards that apply in evaluating each. Another is the inclination and ability to gather factual evidence relevant to one's decisions. Related to this is the ability and disposition to reason accurately in making decisions. Respect for evidence and reason are essential both to personal decisions and the decisions one makes about the kind of society one wants.

In a democratic and socially cohesive society, people must be capable of understanding the impact of their behaviour and decisions on others. In order to do this, they need to imaginatively take the role of another. They need to judge their own actions from the perspective of other people. They need to consider the consequences of the actions they advocate. For this to happen, students need to be able to imagine the consequences of everyone taking the course of action proposed. And they have to be able to judge that proposed course of action in terms of those consequences.

These capacities and dispositions are essential to maintaining a democratic society. They must be developed systematically under the guidance of teachers who have the freedom of expression necessary for the examination of ideas and their implications for action. And if we are serious in valuing the development of these abilities and dispositions, we should include them in provincial assessments in the same way that we include reading, writing, and mathematics.

There are many things we might do to create a more challenging and meaningful school curriculum. We can do it by getting clear about what we are trying to achieve and sharpening our thinking about how the goals might best be achieved. This will permit us to eliminate topics and issues unrelated to the revised goals and objectives and create room for the revisions we want to make.

Take my proposal for a reconsideration of science teaching. I believe we should develop in students a scientific outlook and the sort of scientific literacy they will need to navigate the controversial and complicated issues we face. This would mean rethinking what we teach under the label of science, since what we teach is not science at all, but facts and formulas from biology, chemistry, physics, and geology.

There are many purposes to the science curriculum that are conspicuously absent. Students should understand scientific reasoning. They should be able to think in the ways that scientists think. And they should develop a scientific literacy that enables them to engage in public discussion about such issues as environmental sustainability, cloning, genetically modified foods, and patenting genetic material. I call this the consumer education dimension of science. Students would need to understand the underlying processes as well as the social and ethical implications of such issues.

To consider such issues and topics thoughtfully, students need to think deeply and critically. The problem is, we do not understand what it means to think critically. We act as if "critical thinking" were some generic capacity unrelated to a particular domain. Many people think that critical thinking is a set of tricks people use to get at the heart of some issue or topic. In doing so, they ignore the content-related dimensions of critical thinking. Thinking critically about issues such as the ones raised about genetically modified foods or patenting genetic material requires an understanding of genetics and ethics. Thinking critically about them is different from thinking critically about art or history or about the use of language.

Students should leave school every day having been challenged to reach beyond what they knew that morning and to connect what they have learned to the world around them. We can achieve these goals if they are things we value. If they are things we value, we need to rethink public schooling to focus directly on them. We should not waste our time and students' time on the things we think unimportant or on the things that other institutions should be doing.

## SCHOOLING GONE WRONG

SCHOOLS TEACH LESSONS in addition to those for which teachers plan. When a young man in Toronto was told he couldn't bring his male date to the high school prom, he learned something from the experience. He fought his case in court. Also in Toronto, a young man wearing a T-shirt expressing his opposition to a commercial venture being pursued by his school learned a similar lesson. Someone cut the power to the amplifiers and microphones he and his classmates were using, preventing them from performing during a school-sponsored battle of the bands.

Alan Sears of the University of New Brunswick told me about a francophone school in Fredericton, New Brunswick, that made headlines with its rule forbidding English-speaking on school grounds at any time. School officials believed that the rule would help francophone students retain their language and culture in the predominantly English-speaking Fredericton community. A student who circulated a petition against the rule reported in a local paper that the school's principal went to all of the classrooms to warn students that if their names appeared on the petition they would be punished. Her schoolmates asked that their names be removed from the petition.

My hunch is the young men in Toronto and the woman in Fredericton learned lessons different from the ones taught in their social studies class about exercising one's democratic rights. If we want students to connect what they learn in school with the lives they lead outside of school, our public schools must also practise what they teach.

chapter seven
·····································

# STUDENTS WITH SPECIAL NEEDS


"**S**tudents with special needs" is a catch-all category that includes students of very different backgrounds. Jurisdictions are reasonably consistent about students who have disabilities that impair their mobility, sight, hearing, or socialization or who have intellectual capacities that differ significantly from the norm. But jurisdictions vary considerably when it comes to students who might be labelled "learning disabled" or who are said to have behavioural problems. Students who are hard to teach are often labelled "special" to signal that conventional teaching strategies have not worked well for them or in order to attract additional resources. For some students, the label often depends more on the school jurisdiction than it does on the characteristics of the student.

Canadian public schools accept all students: students with a constitutional right to an education in either English or French, students for whom English is a second language, aboriginal students, students with extraordinary gifts and talents, and students with learning challenges such as from autism or from the parental abuse of alcohol or drugs prior to the student's birth. Today, Canadian public schools educate students who, in previous generations, would have been educated in segregated settings or denied an education. This is an attribute that distinguishes Canadian schools from schools in most other societies.

## LOWERED EXPECTATIONS

CANADIAN PUBLIC SCHOOLS show greater compassion than they have in the past for students with special needs. That is as it should be. But sometimes that compassion gets expressed by lowering the expectations for the youngster who needs additional help. Children with special needs are often capable of much more than their teachers give them credit for. They can achieve more than they do.

The end result of education for most special-needs children should be no different from the result we are trying to achieve for all students. They should leave school in possession of the knowledge and dispositions they need to take a full and active part in their community. Too many do not.

Reduced expectations for these students are not the only reason this happens. For some, the label they are given confirms their identity as someone who isn't able to achieve. Some students do not need to be "pulled out" of their regular class to receive additional help. They would benefit from additional help inside the classroom. Pulling them out from their class cuts them off from the classroom instructional process. It also confirms for them and their peers that they are deficient. Over time, they and their peers often come to feel that the problems they face can never be overcome.

Many students designated as "special needs" would achieve more, and more rapidly, if their needs were identified and addressed early in their school careers. There is an unfortunate tendency among teachers and administrators to interpret the difficulties of children in kindergarten and grade one as developmental problems they will grow out of. Early intervention would eliminate or at least reduce the number of children in grade three who manifest learning difficulties.

In 1999, I asked Stewart Ladyman, superintendent of field liaison in the B.C. Ministry of Education, and Linda Siegel, Dorothy Lam chair in special education at the University of

British Columbia, to undertake a review of special education in British Columbia. I urged them to consider carefully the policies and programs of special education in light of the promise of Canadian public schooling that all students will be challenged to reach beyond the boundaries in knowledge and experience they have previously achieved, something students must do to understand and navigate the world in which they live. Conditions outside of school should not limit a priori what students achieve.

Siegel and Ladyman's review confirmed what a number of similar studies conducted in North America had found. There is confusion about the meaning and implementation of "inclusion" as it applies to students with special needs. Expectations about what students with special needs should be able to accomplish are often nonexistent. Students would achieve greater success if planning and assessment practices were improved.

Nowhere is the information about performance of students with special needs either systematically gathered or analyzed. The preparation of those who work with special-needs students is uneven, and there are few instances of early intervention.

Siegel and Ladyman said that early identification and intervention would reduce the number of special-needs students and the severity of the difficulties they encounter. Student success would be improved if information were more readily shared and services coordinated when students begin school or make a transition from one school to another. But there are, they said, procedural, administrative, and contractual practices that impede the schooling of special-needs students.

Teacher attitudes and expectations, information sharing, and coordination of services are only a few of the factors in addressing the special educational needs of some students. Time and material resources, in-service education, reasonable class sizes, and attention to class composition are other important factors. They should not be ignored if we want to improve the educational and life chances of these students.

## WARRANTY WORK

MANY SPECIAL-NEEDS STUDENTS do not truly warrant the label. Schools spend time and valuable resources repairing faulty work they did the first time around. Or failed to do at all. Some special-needs students are simply regular kids who initially needed extra help.

Last year, my friend Marie's daughter, Emma, was in grade two French immersion. In late September, Marie met with Emma's teacher, who informed Marie that Emma was a struggling reader who would need extra help. The teacher told Marie that, each day when Emma's classmates were reading, Emma and other slow readers would be sent down the hall to the Learning Assistance teacher for help with their reading.

Marie questioned whether this was the best approach to take. The teacher said, "I earned my master's in reading, and I know how it works. I teach reading all day long to kids. I can assure you that this is in Emma's best interest . . . thirty minutes every day in the LAC [Learning Assistance Centre] and she'll be just fine." Imagine that, a French Immersion teacher with master's level specialization in reading unable to address the problems of a struggling reader in her own grade two class of twenty-two children.

Emma's teacher is typical of many of today's teachers. She is well educated and well prepared. My mother's generation of elementary teachers often had only one year of preparation beyond high school. My mother was unusual; she had two years of teacher preparation beyond her high school degree. My mother taught grade one for almost her entire career. Her last grade one class comprised thirty-five students. The school's attendance area included publicly subsidized housing for people receiving income assistance. Many of the children in the area had little exposure to reading before coming to school.

My mother was not given to hyperbole or the "sin of pride." Nonetheless, once, when I asked her about her teaching, she said plainly, "I've never met a child I couldn't teach to read. It may have been difficult for them and for me, but all of the children in my classes began grade two reading at grade level."

I asked her about her approach. She replied, "On the first day of school, I would tell the children that they were very lucky to be in school because they would learn a very powerful secret – they would learn how to read. I'd say, 'Once you learn to read, no one can hide anything from you. It will be very hard, but I will help you. I have never met a child who couldn't learn to read.' Then I would read them a story that I knew they would like."

My mother would not have described herself as a reading specialist. The methods she used were the ones she was taught during her two years of teacher preparation at her "normal school," the name given to the institutions that prepared teachers in those days. "I read to the children every day, often twice a day. Who doesn't like to have someone read to them?" she asked.

"We also used basal readers," my mother explained. "You know, the readers with Dick, Jane, Spot, and all of that. But every child also had a library card. Each week, beginning in September, I would take them to the school library to select their books. In my last few years of teaching, during choosing time the children might select a cassette tape with a story that they could listen to while they followed along in the book."

I asked her whether many of the children struggled with reading. "It varied from year to year, but there were always children who struggled. Some might not have had much opportunity to hear and handle books. Others – even the ones with books at home – struggled too. But they all learned to read at grade level by the end of the year."

My mother's repertoire for teaching reading was eclectic. For children who had difficulty recognizing letters, she had wooden letters covered in sandpaper. "Children having trouble with letter recognition would trace the letter with their finger as they identified the letter. We'd make a game of it. If the letter was identified correctly, the child would keep the letter until the end of the game. We'd count the number of correctly identified letters and chart them on a page in their scribblers."

The priority my mother placed on learning to read meant that she did not always address all of the topics recommended for grade one students. "None of the principals I worked for ever complained that the children were short-changed." Today, it is doubtful that parents and principals would allow teachers the latitude my mother enjoyed. They would demand that all children read and that the entire grade one curriculum be addressed – as unrealistic as that is with the greatly expanded curriculum and increased expectations.

There is little doubt that the conditions under which my mother worked were very different from the ones faced by teachers today. My mother's grade one class was large by today's standards, but the class did not include children confined to wheelchairs or suffering the consequences of parental substance abuse. My mother had the advantage of preparing children for a youth culture that had not yet turned away from reading to electronic media. She and her colleagues enjoyed a measure of respect from the general public and from elected politicians that is less evident today.

Today's teachers have much more education and preparation than those of my mother's generation. The irony is that, despite their greater education and extensive preparation, they believe sometimes they need the help of a range of specialists to teach even the most rudimentary skills.

A variety of factors conspire to undermine in today's teachers the self-confidence and efficacy that teachers of my mother's generation enjoyed. The demands placed upon schools and teachers have grown exponentially. Expecting teachers to address the special education needs of students without providing them with adequate in-service education has contributed to teachers' feelings of inadequacy.

As in Emma's case, special education is often prescribed for students who are having difficulty learning to read, write, and count. But when asked what's "special" about special education, many in the field say that effective special education is nothing more than good teaching.

A big change for elementary teachers has been the inclusion of those students who in the past were segregated or excluded entirely from schools. Most teachers recognize the inherent value in all students, but teachers' usual classroom strategies to reduce differences among students don't always work for students with special needs.

Teachers put students in groups that they think can address the same level of material at the same pace. With exceptional students in the class, the grouping strategy is seldom practical, because the differences among students are too great. Instead, classroom teachers will try to have the exceptional students assigned to specialist teachers who can work with them individually outside of the classroom.

I fully recognize that some youngsters have congenital or acquired conditions that demand additional resources and attention. Children afflicted by autism, children whose cognitive and/or emotional development is severely limited, and children who are seeing- or hearing-impaired, or whose mobility is impaired obviously need "special" measures to ensure they get the maximum benefit from their school experience. And there is no question that they should receive both the additional attention they need and the access to special technologies that will enable them to enjoy success in school and later as adults.

Such children are few, making up only a small proportion of the school-age population. The prevalence of students whose conditions warrant the designation "dependent handicapped" is less than two-tenths of 1 per cent (0.17 per cent) in the United States, where such information has been collected for nearly thirty years. For reasons that are not entirely clear, the Canadian rate is a bit higher, three-tenths of 1 per cent (0.31 per cent) of the school-age population. These children often endure multiple conditions that require the support of what some jurisdictions call "special education assistants." Special education assistants are often workers who have received a modest amount of training to enable them to help with the education of such students.

There are students with physical disabilities in addition to students categorized as dependent handicapped. They comprise slightly more than one-tenth of 1 per cent (0.11 per cent) of the school-age population in the United States and three-tenths of 1 per cent (0.31 per cent) in Canada. Students who are blind or have visual impairments and students who are deaf or hard of hearing account for 0.06 per cent and 0.14 per cent of the Canadian school-age population, according to a survey conducted for the Council of Ministers of Education Canada.

Students with speech and language impairments add another 1.7 per cent in the United States to the population of students with special educational needs. Autism, on the rise everywhere, accounts for another 0.08 per cent. Students with mild to severe intellectual disabilities add less than 2 per cent to the special-needs population (1.75 per cent). And students who manifest emotional and behavioural conditions serious enough to warrant special attention add another 0.78 per cent.

All of the aforementioned students account for less than 4 per cent of the school-age population in Canada. Most jurisdictions count another 4 to 5 per cent of the student population as "special needs." These additional children are described as "learning disabled," a term that includes a variety of learning difficulties.

A combination of factors creates and sustains a system that doesn't always deliver the benefits to students that it should. Part of the problem is the glasses through which we view students with special educational needs. We are an achievement-oriented society that places great emphasis on academic success. The "new economy" depends upon knowledge, and Canadians see themselves as serious competitors. In fact, many believe that Canada's survival depends upon using knowledge to strategic advantage just as we once used our natural resources.

Being achievement-oriented may be a good thing for many, but it places significant pressure on students and their parents. Canadian parents are concerned to provide as many advantages as they can for their children. Parents try to secure for them, by all the means at their disposal, the things they regard as necessary to ensure their children's success.

Unlike times when children largely organized their own activities or played under the watchful supervision of parents, many of today's young children have "play dates" organized by their parents, attend pre-schools, and are enrolled in programs and sports that will cultivate their talents and abilities. Ability, standing out from the crowd, has replaced enjoyment as the primary objective of the lives of many young children.

Parents of children with educational challenges long for a scientific remedy for their children's problems. Medicine has made significant contributions to our well-being, but it has also had unfortunate and unanticipated consequences. One is the belief that there should (or must) be a medical solution to social problems. People do not drink too much, they suffer from alcoholism. They do not abuse drugs, they are drug dependent. As with problems such as addictions to gambling, alcohol, and drugs, we tend to see special education from the medical perspective. One of the unfortunate consequences of this is an increase in the number of teachers who believe that the teaching techniques they have learned are inadequate to address the problems of children who are having trouble learning. The "slow learner" with whom my mother spent more time has become the "learning disabled" student who is sent to another teacher for specialized help.

One family in British Columbia is questioning the way students with learning disabilities are being educated. The family, which is seeking redress through the human rights commission, complains that their dyslexic teenager wasn't taught to read. The parents say the system discriminated against their son because it failed to make him literate despite the fact that teachers and administrators knew he was dyslexic. The family removed their son from public school in grade three and enrolled him in a private school, where the teacher – working with a class of twenty-four students – addressed his difficulty with reading. The student's father argues that reading is a foundation of public education: "You might as well not have public education if you can't teach kids to read."

## PINNING ON A LABEL

A GROUP OF RESEARCHERS from Vanderbilt University and the University of Texas used advanced statistical techniques to answer the question "Is 'learning disabilities' just a fancy term for low achievement?" They compared the reading performance of low achievers who had not been labelled "learning disabled" with low achievers who had been given the label. They found that the reading scores of 73 per cent of low achievers without the label "learning disabled" were above the average reading score of low achievers with the label.

The researchers say that, on the basis of the evidence presently available, "It is difficult to argue persuasively that these students [those labelled 'learning disabled'] have a qualitatively different set of learner characteristics requiring a unique educational response." In the absence of further evidence, they regard the difference between the students labelled "learning disabled" and those not so labelled as being "simply a matter of degree, not kind."

Linda Siegel says the evidence shows that early reading instruction prevents reading failure for many kindergarten children considered at risk. Teachers can promote success for all children at risk of reading failure by using explicit and intensive instruction in the context of a balanced approach to literacy education.

Siegel worked with a group of graduate students and teachers in the North Vancouver School District. The district is committed to early identification and intervention to prevent reading failure. The district's program includes systematic student assessment of pre-reading skills. It also includes a balanced early reading program with small-group instruction in phonological awareness (the ability to identify the sounds that make words and associate those sounds with written words) for the children when they are in kindergarten and phonics instruction in grade one.

The initial results from their longitudinal study indicate that the interventions are successful for the majority of children identified as "at risk" because they exhibit reading difficulties in kindergarten. Siegel points out that the kindergarten phonological awareness training for all children is carried out as part of a variety of literacy activities. The at-risk children receive targeted, direct phonological awareness instruction in small groups in grade one as well.

Siegel and her colleagues believe that the approach taken in North Vancouver reduces the incidence of reading failure in grades one and two for the majority of children. The study also indicates that the North Vancouver program is demonstrably beneficial for children from minority-language backgrounds.

Schooling is hard for many children. Their difficulties create hardships for themselves, their families, and their teachers. Students know when they are not performing as well as their classmates. Parents, appropriately concerned about the educational well-being of their offspring, often seek to have their children "labelled" to obtain the extra help they believe will eliminate or reduce their child's difficulty.

At the same time, school boards and ministries of education try to control the demands for additional services. They establish relatively elaborate procedures for screening youngsters to determine their eligibility for additional help. The screening procedures are costly in terms of time, money, and personnel. The intervention is often delayed by rules that require sophisticated and costly diagnostic procedures before students can qualify for additional resources. The demand for screening almost always exceeds the capacity to carry out the screening in a timely manner. This delays educational interventions.

While students are not ignored, teachers tend to wait until they have been "screened" to plan a unique program to address their difficulties. In the interval, the students continue to perform poorly. They are, in effect, "practising" the errors they are making and not learning more effective strategies to address the tasks they find challenging.

Even teachers who have had coursework in special education prior to completing teacher education programs say they are powerlessness to address the needs of many children. It is my impression that, while the range of children in classrooms has expanded over the past twenty-five years, the range of children that most teachers feel competent to teach has narrowed.

Classroom teachers believe that their specialist colleagues are using more sophisticated techniques to address the needs of youngsters labelled as "special needs." But the secret of special education is coming out. The capacity of special education to identify students experiencing difficulty exceeds the supply of unique methods to address those difficulties. With some notable exceptions – speech and language pathologists, and teachers of the seeing- and hearing-impaired – most special-needs teachers use the same methods that their classroom-based colleagues employ. In fact, most courses in special education imply that the term really means *good teaching applied to students with needs that fall outside the norm.*

This state of affairs is extremely worrisome. The demand for special educational services exceeds the system's capacity. Teachers are feeling increasingly powerless. We are not monitoring systematically the progress of students with special educational needs to see if the out-of-class interventions are actually improving the students' success.

Many of the parents of students who experience difficulty learning are worried. They fear that the challenges their children face will not be addressed and that their children will leave school without the knowledge they need to make their way in the world. The concerns are entirely legitimate.

### WHO GETS THE MONEY?

SOME PARENTS OF SPECIAL-NEEDS STUDENTS have found it helpful to join organizations that provide them with support. These organizations advocate on behalf of parents with school boards and ministries of education, which has led some school boards and ministries to attach funding to students with particular learning characteristics.

Providing additional funding for students with particular characteristics has been a two-edged sword. On the one hand, it has ensured that specific sums of money are reserved for students with special needs. But it does not ensure that the money is provided to the students who most need it. As a result, there are numerous instances of school boards using resources designated for one group of youngsters to provide service to another group.

Learning assistance and special education have become growth industries for some cash-strapped school boards. Attaching funding to students with particular characteristics creates powerful incentives to label youngsters. But the label is a problem if there is no corresponding technology for addressing the condition that gave rise to that label. Labels tend to stick. Too many students suffer unnecessarily the stigma of the label "special needs." They have not benefited from having been identified as "special needs" in the way that they, their parents, or anyone else might reasonably expect.

Attaching funding to students with particular characteristics has also created an atmosphere where the parents of special-needs students are pitted against the parents of the rest of the student population. What parent does not feel their son or daughter is not "special" and deserving of additional attention in some way.

In the United States, Public Law 94-142 required that students with special needs be educated in the "least restrictive environment." Following that example, teachers and parents encouraged Canadian school jurisdictions to hire specialized personnel to assist teachers working with the most challenged and challenging special-needs students. Over the years the number of assistants has grown, and the growth has been more rapid than the growth in the number of special-needs youngsters.

One of my colleagues – an expert in the field of special education – talks about the "profusion of paraprofessionals 'Velcroed' to special-needs students." She wonders whether the provision of such assistance is in the best interest of all the youngsters receiving it. Many students and many teachers benefit from the help the assistants provide. But many students with special educational needs have been abandoned to their special education assistants.

Special education assistants are supposed to work under the direction and supervision of the classroom teacher. Their responsibilities range from assisting students with personal care to assisting the teacher to administer his or her instructional program. Many teachers in whose classes these assistants have been placed seem to have abrogated some of their educational responsibilities.

Some jurisdictions do not make adequate provision for monitoring the progress of students generally and students with special needs in particular. In the absence of such monitoring – and even in its presence – it is often difficult to tell whether students with special educational needs are getting the full benefit of the resources devoted to them. Are students receiving such services learning more than they would if they were not labelled as "special needs"? We simply do not know.

## INCLUSION

LACK OF CLARITY about the meaning of inclusion and poor implementation are a challenge to the schooling of students with truly special needs. Despite some strong policy work, many people continue to misunderstand what inclusion means – and what it doesn't mean. Some of the misunderstanding is the result of misguided advocacy on the part of parents and interest groups.

Parents of youngsters with more profound disabilities want to ensure their child receive the same opportunities as other children. Many of them want their children integrated with their age-peers in the same class all day, every day of the school year. And some parents have difficulty accepting that their children will not progress educationally and socially even when the opportunities they are provided are the same as those given to all others. Some special-needs children require a program that balances integration in classes with their age-group peers with direct, daily help from professionals with specific skills.

A teacher enrolled in a graduate course in educational policy recently described the following situation. The school in which she was teaching was built in the early 1980s, one of the first schools in the region to be constructed with wheelchair access. The school was committed to integrating students with special needs in the regular program in classes with their age-peers. According to the teacher, honouring the commitment worked for most of the eight students with special needs who were attending the school in 2002. But it did not work for all of them.

Two of the eight students suffered from severe disabilities. Their ability to communicate was limited to responses to such basic stimuli as heat, cold, hunger, and pain. They were unable to interact meaningfully with their age-peers. In fact, according to this teacher, the staff was uncertain whether the children knew where they were. The children were completely dependent upon the special education assistants assigned to them for their toileting, feeding, and any other care they required. Nonetheless, as is often the case, these children had been placed in a classroom with their age-peers.

Both students responded well to music and stories and to the stimulation that playing with water provides. But since the classroom to which they had been assigned was designed for more intellectually advanced students, the activities and instruction could not fully accommodate their needs. Intermediate classrooms did not have an area for water play. The opportunities for enjoying music and stories were more limited in an intermediate classroom than would be the case in a primary classroom. "Placing these children in age-appropriate settings without offering alternative programs has done these children a disservice," the teacher told me.

That was the case in Ontario with Emily Eaton. Her parents could not accept that integration in a classroom with her peers was not in her best interests. Emily is a young woman with cerebral palsy. She is unable to communicate through speech, sign language, or other alternative systems. She is also visually impaired and requires the use of a wheelchair because her mobility is restricted.

Emily was identified as an "exceptional pupil." At the request of her parents, she was placed in her neighbourhood school on a trial basis. She was assigned a full-time assistant to attend to her various needs. After three years in her neighbourhood school, the teachers and assistants concluded that the placement was not to Emily's benefit. In fact, they believed that continued placement in the neighbourhood school might actually be harmful to her.

An Identification, Placement, and Review Committee (IPRC) decided Emily should be placed in a special education class. Emily's parents appealed the decision to a Special Education Appeal Board. The appeal board unanimously confirmed the decision of the IPRC. Emily's parents appealed again to the Ontario Special Education Tribunal. The tribunal also unanimously confirmed the decision of the IPRC.

Emily's parents applied for judicial review to the Divisional Court of Ontario. The court dismissed the application. The Eatons then took the case to the Court of Appeal. It allowed the appeal and set aside the tribunal's decision.

The Attorney General of Ontario appealed the decision of the Court of Appeals to the Supreme Court of Canada. The Supreme Court decided that the Court of Appeal erred in finding that the decision of the tribunal contravened section 15 of the Canadian Charter of Rights and Freedoms.

The reasoning of the Supreme Court in Emily's case, and by extension in the case of all students with special needs, is worth considering for what it says about such students and how their needs should be taken into account. The Supreme Court's decision considered exclusion from the mainstream of society and the implications of the meaning of disability. It noted that the meaning of disability differs significantly depending on the characteristics of the individual and the situation. "Segregation," the court noted, "can be both protective of equality" and something that violates "equality depending upon the person and the state of disability."

The Supreme Court observed that the tribunal had tried to determine which placement for Emily would be superior, according to her special needs and educational interests. The tribunal had taken into account Emily's special needs when it concluded that placement in a special class was the best for her. The court also noted that the tribunal had considered the necessity of periodic assessment of Emily's "best interests" so that relevant changes could be reflected in her placement. The Supreme Court commented that "a decision reached after such an approach could not be considered a burden or a disadvantage imposed on a child."

The issue of inclusion is deeply emotional. Despite their good intentions, some parents are unable to accept the judgment of professionals when it comes to their own children. They seek full inclusion – "regular class, all day, every day" – rather than a program better suited to their youngsters' needs.

Education professionals sometimes capitulate to parents who strongly assert their preferences for inclusion, even when they know that it is not in the student's best interest. This makes the teaching situation very difficult for the classroom teacher. Faced with the needs of an entire class of students, the education needs of some special-needs students are left to special education assistants. This sometimes makes the situation worse. Though well intentioned, special education assistants do not typically have the preparation needed to address the educational needs of the student. Deprived of help, some special-needs students languish because their educational needs are not being addressed by the classroom teacher, the special education assistants, or by specialist teachers in a more appropriate setting.

## ABORIGINAL EDUCATION

LET'S BE PLAIN. Canadian public schools have failed the majority of aboriginal students. Their success rates are much lower than those students from other backgrounds. Significantly fewer aboriginal students graduate than do non-aboriginal students. Those who graduate have too often been the recipients of an inferior education. Aboriginal students attend post-secondary education at about half the rate of non-aboriginal students. The situation is a tragedy of enormous proportion.

We all have a responsibility to change the conditions affecting aboriginal learners. The lack of success of many aboriginal learners is caused by racism, pure and simple. Non-aboriginal students who face the same kinds of challenges as confronted by aboriginal youngsters – poverty and the social disorganization that poverty fosters – are more successful.

The state of education for aboriginal peoples makes many people uncomfortable, but not sufficiently uncomfortable to act. In 1999, Paul Ramsey, minister of education for British Columbia, raised the issue at the annual meeting of the Council of Ministers of Education Canada. Ramsey tried to engage other ministers in establishing aboriginal education as a pan-Canadian priority. Nothing happened. There was insufficient political will to address the matter on a pan-Canadian basis. In fact, at a subsequent meeting of deputy ministers designed to review the meeting of ministers, one deputy minister said derisively that British Columbia had tried to highjack the meeting of ministers to pursue "the Aboriginal agenda."

The government of Canada pays for schooling on reserves, but it has failed in its responsibility to aboriginal students. By underfunding schools on reserves, the federal government encourages some parents to move their children from those schools to provincial schools, where the quality of schooling is higher and the services more plentiful. In British Columbia, for example, provincial school boards receive an additional thousand dollars for each student of aboriginal origin enrolled in a public school. The money is intended to provide additional support for such things as aboriginal language and cultural programs, aboriginal home-school liaison workers, and additional counsellors for aboriginal students.

Like a number of provincial jurisdictions, British Columbia has made an effort to address the deplorable state of education for aboriginal learners. The province has been collecting data about aboriginal performance and monitoring school boards' plans for addressing the gap between aboriginal and non-aboriginal learners. Some modest progress has been made on two fronts. The number of students willing to disclose their aboriginal origins has increased, indicating a growing pride in their background. Equally important, the proportion of aboriginal students successfully completing secondary school and continuing their education at the post-secondary level has also been increasing. While encouraging, these improvements are too modest to warrant much rejoicing.

There are many strategies that can be implemented immediately to improve aboriginal success. The first and most important is to address the achievement gap between aboriginal and non-aboriginal students. The effort should begin when aboriginal students enter school, and it should continue as long as aboriginal students differ in achievement from their peers. Primary teachers who recognize children with limited vocabulary should emphasize vocabulary building in their programs. Those who see other signs indicating potential difficulty in reading should emphasize phonetic strategies in their reading programs.

During my time as deputy minister of education, British Columbia sought agreements with school boards and representatives of the aboriginal communities on strategies for improving student success. The Aboriginal Education Performance Agreements asked for a commitment from the parties to a plan that would achieve results, narrow the performance difference between aboriginal and non-aboriginal students, and eventually achieve parity.

Another strategy has been to ensure that aboriginal perspectives are included in the public school curriculum wherever relevant. B.C.'s Ministry of Education launched a number of initiatives to make its curriculum better reflect aboriginal perspectives. The province sought recognition from provincial universities for its First Nations 12 course. The universities approved the course as an equivalent to Social Studies 11, which is a requirement for admission. Our hope was that recognition by the universities would bring additional status to the course and help build enrolment among aboriginal and non-aboriginal students.

British Columbia has also made an effort to develop courses in the aboriginal languages spoken in the province. The British Columbia College of Teachers has developed a certification program for speakers of the aboriginal languages so that they may teach them in B.C. public schools.

British Columbia has also developed material indicating how aboriginal perspectives can be integrated in different areas of the curriculum. *Shared Learnings: Integrating B.C. Aboriginal Content K-10* is a guide for teachers in integrating aboriginal topics in all subject areas at an introductory level. Its purpose is to foster sensitivity to, and respect for, the richness and diversity of the aboriginal peoples of British Columbia.

Yet another strategy is to create the conditions for members of the aboriginal community to become involved in the public schools their children attend. Many aboriginal parents feel uncomfortable approaching teachers and principals about issues affecting their children. They do not feel welcome on school-parent committees and are underrepresented there. Some schools have made successful attempts to reach out to the elders in aboriginal communities, seeking their advice and support for policies and practices that would support aboriginal youngsters. Seeking permission to address elders during band council meetings is one of the successful strategies.

For nearly thirty-five years, various universities across Canada have made efforts to recruit and prepare aboriginal teachers for public school teaching. Despite their efforts and the quality of the programs offered, aboriginal teachers remain underrepresented in the teaching force. We must redouble efforts to prepare and recruit aboriginal people to positions of responsibility as teachers, administrators, and school trustees.

Teachers' unions can support this effort. They could easily waive seniority requirements for aboriginal supply teachers (teachers on call) seeking permanent appointments. The consequences for non-aboriginal teachers would be slight compared with the improvement in the number of aboriginal teachers.

While our schools must address the educational gap between aboriginal and non-aboriginal students, public schools cannot and should not be expected to work in isolation. Aboriginal parents, elders, and community leaders must do their part. Aboriginal children who do not attend school regularly and who live in communities suffering from social problems such as substance abuse will find school success elusive. I am encouraged by the many aboriginal leaders and elders who recognize the importance of schooling and who have dedicated themselves to forging partnerships between aboriginal communities and the public schools that serve them.

### ENGLISH- AND FRENCH-LANGUAGE LEARNING

CANADA DEPENDS on a steady flow of immigrants to maintain its population and ensure a well-educated workforce to pay for the programs, services, and pensions that Canadians have come to expect. Without immigration, Canada's population would shrink rapidly and the dependency ratio – the ratio of children and retired Canadians to the population as a whole – would become unbalanced.

Approximately 45,000 of the 200,000 immigrants that enter Canada each year are students of school age. Canada has a vital interest in ensuring that immigrants learn English or French quickly and well. The possession of one of Canada's official languages is an essential foundation for schooling and work. Canadians of my grandparents' generation may have struggled to learn English and French without the benefit of special programs. Some did not succeed. Even among those who did learn English, their lack of fluency limited their educational and employment opportunities.

Debra Clarke, a teacher in B.C. specializing in students learning English, makes a series of interesting observations. In the past, she points out, in many schools the ratio of fluent English speakers (often mistakenly called "native" English speakers) to non-English speakers was much greater than it is today. Immigrants of previous generations may have been successful learners of English or French without additional help because English-speaking role models surrounded them. They needed to use English to communicate and had many opportunities to practise the English they had learned.

According to Clarke, the situation for non-English speaking students in public schools today is very different. In many urban Canadian schools, non-English speakers outnumber English speakers. As a consequence, there are fewer opportunities to hear and use English. In addition, the need to use English outside of school is much less than in the past because the students live in large communities of people speaking the same language.

Clarke says that the label ESL (English as a second language) may once have been useful shorthand. But today its use is an oversimplification. There is great diversity among learners to whom the label is applied. For example, some students (often from Korea, Hong Kong, and sometimes Japan) began schooling as early as age three or four. In their countries of origin, these students attended school from 8 A.M. to 4 P.M., five and a half or six days a week. Some studied English. In contrast, some of the other students labelled ESL may have had their schooling interrupted or may have never attended school at all. Some refugee students attended school for relatively brief periods (perhaps two hours a day, four days a week), where the language of instruction was neither English, French, nor a language familiar to them.

Clarke also points out that consideration of the need for English- or French-language instruction does not always take into account the children born in Canada to immigrant parents. Many of these children have the same language-learning needs as immigrant children. These children often begin kindergarten without having been exposed to English beyond what they may have heard on television.

Canadian school boards are only beginning to face the challenge of accommodating immigrant students. Clarke says that age-equivalent placement policies are often problematic for students unfamiliar with English or French. A twelve-year-old student who has never attended school and does not have even rudimentary literacy in any language may be assigned to a grade seven classroom.

Clarke points out how the patterns of schooling familiar to Canadians can pose a challenge for students from elsewhere. Canadian schools begin in September. But, Clarke says, large numbers of immigrant students enrol in Canadian schools in the spring because that is when the school year begins in the country of origin.

For Clarke the greatest challenge is that teachers in all subjects and at all grade levels are not aware of the need to teach literacy or are not well prepared to ensure that students acquire the knowledge they need to become literate. The problem is especially challenging for secondary school teachers. They need to be able to address the literacy needs of immigrant students and ensure that their instruction is relevant to the students' level of maturity. More mature students must be engaged in issues that interest them and can also be used as a vehicle for developing literacy. If both factors are not taken into account and the instructional content does not relate to the learners' lives, older learners turn away from school.

Another fairly recent change associated with immigration is a shift in gender balance. In Canada, in general, family preferences for sons are stronger than for daughters. New Canadian families have even stronger preferences for sons than for daughters. Clarke explains that over the last dozen years there has been a shift in the ratio of male students to female students. It is not unusual for a kindergarten or grade one class to enrol a disproportionate ratio of boys to girls. Teachers say this makes a difference in classroom dynamics and management.

Some high school teachers complain that male students raised in strongly patriarchal households do not give female teachers the respect they deserve, though this attitude is not confined to the families of immigrant students. Some teachers also express frustration about families that are content to see daughters complete school but want their sons to pursue professional careers. In a society that values equality, such conflicts can strain relations between schools and families. Outreach to new Canadian families can help ease some of the strains for the newcomers and for the public schools.

## WHAT ARE SCHOOLS FOR?

NOTWITHSTANDING MY CRITICAL COMMENTS in this chapter, our public school teachers respond more capably and successfully than ever before. We should remember that today's schools enrol and provide educational programs for students whose characteristics would – in the past – have seen them educated in a segregated setting or excluded from school. The presence of such children brings us face-to-face with the question: "What are schools for?" They make us conscious that the purpose of public schooling is to maximize the intellectual and social health of *all* members of society. Long overdue, the integration of special-needs students in public schools is a policy consistent with a society that values diversity and treats people compassionately.

# chapter eight

# TEACHERS' WORK, UNIONS, AND PROFESSIONALISM

wo changes have had a substantial impact on teachers and teaching. First, and perhaps most important, is that teacher preparation has improved steadily over the past fifty years. The second factor is that teachers have come to think of themselves as both professionals *and* workers, and as workers they are represented, like other workers, by a union. While the public has generally welcomed the former, it has reacted skeptically – and sometimes angrily – to the latter.

In fact, many people think that teachers are well paid, enjoy generous benefits, and have a relatively easy schedule. There isn't a teacher in Canada who hasn't heard someone say, "I wish I had two months off every summer, two weeks at Christmas, and another at spring break." It is ironic how firmly such perceptions are established in the public's mind. Yet, these perceptions are seldom based on first-hand knowledge about the job of teaching. Most people, including other teachers, rarely observe teachers at work.

## THE REALITY OF TEACHING

THE REALITY OF TEACHING is that it is a management position of considerable responsibility. In a corporate context, no beginning employee would be asked to undertake responsibility for the supervision of others or for tasks as complex as teaching. A person with comparable responsibility in a corporate context would probably require ten or more years of previous experience before being promoted to such a position. Yet on their very first day in the classroom, teachers are thrust into this hidden world to organize people, material, and ideas to accomplish one of society's most important tasks.

Those people who have observed teachers at work are often overwhelmed by the sheer volume of teacher-student interaction, the quantity of paper and material to be managed, the movement of students, and the pacing and sequencing of activity. Talk about multitasking! Managers who are familiar with the impact of absences on workflow might wonder how teachers cope when students are absent. Teachers must ensure that students who have missed school do not fall behind, because when students do fall behind, it makes schooling more difficult for both student and teacher.

Teachers must anticipate the unexpected and respond as if the unexpected were routine. The classroom is a place where the urgent can displace the important. The injury, upset stomach, personal tragedy, or world events can disrupt scheduled lessons.

The activity of the classroom is supported by preparation invisible to others. Even spouses keenly aware of the time it consumes do not appreciate the staggering complexity of the preparation required. Teachers must consider the purposes of the curriculum, the characteristics of the learners, the availability of materials, the time available for instruction, the appropriateness of the methodology, and much more.

A typical elementary teacher prepares for language arts, mathematics, science, social studies, art, music, and physical education, and, in some jurisdictions, a second language. A secondary teacher often has four or more courses to prepare. The contractual preparation time is not sufficient to accomplish the task. Added to their other responsibilities, assessment – making judgments about student work – makes an already demanding job daunting. *You mean you have to read all those papers?*

Few people associate meetings – the métier of middle and upper corporate management – with teaching. But meetings are a necessary part of teaching. Teachers meet to coordinate activities, to review the progress, or to coordinate the program of a student receiving assistance outside the classroom. They meet to plan for the use of shared facilities such as the gymnasium, library, and computer centre. And they meet with parents to explain their programs and discuss student progress. Most, if not all, meetings must occur outside of the time that teachers are responsible for students – before school, during recess and lunch, and after school.

Many teachers sponsor clubs, coach teams, and organize events for the benefit of students. They spend scarce time – for which they are not paid – in extracurricular activities before and after school, during lunch breaks, and even on weekends. Getting to know students in settings outside the classroom often helps teachers to establish rapport. Some students remain in school only because of the opportunity to engage in extracurricular activities.

Extracurricular work is often taken for granted by all concerned – including teachers – which encourages the erroneous impression that these activities are as important as what happens in the classroom. They aren't. We fool ourselves if we believe they are and devalue the educational program and teaching profession in our own eyes, and in the eyes of students. Why should students take their studies more seriously than basketball, band, and working on the school annual if we don't?

Time management, a staple topic in management training programs, is the stock-in-trade of teaching. Teachers manage – and are managed by – time like no other worker. *Please don't forget that Melinda needs her medication before – not after – lunch!* A teacher's day has no elasticity; the student schedule is rigidly fixed. Any disruption of the planned activities will have consequences later in the week, the month, or school year.

In most jurisdictions, curriculum is planned by teachers, Ministry of Education staff, and specialists in curriculum and instruction from provincial universities. They set the goals for any given subject so that the average student working under normal circumstances in 80 per cent of the time allocated can achieve them. This arrangement is based upon professional judgments that, if proven inaccurate, do not usually get corrected until the entire curriculum sequence for the subject area is modified.

"Average students" and "normal circumstances" are in short supply in most Canadian schools. Typical Canadian schools enrol atypical students. Students will misbehave and daydream. They will miss school because of illness and family circumstances. In elementary schools that make use of specialist teachers for particular subjects (music or art, for example), teachers in one class will often schedule a fieldtrip forgetting about another teacher's schedule. At the secondary level, teachers will schedule examinations and papers that prompt students to concentrate their energies on those assignments instead of the lessons taught by the teachers in their other classes. There will be fire drills, snow days, school- or grade-wide assemblies, and other events that will intrude upon the "normal" school day and year.

The time available for instruction is always more limited than the many worthwhile topics available for study. Teachers must select from an enormous range those activities and opportunities appropriate for students with unique characteristics learning in a particular environment. No curriculum guide or set of standards can take into account – except in a very general way – the factors that will affect teaching and learning in a particular classroom. There is no manual that can substitute for the teacher's professional judgment.

The situation might work well enough if we were content to establish general curriculum guidelines and goals and leave instructional decisions to a teacher's professional judgment. But we are not. Teachers are mired in a morass of demands impossible to fulfil in the limited time that students are in school.

The school's formal and informal curriculum is strained to the breaking point. Although the number of hours and days of instruction haven't changed in the past fifty years, the number of additional topics, programs, and courses has. As I mentioned earlier, child-abuse prevention, bully-proofing, anti-racist and multicultural education, career and personal planning, and media studies are but a few examples of the additions made to the formal and informal curriculum of the public school over the past half-century. The added demands and the increased diversity among students make teaching more challenging today than ever before.

Teachers' responsibilities have also increased over the past quarter-century. My mother – who taught grade one for many years – does not recall what has become a common phenomenon: administering medication to students. For her, the administration of provincially mandated assessments was more infrequent and irregular, whereas today, at some grade levels, provincial examinations are universal and mandatory, except for the few students who are exempt. And if a student is exempted from an examination, the teacher must complete a form indicating the reason for the exemption and obtain the approval of someone in a position of authority.

The preparation of report cards is more time-consuming and demanding. Teachers assess a broader range of student work than in the past. Marks are expected to be accompanied by written comments. If children are at risk of failing, they and their parents should be advised and remedial work assigned. Parent conferences are more common. The expanded range of assessment, notification of the risk of failure, and the addition of written comments are beneficial for students and parents, but they have also added measurably to the workload of teachers.

Schools have not made allowances for the increased demands. Teachers are expected to accomplish the traditional goals of schooling as well as address the new topics and issues. They are expected to help a more diverse and challenging student population perform at a higher standard. And they are expected to accomplish all of this within a school day and year that hasn't changed appreciably.

While the quality of schooling in Canada is high, it will be difficult to maintain that standard if the working conditions of teachers do not change to accommodate the additional demands and the complexity of their work. Put simply, teachers spend too much time teaching and too little time preparing for teaching. Although scheduled preparation time has increased, the increase has not been enough.

## TEACHERS' UNIONS

TEACHERS IN CANADA belong to unions that have worked very hard to improve salaries and the conditions under which teachers work. But recently, in some jurisdictions, the hard-won gains have eroded or been eliminated entirely by government legislation.

The Second World War was followed by an explosive growth in the number of students and an increased emphasis on education. Teachers' unions made aggressive efforts to obtain better wages and working conditions for their members. Those efforts paid off. Between 1960 and 1980, teacher salaries and working conditions improved.

Today, teachers' unions in seven of Canada's provinces and three territories negotiate salaries, benefits, and working conditions with government representatives. Sometimes these negotiations are supplemented by negotiations at the school board level for additional fringe benefits or improvements to working conditions. The exceptions are Alberta, Manitoba, and Ontario, where teachers' unions negotiate not with the provincial government but with representatives of local or regional school boards.

Teacher salaries depend primarily upon the extent of their post-secondary and teacher education and the number of years of teaching experience. Beginning teachers with a four-year post-secondary degree (including teacher preparation) will earn from approximately $31,000 in Prince Edward Island to $38,000 in Alberta. Teachers willing to work in more remote regions and in Canada's territories typically receive compensation above these amounts. This reflects market forces and the additional cost of living in such regions.

In other jobs, starting salaries for people with qualifications comparable to those of beginning teachers are typically higher. Graduates with a bachelor's degree in marketing, finance, or advertising make average beginning salaries of $41,000. A bachelor's degree in computer science software engineering usually fetches $50,000. And the Canadian government hires junior lawyers at starting salaries between $45,000 and $66,000.

Devised in the 1970s, the Education Price Index (EPI) charts operating expenditures for elementary and secondary education adjusted for inflation. The EPI shows that, although teachers were successful in improving their salaries between 1960 and 1980, during the last ten years the picture changed. Since 1992, the EPI rose by 13.5 per cent, but teacher salary increases accounted for only 8 per cent. This is dramatic considering that teacher wages typically account for 70 per cent or more of a school board's budget.

That there appears to be a reasonably competent adult in every classroom is misleading. In fact, Canada continues to suffer from an inadequate supply of qualified teachers in most areas of instruction at the high school level and in some areas of specialization (modern languages, special education, counselling) in elementary schools. Part of the problem is that salaries are not sufficiently competitive to attract enough teachers with backgrounds in mathematics, physics, chemistry, modern languages, music, art, technology studies, and a variety of other subjects. If we want teachers who are qualified for the tasks to which they are assigned, we need to make the salaries for those positions sufficiently attractive. The problem is greatest in rural and remote communities. It has an impact on what students learn and the post-secondary opportunities available to them.

Improvements in teacher salaries during the 1960s were followed by more gradual improvements in teacher working conditions. In some jurisdictions, teachers successfully negotiated that a part of their week would be set aside for preparation. Teachers in some union locals obtained recognition for their professional autonomy in their contracts with school boards.

Time for professional development became a feature of some collective agreements. Protocols were established for identifying students with special learning needs or unusual behaviour. In some jurisdictions, teachers' unions secured limits to the size of classes their members could be asked to teach. In other jurisdictions, unions have not been allowed to negotiate class size limits. In 1998, teachers in British Columbia secured student/teacher ratios for teacher-librarians, learning assistance teachers, counsellors, and teachers of special needs and English as a second language students.

Teachers' unions often argued that the improvements they sought in working conditions would also be of benefit to students. Small classes, specification of procedures for ensuring additional support to students facing learning difficulties and other challenges, and additional assistance from teacher-librarians and teachers with specialized knowledge would, they argued, benefit students as well as teachers. These hard-won gains demanded extra resources for which teachers' unions vigorously lobbied at local and provincial levels.

Nonetheless, many people – including some parents and politicians – believe that teachers' unions have too much power. They say teachers are well paid and get generous holidays. Over the past several years, Canadian politicians seem to have declared war on teachers' unions and, by extension, on teachers themselves.

They have resisted demands for giving teachers better pay. Some provinces, such as British Columbia and Ontario, have restricted what teachers can negotiate through collective bargaining, such as class size limits or teachers' preparation time, eliminating such provisions from collective agreements with teachers.

These attacks have had a devastating impact on teacher morale. Many teachers have withdrawn their services from extracurricular activities, activities teachers enjoy and upon which many youngsters depend to help enrich their school experience. The negative atmosphere has precipitated early retirements among those who can afford them and even among those who cannot.

The impact of all this on recruitment of new teachers is unclear. The number of applicants to teacher education programs has not diminished. One wonders why people are still attracted to teaching under the current conditions.

There is a palpable malaise among Canadian teachers that appears to be spreading. They increasingly feel they are neither respected nor appreciated. In a recent meeting of the board of the Canadian Education Association, Doug Willard, president of the Canadian Teachers' Federation, said, "Teachers were asked to do their part in addressing inflation with a promise – sometimes expressed, sometimes implied – that, when inflation was under control, they would enjoy fair compensation.

"By the time that inflation was under control, politicians and the public had become concerned about the deficit and rising debt. Again, teachers were asked to do their part – to moderate their salary demands with the promise that their demands would be addressed when the deficit was under control. Teachers moderated their demands and witnessed the society granting large salary increases to politicians, civil servants, physicians, and nurses. They felt devalued when their demands were diminished in favour of the demands of others."

"If that wasn't enough," said Willard, "teachers found that gains they had negotiated – in establishing limits to class sizes, in securing time to prepare for teaching and do marking, and in establishing procedures for the evaluation of their work – were eliminated by the action of provincial legislatures. On top of that, teachers in Ontario were told they have not maintained the currency of their knowledge and must prove they deserve to maintain their professional standing through re-certification."

According to Willard, "Teachers feel insulted and they are demoralized. And it is no wonder they feel betrayed. They played by the rules only to have the rules changed without their consent. They don't think that's fair and neither do I."

Leaders of teachers' unions are no less ideological than school trustees or members of provincial legislatures or parliament. To maintain their positions – and some have enjoyed a longevity that is the envy of politicians everywhere – they are carefully attuned to the preferences of their fellow activists. This is, in part, the reason that teachers' unions often appear to resist changes to education unless they improve the salary and working conditions of teachers. Even when they have supported changes, teachers' unions have often responded "yes, but . . ." to the changes, complaining, often with justification, that there are too few resources and too little time to implement the changes sought.

## WORKING CONDITIONS

A CENTRAL QUESTION is whether the provision of educational services such as learning assistance, the assignment of teacher-librarians, and limits to class sizes should be negotiated as part of the collective bargaining process or be determined by government policy? Class size limits and educational support services such as the number of teacher-librarians or learning assistance specialists should be matters of concern for every citizen. The presence or absence of these limits and specialists affect the quality of education.

There are several difficulties in setting class size and staffing provisions by public policy. Public schooling is too often only a concern of parents, who, as a group, make up a rather small and diminishing segment of the population. If left as matters of public policy, limits to class sizes and the number of specialized educational staff would have to compete with other priorities for public and political support. Indifference on the part of the general public toward education and an aging population do not bode well for improving the conditions under which students learn and teachers teach.

Governments – with few exceptions – are unwilling to legislate or regulate such matters as class size and the number of specialist teachers. This leaves those matters open to the incursion of competing political interests. Teachers' unions argue that it is preferable to protect them by allowing them to be negotiated through the process of collective bargaining. Their inclusion in collective agreements does not ensure their longevity; what is bargained can be undone in subsequent negotiations. But it does ensure that, so long as the parties that signed them respect agreements, such provisions will endure for the duration of the contract. This will give a measure of stability to the workplace.

### SCHOOL WARS

WITH SOME RARE EXCEPTIONS, relations between teachers' unions and governments across Canada have been poor for much of the past fifty years. Conditions in the postwar period helped teachers' unions achieve some of the goals they had previously worked toward without much success. Furthermore, in the late 1960s and early 1970s, a cadre of teachers' union leaders (mostly males) emerged who wanted to use public schooling as a means of achieving social justice.

With the fervency of soldiers, teachers have engaged in combat with governments in what became known in some quarters as "school wars." The conflict between Ontario's teachers and the Ontario governments of NDP Premier Bob Rae and Conservative Premier Mike Harris dominated the attention of central Canadians for much of the 1990s. Less well-known nationally, the continuing conflict between the British Columbia Teachers' Federation (BCTF) and successive governments in that province have been just as volatile.

Attributed to disagreements about the funding of education, the differences between the BCTF and various governments in British Columbia have created strained relations and from time to time developed into full-scale warfare. Governments are determined to exercise their authority over education, and the professional body is equally determined to increase its autonomy.

The most recent conflict between the BCTF and the Liberal government of Premier Gordon Campbell is another in a long series of battles. The conflict is attributable to differences regarding the nature of education, the part education plays in the lives of citizens, and about the relationship between citizens and the state. Strong ideological differences separate the two sides.

To a great extent, the conflict is a consequence of the teachers' union's disagreement over the years with the individualistic and corporate values espoused by some of B.C.'s conservative governments. Where such governments have emphasized the individual, the BCTF places primacy on the group. Instead of competition, the BCTF emphasizes co-operation and collective action. Where conservative governments see inequality as inevitable, the teachers' union sees it as a condition that may be overcome, at least in part, by education and through democratically produced social changes.

Recent battles have seen the B.C. teachers' union square off over the government's elimination of hard-won working conditions. The current Liberal government has proclaimed that education is an essential service that should not be disturbed by union job action. In the past, like the battles between Ontario's public sector unions and the government of Bob Rae, teachers in B.C. have fought NDP governments that introduced accountability measures. These measures included annual assessment of reading, writing, and numeracy, and using school accreditation as a means of promoting school improvement.

A particularly graphic illustration of the underlying ideological differences between teachers' unions and some conservative governments can be seen in the conflict that erupted when the Social Credit government introduced a new school act in 1989. Back in 1974, the BCTF had adopted a statement of the purpose of education. According to the statement, the purpose of education was "to foster the growth and development of every individual, to the end that he/she will become a self-reliant, self-disciplined, participating member with a sense of social responsibility within a democratic society." Fifteen years later, the Social Credit government said, "[T]he purpose of the British Columbia school system is to enable learners to develop their individual potential and to acquire the knowledge, skills, and attitudes needed to contribute to a healthy society and a prosperous and sustainable economy."

The two statements set the competing ideologies into relief. Both focus on the individual, but each views the individual differently. The government's statement places emphasis on the individual's economic contribution, regarding education as an investment in human capital. The BCTF's statement gives emphasis to the individual as socially responsible citizen obliged to bring about changes democratically.

Like its brother and sister unions across the country, the BCTF has advanced a number of policies over the years that expressed its views about schooling. Those policies have included: support for federal and provincial affirmative action for women; opposition to membership in organizations that limited membership on the basis of sex, race, or creed; encouragement of French-language instruction for both English- and French-speaking students; condemnation of racial discrimination; support for the establishment of a dental health program for students; support for the provision of family planning information and services; support for negotiated Indian land claims settlements; support for minority and aboriginal language instruction; and support for provincially established preschool education centres. Like its provincial counterparts across the country, the BCTF has opposed: any reduction in expenditures for public education; funding private schools from the public purse; provincial examinations; recognition and support of home-schooling; legislation establishing a college of teachers; and the elimination of local bargaining with school boards.

Teachers' unions have fuelled the perception that they have too much power. Some people see sponsorship of social justice initiatives as inappropriate for an organization of teachers. Their opposition to bodies such as colleges of teachers is interpreted to mean that they are opposed to the regulation of their profession. They resist recertification, an attempt to ensure that the knowledge and practices their members employ are current. And, in the eyes of a society that only tolerates unions at best, they are guilty simply for doing what unions were established to do: protect their members and advance their interests.

Demands for increased competition and choice in education reflect frustration with the apparent unwillingness of public schools to monitor and adjust their approaches to student and school improvement. The demand for traditional schools and specialized schools within the public system is symptomatic of attempts to introduce market forces. This demand will continue to increase until public schools and teachers become more self-regulating.

## TEACHER PROFESSIONALISM

CANADA ALREADY HAS TWO self-regulating professional organizations, the Ontario and the British Columbia College of Teachers. They are loosely patterned after a similar institution in Scotland. It is ironic that, although both organizations originated from ideas advanced by teachers' unions, the same unions in both provinces have opposed the colleges.

In 1974, in an initiative similar to the one proposed in the late 1960s by their colleagues in Ontario, the British Columbia Teachers' Federation proposed a "teaching profession act." The submission, produced by a BCTF task force, argued that the main purpose of such an act "should be to assign to the teaching profession a major role in guaranteeing the quality of teaching service." The task force believed that the BCTF should retain autonomy governing its own internal operations. It proposed that a "teacher certification board" independent of government be established. The board should have "major representation" from the BCTF and representation from the "public-at-large, the minister, and institutions, associations or agencies concerned with the preparation, training or certification of teachers." The Social Credit government of the day took no action on the BCTF's proposal.

More than a decade later, another Social Credit government proclaimed the Teaching Profession Act (1987), establishing Canada's first college of teachers and giving it the power to introduce and enforce professional standards related to training, certification, discipline, and the professional practice of teaching. The legislation was not entirely motivated by a concern for the public's interest in high standards for the teaching profession.

The effect of establishing the college was to eliminate compulsory membership in the British Columbia Teachers' Federation. Under previous legislation, every person who was a teacher on November 29, 1973, or thereafter was required to be or become a member of the BCTF as a condition of employment. By establishing the college and removing the historical recognition of the BCTF, the government attempted to separate the professional concerns of teachers from their economic concerns.

Following its 1974 mandate to take a broad view of education, the BCTF had adopted positions about issues that were perceived by some of its own members to be beyond the

professional purview of the organization. Taking a stand on political and social issues set the BCTF apart from medical and legal
professional organizations in British Columbia. The federation
took an explicitly partisan stance toward the Social Credit government and its political orientation. The government's philosophy of privatization suggested that it should rid itself of the
branch responsible for teacher certification. The Teaching
Profession Act did so in a way that would prevent the BCTF from
exerting direct control over entry to the profession, professional
preparation, and the judgment of competence.

In addition, the Social Credit government permitted teachers
to organize under the terms of the Industrial Relations Act
(1987). The minister of education announced the provisions of
the legislation at a meeting with superintendents, secretary treas-
urers, and teacher association presidents in Richmond, B.C., in
April 1987. He said that, in offering teachers the option of either
forming an association or unionizing, the government was
responding to a long-standing request from some teachers that
they be granted expanded bargaining rights and from others
that wished to see themselves as professionals. The inference
was that unionism and professionalism were incompatible.

The BCTF reacted strongly to the introduction of the Teaching
Profession Act and the inclusion of the federation under the
Labour Code. It launched two provincewide job actions: a one-
day study session and involvement in a provincial general strike.
Although the Industrial Relations Act granted teachers long
sought-after expanded bargaining rights, the legislation was itself
an attack on labour. The Teaching Profession Act was interpreted
as a direct attack on the BCTF; it both eliminated compulsory
membership in the BCTF and established a college of teachers with
a mandate that intruded into the domain of the federation in the
area of professional development.

In April 1987, the BCTF distributed a two-page circular to its
members addressing the question "Why Don't Teachers Want a

'College of Teachers'?" The circular spelled out the federation's "eight good reasons" under headings that proclaimed:

1. It will be divisive and disruptive. Education will be the loser.
2. Freedom of association: Teachers' structure should be agreed – NOT IMPOSED.
3. A college isn't needed. The job's being done.
4. Cost and bureaucracy will be added to education.
5. Professional certification: There is a better way.
6. The college puts teachers in double jeopardy.
7. All other provinces agree: A college isn't necessary.
8. It won't work.

The BCTF held a representative assembly in May 1987. The representative assembly approved a motion by Bill Broadley, a former BCTF president who would later become the first chairperson of the British Columbia College of Teachers, establishing the federation's strategy toward the college. The motion proposed:

That the BCTF participate in the College of Teachers:

1. To elect board members who feel a responsibility to teachers' needs as expressed through the BCTF.
2. To ensure that individual teacher rights are protected against arbitrary and unfair action by the college.
3. To ensure that the scope of activities of the college is limited to certification and setting of standards for teacher education, leaving professional development to the BCTF.
4. To ensure that the fees charged by the college are limited to those required to carry out only certification and setting of standards for teacher education.

The BCTF ignored the fact that the Industrial Relations and Teaching Profession acts granted the seventy-five local associations the right to seek union status with expanded bargaining rights and established teacher control over teacher certification. The federation focused almost exclusively on what it perceived to be an attempt by an ideological adversary to dismantle the BCTF.

In the ensuing sign-up and certification drive, necessitated by the end of compulsory membership, the federation called for teachers to resist this attack on its collective voice. Prompted by a puzzling decision by government to make the alternative "association option" singularly unattractive, all seventy-five local associations chose the union option, and some 98 per cent of the teachers in British Columbia rejoined the BCTF.

The membership of the College Council, the governing body of the British Columbia College of Teachers, was set out in the Teaching Profession Act. The council had twenty members: fifteen elected by teachers and five appointed by government (of whom two would be representatives of Cabinet, two representatives of the minister of education, and one representative of the deans of education). To ensure that persons sympathetic to its point of view were elected to the College Council, the BCTF identified and endorsed candidates in each of the fifteen zones from which the teacher members would be elected. In each zone, the federation's endorsed candidates were successful. Bill Broadley, a former president of the BCTF, was elected chairperson of the College Council, and Debbie Gregg, a teacher activist from Coquitlam, was elected vice-chairperson. The council hired Doug Smart, a teacher from Prince George and former vice-president of the BCTF, as the registrar of the college.

The government plan to substantially weaken the BCTF by ending compulsory membership and by presenting teachers with a choice of belonging to an association or union failed. In fact, the plan had an ironic outcome. Despite the ideological gulf between teachers and the Social Credit government of the day, teachers secured from that government many, if not all, of the elements central to their professional authority.

In creating a teacher-dominated College of Teachers, the Teaching Profession Act gave teachers control over entry to the profession, the preparation of its members, and the judgment of their competence. With certification under the Labour Code, the BCTF gained the ability to bargain the material conditions and terms of the employment of teachers, including their professional autonomy. The BCTF used its considerable organizational ability to make sure its members were elected to all of the fifteen elected positions on the council of the British Columbia College of Teachers. They then passed a resolution calling for the elimination of the college itself! Needless to say, the government ignored that resolution.

The Ontario College of Teachers was proposed by a Royal Commission established by Bob Rae's New Democrats and passed by Mike Harris's Conservative government in 1996. Like their colleagues in British Columbia, Ontario's teachers opposed the establishment of a college of teachers and have resisted most of the initiatives it has undertaken, including mandatory recertification and teacher testing. The opposition of teachers' unions to the B.C. and Ontario colleges continues to fuel public perceptions that the unions are disinterested – if not openly hostile – to attempts to regulate the profession in the public interest.

Teachers are unlikely to build sympathetic support for their interests so long as they are perceived – rightly or wrongly – as being hostile to regulation of the profession in the interest of the public. Teachers' unions should modify their stance toward the Ontario and British Columbia colleges of teachers. They should treat them as institutions with different but complementary functions. The colleges in Ontario and British Columbia have helped to increase public confidence in the teaching profession by establishing standards for the preparation of teachers, the maintenance of their certification, and the suspension or revocation of certificates.

## RELATIONS WITH PARENTS

IN MANY JURISDICTIONS, the relations between teachers' unions and parents are poor. Conflicts have flared up on a number of fronts. Canadian teachers' unions have resisted the demands for greater accountability and parents' desires to play a larger role in the education of their children. Unions are cautious about parents volunteering at the school their children attend, participating on parental advisory councils, or advocating on behalf of their children. At issue is power. Any increase in the amount of influence that parents exercise is perceived as a decrease in the power exercised by teachers.

The presence of parent volunteers in schools makes some teachers feel uncomfortable and vulnerable. They already feel they are subject to too much scrutiny and regulation. Teachers do not want volunteers who are able to observe them work. They do not want to share their staff lunchroom with volunteers who would be privy to conversations about students, conflicts with administration, or union business. In addition, work that is performed by volunteers threatens teachers' or support workers' jobs.

The participation of parents on school councils diminishes the influence of staff members. Even though the bodies are typically advisory, parent involvement makes it necessary for staff to justify their recommendations in a way that isn't otherwise required.

The "accountability agenda" – the demand for student testing and public reporting of results – was slower coming to Canada than to some other countries. By the time Canadian politicians realized they could not resist, the accountability movement was well underway in the United States and Britain. Nonetheless, Canadian teachers' unions acted as if they believed they could resist what their colleagues in other countries could not.

Teachers' unions might have approached the accountability issue strategically by suggesting indicators by which student achievement could be judged. They might have helped to construct the means of gathering and interpreting relevant data. But they didn't. Although they had plenty of advance warning, teachers' unions fought a rear-guard defensive and lost.

When the Ontario and British Columbia governments declared war on teachers, teachers' unions reacted in ways that alienated parents and students. Teachers' unions withdrew their support for extracurricular trips, student clubs, athletics, music performances, and the like. Although the frustration and anger were understandable, teachers' actions were not strategic. Limited in the options available to them, teachers seemed to attack their natural allies: students and parents.

Withdrawal of support for extracurricular activities might not have alienated students, parents, and the general public if teachers' unions had enjoyed a reservoir of parental support. But they did not. By opposing increased parental involvement (for example, more parent volunteers in schools and greater parental consultation), teachers had little reserve of goodwill.

In most of their relations with parents, teachers' unions have it all wrong. Parents are natural allies with teachers in many areas. Most parents want better learning conditions for their children, and as teachers' unions have successfully argued in the past, better learning conditions often mean better working conditions in the form of smaller classes, additional support, more resources, and the like.

There will be times when the interests of parents and teachers conflict. Teachers' unions have an obligation to defend teachers when parents or administrators lodge complaints against them. Teachers have a right to be represented by their union when they are accused of neglecting their duties, incompetence, or unprofessional conduct.

Parents are more likely to accept teacher professional autonomy if they think teachers' unions share some of their goals. But as long as teachers' unions are seen as opposing increased parental influence of any kind, parents are likely to be unsympathetic even in areas where their interests intersect.

The same might be said about the relations between teachers' unions and administration. Because of the hierarchical relationship between administrators and teachers, there are likely to be fewer places where their interests intersect, but there are some. One particularly important area is funding for public schools.

Teachers' unions must be more strategic in their approach to both teachers and administrators. If they persist on the path they seem to have chosen, they will continue to be marginalized. Governments hostile to teachers' unions will be able to use the conflict between teachers and parents to justify their interventions. The contributions that teachers' unions have made to public schooling are considerable, but as recent events in Ontario, British Columbia, and Alberta have proven, their lack of practical strategic vision has put the unions at risk.

## IMPROVING TEACHING

TEACHERS COULD IMPROVE their image with parents and the public if they were seen to be concerned with improving teaching. Teachers' unions support professional development for their members and provide specific programs to help teachers who need it. But these initiatives are not very visible to the public. The attention that professional development gets is largely negative because it is seen as a disruption to students' school attendance, requiring parents to make alternative arrangements for the supervision of their children.

Unfortunately, most members of the public do not see helping poorly performing teachers in compassionate terms. Parental and public sympathies overwhelmingly favour students over struggling teachers. Rather than letting a poorly performing teacher remain in the classroom while working to improve with the help of the union, they would prefer to see him or her replaced.

There is a way both to safeguard the progress of students *and* provide help to teachers who need it. Teachers' unions and school boards should be prepared to share the cost of a substitute teacher (a supply teacher or teacher on call) while the teacher needing help to improve receives such help.

Teaching would also be improved if there was an ethic of helpful peer criticism within the profession. One obstacle to such an ethic developing is teachers' reluctance to being observed by other adults. Most teachers would sooner remove their clothing in front of their peers than teach in front of them.

An ethic of helpful peer criticism is unlikely to develop for a number of reasons. Musicians, artists, dancers, and actors are accustomed to criticism of their work in ways that other professionals are not. Although it is sometimes difficult to receive criticism, most musicians and artists believe it improves performance. In the arts, two conditions help account for the development of constructive peer criticism. First, the preparation of musicians, actors, and so on typically involves sessions during which they expect to receive feedback from their peers and mentors. Second, their work – or at least the product of their work – is publicly displayed. These conditions are absent in teaching.

Although teaching is done in public, the audience is almost never made up of one's peers. In fact, the audience for teaching is largely made up of persons whose status and powers are considerably less than that of the teacher. This is true even during the period of teacher apprenticeship that is referred to as "student teaching." Beginning teachers are mentored by supervising classroom teachers and the person from the college or university assigned to assist and evaluate them. But rarely do beginning teachers perform for other beginning teachers. As a consequence, there is little opportunity to benefit from observing the work of other teachers and from the helpful criticism that one's peers might provide.

This situation doesn't change much after one is hired. As I said before, the work of teachers is performed almost exclusively to an audience of subordinates. If other adults observe teachers – and the occurrence is extremely rare – they are likely to be supervisory personnel obliged to evaluate the teacher's suitability.

The majority of school principals simply do not see regular classroom-based instructional supervision as part of their role unless it is for the purpose of evaluating the teacher. This is unfortunate for at least two reasons. First, it does not help support good teaching and improve the overall quality of teaching. Second, it does not diminish the distance between principals and teachers.

Schools are not organized to facilitate peer observation. Almost all teaching occurs simultaneously. The few teachers who are not engaged in teaching are usually involved in preparation for teaching. That preparation almost never involves peer observation.

To ensure that their members treat one another with respect, teachers' organizations have adopted codes of conduct that implicitly discourage helpful peer criticism. The codes often say something like the following from the code of ethics of the British Columbia Teachers' Federation: "The teacher directs any criticism of the teaching performance and related work of a colleague to that colleague in private, and only then, after informing the colleague in writing of the intent to do so, may direct in confidence the criticism to appropriate individuals who are able to offer advice and assistance." Such clauses have an unintended chilling effect. Teachers are reluctant to provide their peers with helpful criticism because they fear accusations of harassment or charges that they have violated the code of ethics.

Beginning teachers should become comfortable with being observed. This could be accomplished by including the practice of peer observation in teacher education programs. Teachers at all levels of experience should learn how to give constructive criticism. This requires providing sufficient time for teachers to observe one another, the development of the ability to give and receive feedback, and the establishment a professional environment supportive of such practices. Codes of conduct should not be interpreted or used as means of silencing constructive peer criticism.

School accreditation is a practice that seeks to encourage the members of a school to engage in self-study, to set goals for improvement and the means for achieving them, and to monitor progress toward the goals established over time. Although there is often provision for external evaluation, the primary benefit of school accreditation is the self-study component. Practices like accreditation seek to inculcate among those responsible an ethic of self-regulation rather than impose regulation externally. Teachers' union opposition to school accreditation diminishes its potential as a means of collective self-study and self-improvement. It also reinforces the impression that teachers are disinterested – if not opposed – to improvement.

## FOSTERING PUBLIC SUPPORT

BY VIRTUE of their education and preparation, teachers have legitimately argued for compensation equal to that of similarly well-educated professionals. Those arguments have not always had the success that teachers would have liked. But they have helped improve the economic situation and professional standing that teachers currently enjoy.

However, teachers' unions undercut their claims for decent pay and professional autonomy when they oppose efforts to guarantee that teacher knowledge and practices remain current. Teachers' unions have seriously misjudged the depth of concern that parents and other members of the public have about such issues. They would do well to advance proposals that would ensure their members continue to enhance their knowledge of their disciplines and of appropriate teaching methods.

Teachers' unions that oppose certification linked to areas of specialization also do themselves and their members a disservice. "Endorsed certification," as it is sometimes called, provides recognition that a teacher's specialized knowledge is taken into account in the assignment of their teaching responsibilities. In places where endorsed certification operates, only teachers with the proper endorsements on their certificates may apply for and be assigned teaching responsibilities in those areas.

Some teachers' unions and school boards have argued that endorsed certification limits their ability to staff small, remote schools. Without proper endorsements, teachers are unable to assemble a sufficient number of classes to equal a full-time teaching assignment. School boards in some areas think the endorsed certification limits their ability to recruit teachers because they cannot provide some teachers with full teaching assignments.

While the problem is a real one, there are other ways of addressing the matter. Endorsement should work as an incentive for teachers to increase the breadth of their background so that they can teach in several fields. Teachers who are working toward an endorsement can be given temporary letters permitting them to instruct in that area while they complete the necessary study.

The logic that "a teacher is a teacher is a teacher" undermines claims for better economic conditions and greater professional autonomy for teachers. It also undermines confidence in teachers and their preparation among students, parents, and the general public. Teachers' unions should seek ways to address the issue and strengthen their demands for recognition of teachers' considerable knowledge and experience.

Teachers' unions improved the status of teachers, their salaries, and their working conditions. The approaches used to achieve these gains no longer work as well as they did between 1960 and

1980. The approaches need to be reconsidered in light of the changes that have occurred in Canada and in public schooling.

A more strategic approach is called for. Teachers' unions should build and maintain strategic alliances with parents, principals, school trustees, and ministries of education. They should develop a reservoir of public support and goodwill upon which they can draw for support for their own interests and in the interest of public schooling.

Parents are teachers' natural allies. Many of their goals are similar. The coincidence of parental and teacher interest should be cultivated and reinforced. Most – but not all – improvements in working conditions are also conditions that improve learning. Parents want teachers who are well qualified and experienced. They want reasonable class sizes so that their children receive the attention they need and have their work returned promptly with helpful comments. They want sufficient resources to ensure their children's education is supported and their children enjoy their schooling. There are similar opportunities for strategic alignment of interests among teachers and school principals, district administration, and school trustees.

Many teachers' unions do not think strategically. They resist initiatives that would build a reservoir of public support upon which they might draw when conflicts arise. Too often they act as if they are the only group that can speak authoritatively about education.

·······························

# chapter nine

# CLIENTS, COMPETITION, AND CHOICE

## THE CALL FOR CHOICE

THE CALL FOR EDUCATIONAL CHOICE in Canada is fuelled by widely held misperceptions. Canada's proximity to the United States has always meant that ideas current across the border get prominence here, even if they do not apply. The philosophical differences discussed earlier are an example of the way that ideas about education travel across borders and influence the character of Canadian education.

For fifty years, "school failure" has been a staple of educational politics in the United States. The ultra-conservative Heritage Foundation is a cheerleader for the introduction of competition within American public school systems and between the public and private systems. The Heritage Foundation says that "American business understands well that the nation's public schools are like a money-losing industrial giant that cannot produce a product that satisfies its customers. Leaders of America's major companies understand too that the nation's schools must improve if the United States is to remain competitive in world markets." The authors of this Heritage Foundation paper urge business leaders to "recognize in the education structure what they would in a failing sector of the economy."

There are a number of common themes in the rhetoric of American school failure. One is that the public system is a bloated, bureaucratic monopoly. A second is the increase in the cost of public education resulting from such initiatives as class size reduction and better pay for teachers. Conservative groups claim that high cost and low quality are characteristic of all American public schools. They believe that giving parents choice will address high costs and low quality and that the cost of public education will decline if parents choose private schools. The quality will improve, they argue, by forcing schools to compete, rewarding successes and punishing failures.

According to the Heritage Foundation, "An industry that is an uncompetitive monopoly, in which customers have no right to choose who will supply them, and in which tenured managers and unions determine who will work in each firm, will be an industry with angry customers and an expensive, low-quality product." This, says the Heritage Foundation, "is the real problem of America's schools."

Though typically more muted than in the United States, Canadian conservative groups make the same arguments. For example, the Fraser Institute argues that "the Canadian system of public education is inefficient and inadequate. . . . Over the past 30 years, our Ministries of Education have tinkered with a variety of reforms, including smaller classes and higher salaries, in an effort to improve the public education system. In doing so, they have tripled the real cost of education."

Just before the start of the school year in 2002, the *Globe and Mail* ran a story under the headline "FUNDS FAIL TO FUEL HIGHER TEST SCORES: A BOOST IN MARKS NOT GUARANTEED." The story reported the results of what appeared to be a politically motivated and simplistic analysis of the relationship between school board spending and student achievement as measured by the School Achievement Indicators Program (SAIP).

The report said that the provinces and territories with the four highest-operating expenditures per pupil were not among the top performers on the SAIP achievement tests in mathematics and science. Education reporter Kim Honey said the research "showed that the more school districts spent in British Columbia, the worse their students fared on B.C.'s Foundation Skills Assessment."

At first glance, it seems plausible that school board expenditures and achievement should be related. But with a closer look, the reasons why they are not related become clear. School board expenditures are based on the cost of many factors (explained in more detail in Chapter 10). The following table illustrates the problem with the kind of analysis reported in the *Globe and Mail* article. It shows the 1995 per-student expenditures for elementary and secondary schools in each province and territory and the average for Canada. It also shows the relationship between a province or territory's expenditure and the Canadian average. For example, in 1995, Manitoba spent $6,660 per student, almost exactly the average per student expenditure for Canada as a whole. The Northwest Territories spent $19,913 per student, nearly three times the Canadian average. By the reasoning used in the study reported by the *Globe*, students in the Northwest Territories should have achievement well beyond the Canadian average.

A similar range of expenditures exists within provinces. The costs of operating schools differ from school board to school board. Some school boards spend more on heating and light, more to attract teachers and administrators, and more for transportation. Teachers are compensated for the number of years of teaching experience. School boards that have a larger number of experienced teachers have higher salary bills than ones with less experienced teachers. Urban districts such as Vancouver and Toronto have large populations of immigrant students requiring additional assistance to learn English. Other districts have no ESL students. Spending more money for heat, light, transportation, ESL classes, and teacher salaries cannot translate into better student achievement scores in mathematics and science.

The *Globe and Mail* article concludes with the statement that, "Despite a 23-per-cent increase in expenditures per pupil in the

**Per-Student Expenditure for Elementary and Secondary
Education (1995) for Canada, Provinces, and Territories**

|  | $Canadian | % Canadian Average |
|---|---|---|
| **Canada** | **6,677** | **100%** |
| Newfoundland and Labrador | 5,516 | 83% |
| Prince Edward Island | 4,761 | 71% |
| Nova Scotia | 5,394 | 81% |
| New Brunswick | 5,120 | 77% |
| Quebec | 7,063 | 106% |
| Ontario | 7,617 | 114% |
| Manitoba | 6,660 | 100% |
| Saskatchewan | 5,507 | 82% |
| Alberta | 5,520 | 83% |
| British Columbia | 6,399 | 96% |
| Yukon | 15,327 | 230% |
| Northwest Territories | 19,913 | 298% |

*Source: Table 3.23 – Canadian Education Statistics Council (2000) Education Indicators in Canada: Report of the Pan-Canadian Education Indicators Program 1999.*

past 20 years, 'standardized test scores have remained relatively stagnant.'" The research wants the reader to connect increased expenditures with better results in science and mathematics. But there is no necessary reason why the two should be connected. Almost everything is much more expensive today than it was twenty years ago.

There are many reasons for increased expenditures for public schools. Supplies are more expensive, staff members have higher salaries, and, until recently, the number of pupils was increasing. Let me illustrate the logical error with an analogy. The cost of gasoline has risen dramatically over the past twenty years, but my car's mileage has not improved!

Those who seek to reduce expenditures for public schooling use statistics selectively. Ignoring considerable evidence to the contrary, conservative groups such as the Fraser Institute say that, "Despite their variety and expense, these reforms have failed to improve student achievement, and failed to solve the problem of mounting public frustration with the education system." As we will see later in this chapter, the Fraser Institute ignores the evidence when it states, "[I]f the Canadian education system supported greater parental choice, student achievement would improve."

## THE CONFLICT OVER CHOICE

FOR MUCH OF THEIR HISTORY, Canadian public schools have been seen as serving the needs of the larger society through the development of citizens. A balance between the needs of Canadian society and the needs of the individual was achieved and maintained. But Canada's emergence as an advanced industrial society and the changes that followed seem to have tipped the balance in favour of the individual.

Now, many Canadian parents are seriously questioning whether public schools can deliver on the multiple visions they have for the education of their children. Economic competition, social diversity, and changes in other institutions have prompted some Canadians to question the broadly based general education traditionally offered by Canadian public schools.

Parents worry about the welfare of their children. They know that their own well-being and that of their children are connected to the quality of the schooling their children receive. Parents want their children to grow up well educated and able to find meaningful work. Increasing economic uncertainly is one reason parents wish to choose the schools their children attend and the programs they pursue.

Many parents are concerned about the increasing diversity in the student population. With the inclusion of students with special educational needs, a growing aboriginal population, and significant numbers of students of colour among the student population, the altered role of schools concerns some parents. While passing on Canadian cultural values to the next generation has always been a significant role of public schooling, it was less conscious a mission when the similarities among students outweighed their differences.

Some parents seek refuge from the debate about whose culture and heritage public schools transmit. They want to educate their children in schools with a special focus, in private schools catering to particular interests, or through home-schooling.

In many jurisdictions – most notably Ontario, Alberta, and British Columbia – governments are retreating from the core Canadian value of trying to achieve equality. They are saying that *inequality* fuels the competition leading to economic progress. Provincial governments in those jurisdictions have generally been reducing the role of government. They believe that governments should not provide all the social, health, and education services Canadians have come to expect in the postwar period.

Canadians remain largely supportive of public schooling, but many no longer believe that society in general and schools in particular will assure opportunities for all. In the face of what appear to be limited opportunities, Canadians are increasingly inclined toward a competitive model of society and schooling. They seek market mechanisms to influence change in public schooling. They want to be able to choose schools and programs as they might an automobile, a restaurant, or a fitness centre, and an increasing number are moving their children from the public to the private system or schooling them at home, while arguing that their choices should be subsidized from the public purse.

Canadian politicians increasingly reinforce the mistaken idea that public schooling is primarily a commodity for individual consumption rather than a process designed to benefit society. They do it when they seek to sell the provincial curriculum to other jurisdictions or establish schools beyond Canada's borders for persons who are not Canadians. And they do it when they talk about offering more choice of schools and programs. Choice in itself is not a bad thing, but when politicians talk of choice without talking about the social benefits of schooling, it reinforces the consumer mentality.

## CHOICE WITHIN PUBLIC SCHOOLS

PUBLIC SCHOOLS HAVE RESPONDED WELL to the demand for choice. School boards have the authority to implement innovative school programs and services that offer flexibility and options to parents and students. For example, there are traditional schools that focus on back-to-basics and alternative schools that cater to secondary school students who left the school system early. Additionally, courses offered by outside agencies may be awarded credit through equivalency. In some jurisdictions, students may challenge courses for which they feel they have already attained the key objectives, and schools may offer guided independent study for secondary school credit.

With minority-language rights enshrined in the Constitution, French-speakers outside of Quebec and English-speakers in Quebec have the choice of attending schools in which French or English is the language of instruction. Three Canadian provinces – Alberta, Saskatchewan, and Ontario – and all three territories make provision for constitutionally protected denominational schooling with separate school boards.

Status Indians have increasingly exercised choice of schools. Despite living on reserve lands that have their own schools, many send their children to public, separate, and private schools for their education. Others have migrated from reserve lands, in part to obtain educational services not provided as fully in schools located on reservations.

Local school jurisdictions implement provincially prescribed curricula and local electives, develop a variety of school organizations (middle and alternate schools, for example), and implement alternative scheduling (year-round schooling). Provinces make provisions for parents who wish to educate their children at home, allowing them to provide their children with an educational program that conforms to the parents' philosophy and reflects outcomes the parents wish to achieve.

Early and late French immersion are popular choices within public and separate school systems. Heritage-language programs have been established and have grown in response to requests from parents. Advanced Placement and International Baccalaureate programs are popular offerings at senior levels in secondary schools.

Alternative "schools" – which are often programs appended to public and separate schools – provide choices for students within the public and separate school systems. Schools with particular curricular emphases – such as fine arts, performing arts, or Montessori – are increasingly common features of public and separate school systems. Distance learning – whether by correspondence or by means of newer technologies – has always figured prominently in Canada wherever geography and difficult climatic conditions made school attendance impractical or impossible. Challenging university-oriented programs such as International Baccalaureate and Advanced Placement are widely available.

There are many reasons why parents want more choice. Some want their children to have a course, program, or opportunity unavailable in their neighbourhood school. Some want a particular teacher or teaching approach for their children or want to avoid a teacher or an approach. A few want to avoid contact with people from backgrounds different from their own or ideas with which they do not agree. Others want choice to stimulate school improvement through competition among schools. Most school boards produce brochures and maintain Web sites describing their schools and the programs offered. Most boards permit students to transfer to schools other than the one to which they have been assigned, if space is available.

Some parents seek programs that emphasize the basics, while others want specialized enrichment programs with a focus on the arts. Some parents want schools to reflect better society's diversity, while others prefer schools that emphasize discipline and "traditional" values. Still others want their children sheltered from society's problems, while others want those problems to be the object of their children's study. A small minority of Canadians provide schooling to their children at home, with varying degrees of provincial support and regulatory control.

The capacity of schools to differentiate programs (gifted, career prep, learning assistance, mini-schools, outdoor programs, and so on) is also part of the system's attempt to retain parents who might otherwise move to private schools. I suspect that few, if any, private schools offer the array of programs found in public schools.

School choice may be an unanticipated by-product of the success of universal public schooling. Initially confined to what we have come to regard as elementary schooling, universal public schooling eventually supplanted selective secondary schools. Having achieved near universality, Canadians seeking to ensure the economic success of their children may simply be looking for other ways to differentiate their offspring from the mass of children with whom they must compete.

## OBSTACLES TO CHOICE

THE CHOICES AVAILABLE to parents depend upon the school jurisdiction in which they live and the resources available for the support of public schools. Some programs are not offered because of the governance structure. For example, charter schools (see page 187) are not permitted under the School Act in British Columbia. In rural and remote regions across Canada, there are often no alternatives among which to choose, because schools are too small and residences too isolated for the development of different programs. Financial resources also limit the range of choices schools are able to provide. Low student enrolments make the provision of some opportunities too costly.

Flexibility and choice are also constrained by obstacles between and among school jurisdictions. Legislation typically

gives authority for school boards to provide educational programs to children residing within their boundaries. There are
some people who favour policies that would enable parents
to select the schools their children attend without regard to
boundaries. On the other hand, many parents value their neighbourhood schools, and the priority accorded persons living in
the school's catchment area. If the number of parents choosing
a school exceeds the capacity of the school, there will likely
be dissatisfaction among the parents whose preferences are
not accommodated.

Such was the case last fall in the borough of Kensington in
London, England. Peter Wilby, a columnist writing in the *New
Statesman*, describes one of the unintended consequences of ex-
British prime minister Margaret Thatcher's breakup of the Inner
London Educational Authority. Ellie Sherman Smith – an
eleven-year-old student with neither learning difficulties, a poor
disciplinary record, nor a physical handicap – could not be
accommodated in the one school in her borough. The law says
that a local education authority has a duty to find every child
a school place, but they could not find a place for Ellie. Nor could
schools in the adjacent boroughs accommodate her.

Wilby says that Kensington takes "a somewhat insouciant attitude" to its duty to place Ellie. The borough says, "We do our
very best to place as many children who live in the borough as
possible." Wilby's piece ends, "Well, thanks. But any doubts about
whether an 11-year-old should receive full-time education were
supposed to have disappeared early last century."

### OTHER KINDS OF CHOICE

CHARTER SCHOOLS AND VOUCHER PROGRAMS are choices that
have polarized communities. Charter schools are funded by government with local parent committees instead of school boards
or government deciding the school's philosophy or focus. There
are ten charter schools in Canada, all located in Alberta. The ten

include: two schools with a focus on "the gifted and talented"; one with a focus on English as a second language; one "traditional" and one "back to basics" school; a school with a focus on mathematics and science; one for students "at risk"; one with a focus on the Suzuki philosophy of music; a school with a focus on "academic and personal excellence"; and one with a focus on "learning styles."

Voucher schemes take many different forms. The common ingredient is that parents are able to take the money (in the form of a voucher) that government provides for neighbourhood public schools and use it instead to pay for any public or private school their child attends. Thus far, no Canadian provinces offer vouchers.

Parent-funded and government-subsidized private religious and independent schools are familiar features of the Canadian educational landscape. And although the proportion of students in attendance in such schools has grown over the years, it typically constitutes only a small fraction of the total school-age population.

Parents in Ontario sought to extend school choice to private Christian and Jewish religious schools in 1996. That year, the Supreme Court of Canada heard a case brought by a group of parents whose children attended Christian and Jewish private schools. The parents argued that the failure of the Province of Ontario to fund the schools their children attended violated the Canadian Charter of Rights and Freedoms.

They said that the non-funding of their schools by the province violated two provisions of the Charter: their guarantee of freedom of religion and their guarantee of equal protection and equal benefit of the law without discrimination. In making their case, the parents of the students attending Christian and Jewish private schools compared themselves to Roman Catholics whose schools receive full public funding under the terms of the Constitution Act.

The Supreme Court rejected the parents' claim. Under the terms of subsection 93(1) of the Constitution Act, the Province of Ontario is required to fund Roman Catholic separate schools. The court said that Ontario's funding of Roman Catholic separate schools (but not other religious schools) did not violate the equality provisions of the Charter. The court reasoned that the decision by Ontario to fund Roman Catholic schools is exempt from challenge under the Charter because the Charter exempts from challenge all rights and privileges "guaranteed" under the Constitution in respect of denominational, separate or dissentient schools. It also held that Ontario's decision was also "immune" from review because it was made in accordance with the provincial legislatures' power to make laws about education granted at the time of Confederation. In essence, the court said that one section of the Constitution couldn't be used to interfere with rights protected by a different section of the Constitution.

The Supreme Court also ruled that freedom of religion guaranteed by the Constitution was a protection against governmental interference in the practise of one's religion. As such, it did not oblige Ontario to subsidize religion by, for example, funding religious schools. It was the court's view that the parents had the option of sending their children to publicly funded non-denominational schools without charge. The fact that they paid tuition to send their children to private religious schools was a result of their religious choice and not a result of interference by Ontario in the practise of their religion.

### SEARCHING FOR CERTAINTY

IN 2000, the *National Post* newspaper commissioned COMPAS, Inc. to ask Canadians a number of questions about various dimensions of education. With the permission of COMPAS, I was able to re-analyze that data to see what it revealed about the issue of choice. The picture that emerges is an interesting snapshot of what the Canadians surveyed believe.

Canadians were asked whether parents should or should not be allowed to send their child to any school within a government-funded public system and not just the one assigned to their neighbourhood (i.e., open-boundary choice). Seventy-four per cent said that the practice should be allowed, 22 per cent said the practice should be prevented, and 4 per cent said they didn't know. I did further analysis of the COMPAS data to understand as much as I could about who supported and who opposed open-boundary choice of government-supported schools. I was not surprised about what I found.

COMPAS had asked the Canadians polled to compare today's education to the education they had received. Canadians who were not sure about the quality of public schools – who felt that today's schooling was either "somewhat better" or "somewhat worse" than the schooling they had received – generally supported open-boundary choice for parents. My feeling is that, consistent with Darrell Bricker and Edward Greenspon's argument in their book *Searching for Certainty,* these Canadians are searching for greater certainty in education. They think parents may find certainty if they are not restricted to sending their children to their neighbourhood school. This is ironic, since Canadians typically think that the school in their local neighbourhood is doing well, even if they think that other schools are not!

Residents of Quebec are consistent with the rest of Canadians in wanting choice. La Charte de la langue française (the Charter of the French Language) establishes French as the language of instruction in Quebec from kindergarten to secondary school in all schools receiving support from the province. An exception is made for students whose parents, if Canadian citizens, received their elementary instruction in English in Canada. These students may be instructed in English.

Given that most Québécois feel strongly about protecting their French heritage and language, the results of the COMPAS survey were surprising. The survey included 197 residents of

Quebec who overwhelmingly (81 per cent) approved of allowing parents to send their children to either an English-language
or French-language school regardless of the language spoken by
the child's mother! Only 15 per cent of Quebec residents dis-
approved and 4 per cent did not know. Even a majority (65 per
cent) of Bloc Québécois–aligned respondents supported the
proposition, albeit less enthusiastically than respondents aligned
with the federal Liberal party (94 per cent).

I looked more closely at who supported or opposed the idea
of English-language instruction in Quebec and was a little less
surprised. I found that persons who responded to the survey in
English, who said they were Protestants and Liberals, were much
more likely to favour giving parents such a choice. Persons
responding in French, who said they were Catholics and affiliates
of the Bloc Québécois, were much more likely to be opposed.
But there is still general enthusiasm for language choice in
Quebec education.

The COMPAS survey also tried to gauge support for an arrangement that would enable parents to send their children to any
private (i.e., parent-funded) school and have the tuition paid
with the money that government would have otherwise given
to a government-funded school. This voucherlike arrangement
was supported by 57 per cent of respondents and opposed by
36 per cent; the remaining 7 per cent was uncertain. Again,
respondents uncertain about whether education today was better
or worse than the schooling they received were overrepresented
among those favouring the voucher arrangement.

All taxpayers pay for government-funded public schools. It
does not matter whether they send their children to such a school
or to a parent-funded (private) school or have no children at all.
Most Canadians believe that the cost of sending children to
parent-funded schools should be offset by providing parents with
some tax relief (43 per cent) or full tax relief (21 per cent); 32 per
cent of Canadians were opposed.

Sixty per cent of the respondents in the COMPAS sample were parents, to whom particular questions were directed. Most parents (70 per cent) liked the option to send their children to charter schools, while 24 per cent were opposed. Roman Catholic parents, parents living in Atlantic Canada, Quebec, or Alberta, parents of children attending school in a separate (Catholic) school system, and parents whose children had received help from an educational psychologist were among those most likely to support charter schools. Conversely, Protestant parents, parents living in Ontario, parents whose children had never attended a separate (Catholic) school, and parents whose children had never received help from an educational psychologist were among those most likely to oppose charter schools. It isn't surprising that parents whose children are attending religiously oriented schools or are having difficulty would be open to alternative forms of schooling.

Personal finances seem to be the main barrier to Canadians choosing private schools in preference to public schools. COMPAS asked parents whose children had been educated entirely in public or separate schools, as well as parents whose children had attended private schools at some time during their schooling, whether they would have sent their children to a private school if money were not an obstacle. Only 25 per cent of parents whose children had received all of their schooling in a government-funded public or separate school said they would send their child to a private religious school if they inherited "a lot" of money. Forty-one per cent of the same group said that they would send their child to a parent-funded, non-sectarian private school.

Not surprisingly, parents whose children had all of their schooling in separate schools were most in favour of sending their children to private schools if money were not a barrier. Conversely, parents of children who had all of their education in public schools were most likely to oppose sending their children to private schools.

## THE CHALLENGE OF CHOICE:
## WHAT THE RESEARCH SAYS

THE SUPPORT FOR CHOICE among Canadians with and without children appears consistent with the changes in values of the past fifty years. Canadians are increasingly meritocratic and assertive, less confident in both governmental and non-governmental institutions, and more willing to pursue goals through alternative forms. They are more individualistic than previous generations. They are more apt to regard education as a consumer good of benefit to the individual rather than a social process of benefit to the society as a whole.

Most of us buy things without doing much research. Many items are purchased on impulse. For the others, we typically rely on advertising or the recommendation of friends. Although parents may have a consumer orientation toward schooling, I doubt seriously whether those who support school choice are any more inclined to consider the evidence about schools than they are with any other consumer good.

What leads me to this conclusion is the research conducted over the past fifty years about school choice, vouchers, and charters. Advocates of school choice – such as the Fraser Institute – argue that competition among schools will increase if market forces are introduced into the educational arena. Competition for students will, according to the advocates, heighten the awareness of teachers and administrators to parental concerns, make them more accountable to parents, and improve the quality of schooling.

Charter schools are thought to be more "innovative," "focused," "energetic," and "responsive" to the needs of the students who attend them. It is claimed that students attending voucher schools in preference to government-funded schools learn more. Organizations such as the Fraser Institute claim that government-funded schools also improve because they are forced to compete with voucher schools, requiring them to offer both a wider variety and better quality programs.

Critics have expressed many concerns. They argue that this sort of choice will not deliver on the promise of improved education. They say that charter and voucher school options will increase segregation of students from different backgrounds and erode the public school's capacity for socializing students for democratic citizenship.

The impact of charter schools in the United States on student achievement has been studied at the RAND Corporation and the Evaluation Center located at Western Michigan University. In general, researchers find a mixed picture, with some positive and negative results. This is surprising, given that the charter school movement is more than ten years old in the United States and eight years old in Alberta, but the studies point out that more research is required.

Part of the problem may be that the politicians who approved of charter schools did not seek to evaluate their impact. This suggests a number of things about the way politicians address issues of school choice. Choice seems more of a dogma than something worthy of careful scrutiny. By "giving people what they want," politicians are able to shift responsibility about issues of quality from themselves to the individual consumer – something consistent with the general philosophy of organizations like the Heritage Foundation in the United States and Canada's Fraser Institute.

Although some have claimed that parents will rationally seek to maximize educational benefits for their children by exercising the opportunity to choose the schools their children attend, the research indicates that parents choose schools on other grounds. The Fraser Institute, one of the main advocates for school choice in Canada, has said there are countries from which we might learn some lessons about school choice. Consider, then, what happened in Scotland when parents were given the chance to choose the schools their children attended.

Beginning in 1981, Scotland gave parents the right to request that their children attend a school outside the school attendance areas to which they had previously been assigned. The legislation required that Educational Authorities – bodies responsible for schools in their region – publish brochures providing information about each school (including examination results), required that they take into account parental requests, and limited the grounds for refusing a parent's request to send their child to the school. This experiment in school choice was the subject of considerable research.

One group of researchers interviewed more than six hundred parents who chose the school their children attended in three Educational Authorities in Scotland. Rather than seek the best school for their children, parent choices were fuelled by a desire to *avoid* the school in the area to which they had been previously assigned. Parents were more apt to consider a school's general reputation and how close it was to their home than they were educational factors such as examination results. In other words, they based their decisions on hearsay and convenience rather than evidence.

Before school choice was introduced, Scotland had replaced its system of selective grammar schools with comprehensive secondary schools. In 1982, the first national cohort of Scottish pupils entered the comprehensive secondary schools that had been introduced during the two preceding decades. Frank Echols, a sociologist at the University of British Columbia, and Doug Willms, a sociologist at the University of New Brunswick, studied the parents of students in the first national cohort who exercised choice. They found that those who chose were better educated and better off than those who did not choose the schools their children attended. Moreover, parents tended to choose the older, previously more selective schools whose pupils were of more advantaged backgrounds and had higher academic achievement.

Willms and Echols found that parents did not make the best choices for their offspring. When choosing among the previously more selective schools, parents were unable to differentiate those that were more or less effective. Instead, they choose schools whose socio-economic compositions and examination results were marginally higher than the schools to which their children had been previously assigned. They did not necessarily choose schools that would maximize their children's educational advantage. They inferred that, because children with higher examination scores attended the schools they selected for their children, that the school had caused the higher examination scores.

Echols and Willms also analyzed the data from Scotland to try to understand parental motivation for their decision whether or not to choose. Most parents (90 per cent) did not exercise a choice. Those who did tended to live in urban areas. More advantaged parents considered more factors in making their decisions than less advantaged parents.

Despite having a wide range of schools from which to choose, more than 60 per cent of the parents requesting a placement considered only one alternative to the school to which their children had been assigned. The advantaged parents paid more attention to the information provided by teachers and school administrators and to direct observations made from their visits to the school than did less advantaged parents. Less advantaged parents were more concerned about the reputation and the disciplinary climate of schools.

The Scottish experience confirms another of the concerns voiced by critics of school choice. Echols and Willms found that social class segregation between schools increased substantially with the introduction of choice.

It is not particularly surprising that choice appears not to improve performance. If parents do not choose schools to maximize educational advantages for their children, such advantages are not likely to occur.

After reviewing the evidence about the impact of charter schools on student achievement, researchers, as I have said, observe that the evidence is scant and conflicting. They conclude that "our knowledge of charter schools' impact on student achievement is still in its infancy, in spite of the fact that the movement is now ten years old."

Chile is another of the countries from which Canada might learn about choice and competition. Researchers examined Chile's use of vouchers in its nationwide school choice program. They used test scores and the rate of grade repetition, and compared the grade at which students were enrolled with where they should be in relation to their age. They "found no evidence that the large reallocation of students from public to private schools improved average educational performance in Chile."

As mentioned above, researchers in many places are finding that parental choice leads to increasing economic and ethnic-group segregation. Economically advantaged families have resources such as time and transportation that enable them to choose, so they are more apt to do so. And the schools they are likely to choose are those with student bodies from families much like their own. As a consequence, choice produces higher concentrations of children from advantaged backgrounds in some schools and increasing concentrations of less advantaged students in the schools from which the more advantaged children have departed.

Doug Willms points out that, for poor students living in poor communities, there is a double disadvantage. There is the disadvantage that comes from their own poverty and the additional disadvantage from the influence of their peers who are also poor. When choice, charters, or vouchers skim the most able students from the peer group, this increases the similarities among the remaining students. When most of the students who are left behind live in poor circumstances, their segregation amplifies and reinforces their difficulties.

School success is influenced by the advantages that economics can provide. Economically advantaged families have more books, make more visits to libraries, and more trips to interesting places than less advantaged families. Parents in advantaged families have more time to talk with, and read to, their children than parents with fewer resources. Children from more affluent backgrounds come to school with better-developed vocabularies and richer experiences on which to draw than children from less advantaged families. Schools try to overcome these differences by closing the gap between less advantaged and more advantaged students.

Students from disadvantaged backgrounds are more susceptible to the influences of their advantaged peers than vice versa. Children with well-developed vocabularies and strong interest in reading are good models for children with less developed vocabularies and less interest in, and experience with, reading. The loss of high-ability students from a school tends to lower the performance of the students who remain in the school after the choosers leave. Advantaged students who change schools do not benefit as much as people imagine. Even in those studies showing a benefit, the impact on academic achievement is small (about 3 per cent).

The United States is another of the countries, according to the Fraser Institute, from which Canada is supposed to learn. In 1999, researchers studied the ethnic composition of fifty-five urban and fifty-seven rural Arizona charter schools. They found that nearly half of the charter schools exhibited evidence of substantial ethnic separation "large enough and consistent enough to warrant concern among education policymakers." They observed that students who attend schools segregated along ethnic lines do not get the benefits of integration with students of a rich variety of backgrounds.

Inclusive schools – schools that have a healthy mix of children from the local neighbourhood – enjoy a balance of what they refer to as neighbourhood political support. "Ethnic and class-based separation," the researchers argue, "polarizes the political interests which look out for neighbourhood schools, which results in further disparities in resources, quality of teachers, number of supportive parents, and the like. Schools without political support struggle, and the students suffer."

Increasing school choice has the capacity to fragment Canadians, reduce the influence that Canadian schools exert on the transmission of common values, and diminish social cohesion. But, so far, school choice in Canada has not gone as far as in other countries.

## THE VOLATILE POLITICS OF
## SCHOOL CHOICE

PROVINCIAL JURISDICTIONS have exercised significant control over the growth and conduct of alternatives. Where choice in the United States is often seen as an expression of individual rights, the Canadian view – albeit influenced by views prevalent in the United States – is that choice ought to be accommodated within a framework of regulatory and financial control designed primarily to ensure equality among alternatives. Politics, however, sometimes gets in the way.

Under the Social Credit government of the late 1970s, B.C. private schools began to receive government financial support. The support was based on a proportion of the public school per-pupil funding. In 2001, the New Democratic government in British Columbia attempted to change its formula for distributing funds to independent schools. In 1998, the NDP government had reduced class sizes in public schools. Class sizes in private schools did not change. However, because more public school teachers were hired and public school funding increased, the private schools benefited financially.

The NDP government tried to limit passing on funds to independent schools for class size reductions it did not make. The attempt, opposed by the association representing independent schools, was denounced even from the pulpit of the Catholic Church. The government received an estimated twenty-three thousand form letters opposing the change and withdrew its proposal.

Later that year, the Liberal party formed the government in British Columbia following a landslide election promising a "new era of hope and prosperity." Although it denies that vouchers and charters are in the offing, the government's first throne speech promised changes to the School Act that would provide for increased flexibility and choice for parents and students.

The Freedom Party of Ontario "supports the right of taxpayers to direct their education taxes to the school(s) of their choice, including private options. Within the public system, we propose clear education standards and objective student evaluations, with emphasis on basics, including direct instruction, the systematic use of phonics to teach reading, standardized testing, and effective standards of discipline." The Freedom Party of Ontario would "allow taxpayers to direct their education taxes and send their children (or themselves) to the school of their choice, public or private" and "separate the state from the direct provision of education." The governing Conservative party in Ontario did not go as far as the Freedom party might have liked, but it did propose a system of tax credits to offset the cost of private schooling previously borne entirely by parents.

There is evidence, in recent years, that the delicate balance between the accommodation of parental choice and the maintenance of equity is shifting. To the extent that the COMPAS/ *National Post* findings represent the opinion of Canadian parents, the following observations seem warranted. (1) The numbers of parents whose children attend public and separate schools but would rather their children were schooled in private religious or private non-sectarian schools is surprisingly high. (2) Governments contribute to the migration of children from public to private schools by eroding confidence in public schooling through unwarranted criticism and by increasing financial support for private and home-schooling. I agree with writer and philosopher

John Ralston Saul, who, in a 1999 address at the University of South Wales, said, "The wilful undermining of universal public education by our governments and the direct or indirect encouragement of private education is the most flagrant betrayal of the basic principles of middle-class representative democracy in the last fifty years."

Competing and unrealistic expectations for schools create confusion among those responsible for carrying out the work of the school. They sow the seeds of disillusionment among parents and the general citizenry. Many parents regard themselves as consumers or clients. The public school cannot continue to accommodate the increasingly vast array of choices that parents seek and still remain universal and public.

Policy-makers need to consider the impact of increasing school choice on student achievement. The outcomes of schooling are influenced by a number of factors, including the composition of the school's student population. As I mentioned earlier, expanding school choice will likely increase socio-economic segregation. This, in turn, will make it difficult to prevent increasing disparities in educational outcomes for the students left behind, including those of high ability.

One purpose of promoting choice is to promote excellence through competition among schools. Where such competition exists, however, it doesn't appear to have much to do with improving the quality of programs. What does seem to happen is that it causes schools nearby to try to differentiate themselves from one another. Parents seeking schools they think will improve their children's academic success may find that they have been attracted to schools offering programs different from – but not better than – the ones offered by schools in their catchment area.

If improved test scores on large-scale student assessments is a goal of school choice, increasing choices – where choices mean alternative programs or opportunities – will not produce the desired outcome. Diversification in education is not the same thing as improving the outcomes of schooling. While no doubt some schools will emphasize traditional academic goals, others will emphasize music, art, citizenship, or other goals. You can't judge programs with different goals by the same standard.

We live in a highly mobile society. School variation makes transitions from one school or system to another more difficult. That is why there has been pressure upon provincial jurisdictions to ensure that students achieve common standards, and that teachers are able to transfer from one area to another without unnecessary difficulty. Dramatically increasing school choice – where choice is primarily programmatic – will exaggerate differences and make the achievement of common standards and transferability more difficult.

Public schooling in Canada has shown itself to be as elastic as it has been successful. But there are limits to the elasticity of our public schools. Changing demographics and family circumstances, the assumption of tasks previously performed by families and other community agencies, an increasingly diverse student population and an equally diverse and crowded curriculum, changing values, and competitive expectations are placing unprecedented demands upon public schools. Expanded opportunities for school choice might seem an appealing way for politicians and educational leaders to manage these demands. The danger is the precarious balance that public schools have achieved between serving individual and societal needs will be upset in favour of the individual. Seen in the larger context of an increasingly individualistic and consumer-oriented society, this would accelerate the growing fragmentation and alienation in Canadian society.

Canadians would be wise to think carefully about the consequences of expanded school choice for themselves and for Canada. They have every reason to hold high expectations for their public schools, but they should not turn to the economic marketplace for solutions. The "rational consumer" is a fiction of economic thought. Parents' inclination to lobby for a wider choice of schools is more ideological than practical. Most of us, in fact, are irrational consumers. The proportion of people who research the options available to them in any area of consumption is tiny. Among those who do such research, it is often done to find evidence that confirms decisions already made.

If Canadians were more practical about looking in the private sphere for solutions to public issues, they would find that quality is not a result of competition, but of price. Competition leads to advertising that consumes significant resources to increase market share, it rarely leads to quality improvements. Not surprisingly, higher quality is typically associated with higher cost. If we want better public schools, we will have to spend more money.

Competition for market share often involves offering features – colour, labelling, finishing touches, and the like – that are unrelated to the basic function of the product. Many of us are attracted by such features. I know I am. But those features do not make the product perform any better than its near-price competitors.

Increasing public school choice is unlikely to bring dramatic positive change, and it could upset the balance between the social and individual achievements of public schooling. School choice does not deliver on the promise of improved outcomes, showing mixed results as far as student achievement is concerned. There are some small improvements – three or four percentage points – for the students whose parents have exercised choice, and a small drop in performance for those students who remain in the school when the "choosers" leave. But one thing is undoubtedly accomplished – increased economic and social segregation.

·······························

# chapter ten

# FINANCE AND GOVERNANCE

n 2002, cash-strapped Ontario school boards openly rebelled against alleged provincial government parsimony toward public schooling. The Ottawa, Hamilton, and Toronto school boards refused to submit balanced budgets in defiance of provincial government regulations requiring them to do so. In a counteroffensive, the minister of education appointed an auditor to examine the school boards' books. Trustees called the auditor a "government stooge" and alleged that he talked about children as if they were products on an assembly line. The provincial government withdrew the three school boards' authority and appointed an administrator.

## WHO PAYS AND HOW MUCH?

OFTEN FRAMED AS CONFLICTS between the forces of good and evil, conflicts about the funding and governance of public schooling are as old as Canada itself. As early as 1846, Egerton Ryerson, the Methodist minister who had advocated so vigorously for free, universal schooling, was arguing with equal vigour for a strong central educational authority vested in the hands of government. He said, "If 'it is the Master which makes the School,' it is Government that makes the system. What the Master is to the one, the Government is to the other – the director, the animating spirit of it."

Ryerson was worried about the "isolated, independent, Democracies" that were administering education. In particular, Ryerson was concerned that local school jurisdictions might misappropriate the monies allocated for education to some other purpose. "If it is the duty of Government to legislate on the subject of Public Instruction," Ryerson said, "it must be its duty to see its laws executed."

Upon confederation, the British North America Act, 1867, gave the provinces the sole responsibility for making laws about education. The provinces, in turn, created strong centralized departments of education to oversee the local school jurisdictions responsible for the day-to-day operations of the school or schools. Provincial governments maintained tight control over the operation of the province's schools. The provincial departments of education determined the method and extent of financing education. They established school boards. They set the curriculum and examinations. They determined the criteria used for teacher certification and reviewed the qualifications of those who wished to teach. And, in some jurisdictions, they even selected and appointed all administrators above the position of principal.

Ryerson's concern about school trustees' use of funds was justified. The Depression created financial havoc for many Canadian school boards and jeopardized local governance. Citizens whose school taxes were in arrears were ineligible for election, which often made it difficult to find eligible people willing to stand for office, which in turn made it hard to elect local school boards. As a consequence, provincial governments were often forced to appoint an official trustee to administer the affairs of the local district. British Columbia was typical of the situation prevailing throughout Canada. In 1934–35, 182 of the province's 752 school districts had official trustees. In the following ten years, the province reduced the number of school boards. By 1944–45, when there were 525 school districts, 204 of them were administered by an official trustee.

Today, with the exception of Quebec, Manitoba, and Saskatchewan, the Canadian provinces provide money to finance what their departments of education determine to be core services and capital facilities for the provinces' schools. The money comes from general revenue. In Quebec, the province provides 85 per cent of the funding for public schools and the remaining 15 per cent comes from local property taxes. In Manitoba, the province provides approximately 60 per cent of the funding through general revenue, and the remainder is raised through a school board levy on property. In Saskatchewan, the province provides 40 per cent from general revenue, and the remainder comes from local property taxes.

Provincial governments are wise to assume responsibility for funding public schools. It is consistent with the principle of equalization – fairness to all regions – that distinguishes Canada from her closest neighbour. In the United States, where local taxes pay for public schools, the inequities among school boards in their ability to provide for public schooling is a disgrace.

The cost of education rose rapidly after the Second World War. Canada's population escalated. Talk about the importance of staying in school to get good jobs and further education helped school retention rates improve. Schools and teachers were needed in unprecedented numbers, and teachers were better educated and better prepared than ever before.

Beginning in 1950 and continuing until the mid-1980s, expenditures for public schooling consumed larger and larger proportions of provincial and municipal budgets. Between 1950 and 1970 in Ontario, a period when provincial education was still partially funded by property taxes, the share of the provincial budget consumed by education doubled, from 16 per cent to 32 per cent. At the same time, the proportion of property taxes devoted to education also doubled, from approximately 29 per cent to 59 per cent.

Teachers' unions won dramatic improvements to salaries and working conditions between 1950 and 1980, as their education and qualifications increased. Rapidly expanding student populations and a shortage of qualified teachers helped fuel arguments for much-needed improvements. People began to see that education was increasingly important to the long-term economic well-being of society. The population grew more receptive to teacher demands for improvements. Two other conditions also contributed to successful teacher bargaining. One was the ability of local school boards to raise revenue through taxation on property; the other was local bargaining.

Teachers and trustees were often neighbours and friends in local communities. They saw one another at the service station, in local shops, or at the arenas where their children played hockey and learned gymnastics. Teachers, respected members of their communities, were represented by increasingly sophisticated unions that used negotiated settlements in one school district to lever – "whipsaw" – contract improvements from other school boards. The system was successful for teachers as long as school boards retained the right to raise revenue at the local level through taxation on property. But it was not a system that could continue indefinitely in the face of rising educational costs. Another problem was the inequality among school boards in terms of their capacity to raise revenue from property taxes.

Government spending has dominated the public agenda since the mid-1980s. In a speech to the Economic Club of New York in 1984, Conservative Prime Minister Brian Mulroney stated what would become a recurrent theme for Canadians. He told the Economic Club that, at Canada's centennial celebration in 1967, the public debt was $4,000 for every Canadian family. By 1984, it had reached $24,000 per family and, if unchecked, it would reach $54,000 by 1990.

Between 1990 and 2000, nearly every jurisdiction in Canada was reducing expenditures for education. The *Globe and Mail* called British Columbia a renegade because it was the only province to increase appropriations for education throughout the decade. Even so, school district amalgamations and centralization of finance at the provincial level were inevitable responses to increasing provincial costs.

Now, cash-strapped school boards in British Columbia are being forced to engage in entrepreneurial activity to raise the funds they need to provide basic services to students. Instead of providing sufficient funding to school boards to meet the costs of educating the students for whom they are responsible, the B.C. government has told school boards they can establish businesses to make up the shortfall in revenue.

The direction does not bode well for public education. Entrepreneurial activities divert time and human and material resources away from the main focus on public schooling. School boards are not adept at or well suited to such activities and they cannot compete in the marketplace on an equal footing. That's why most provincial governments have eliminated the use of local property taxation as the major source of revenue for public schools and introduced complex formulas to ensure equity across school boards.

School boards that are successful in the marketplace will be able to offer programs and services that unsuccessful boards cannot afford to offer. This will increase inequalities in the provision of educational services. The biggest problem with school boards raising additional resources through entrepreneurial activities is that, if they are successful, it may prompt provincial governments to reduce further their contributions to public schooling.

#### HOW PUBLIC SCHOOL FUNDING WORKS

PROVINCIAL AND TERRITORIAL GOVERNMENTS still devote significant financial resources to public schooling. The money flows down through the chain of command. Provincial cabinets and treasury boards establish the province's budget and the amounts allocated to each ministry. Ministries of education establish priorities within the amount allocated to them and allocate monies to school boards. School boards determine their spending priorities, identify other sources of revenue, establish their budgets, and allocate funding.

There are fundamentally two ways of deciding how much money should be allocated to public schools in any given year. One is to determine the cost of all of the elements required to run and maintain schools during the year. For example, it would be necessary to calculate the number of teachers needed in any given year and multiply that figure by the salaries and benefits for each one. The same process would be carried out for each and every item required. For example, in order to budget for pencils it would be necessary to determine how many would be needed per pupil multiplied by the number of pupils, then that quantity would have to be multiplied by the cost of the pencils, including the appropriate taxes and the cost of distributing them.

There is a second way of deciding how much money should be allocated to public schools in any given year. Provincial governments can determine merely the lump sum of money available for allocation in any given year, depending upon revenue projections and the government's priorities. That sum is then divided among school boards according to formulas. It is less time-consuming, but this method does not ensure that the funding provided is the funding needed. Over time, governments concerned that they are providing adequate funding must determine the true costs of the goods, services, salaries, and the like for which public schools must pay.

Determining exact costs is a troublesome process. Some people advocate "zero-base" budgeting. For public schooling, this would involve beginning the budgeting process afresh each year ("zero-base"). School boards would need to determine annually the exact nature of the programs and services they were required to offer or wanted to offer in the coming year. In addition, school boards would also need to identify the administrative costs as well as the costs of maintaining and operating their physical plant, buses, and the like. Once all of these requirements were specified, school boards would then need to determine the cost of everything they needed to operate for the coming year.

Because "zero-base" budgeting is time-consuming and costly, school boards and other agencies typically begin the budgeting process using the expenditure patterns for the current year as the starting point. In doing so, they are assuming that all of the conditions that prevail in the current year will apply in the year to come. If they do not anticipate offering any additional programs and services, they just budget for any additional cost increases anticipated for the commodities, staff, and services.

### ADJUSTING THE FUNDING FORMULA

PROVINCIAL GOVERNMENTS typically want to ensure that school boards in remote regions are able to provide the same education as do school boards in more accessible regions. They recognize that costs such as heat and transportation vary in different communities, and relevant differences must be taken into account to ensure equity across school boards.

In British Columbia, for example, the number of students served by school boards differs dramatically. The number of students in the sixty school boards ranges from approximately 350 students to nearly 60,000. The school board with 350 students is located in the northern region of the province more than 1,300 kilometres from a regional transportation centre, and its students are dispersed among small towns located in an area about two-fifths the size of France! The distance from a regional transportation centre makes the cost of shipping goods and services to the district more expensive, and the distances between towns make travel for the superintendent and maintenance crews very expensive. The temperatures are very low during the winter months, and daylight is limited for much of the school year. These factors make the costs for this district greater than for districts located in warmer regions where daylight hours are longer. The cost of providing public schooling in this district with 350 students is almost 2.5 times the provincial average.

The district with 60,000 students is located far to the south in a relatively compact area near the province's main regional centre. It operates many schools and each school enrols many students. Transportation is less costly per student, as are heating and electricity.

To compensate for such variations, provinces develop formulas that take into account the differences among districts. These formulas are designed to ensure that districts are not disadvantaged because of their location or because of other relevant differences, but they are not necessarily perfect. Controversy arose in Ontario during recent years because some districts – including Toronto, Hamilton-Wentworth, and Ottawa – said that the formulas used by the province did not take into account relevant circumstances that made public schooling in those districts more costly than the formula recognized.

## "TARGETING" AND "CAPPING" FUNDING

FUNDING FOR PUBLIC SCHOOLING is further complicated by the establishment of funding "targets" and funding "caps" (maximum capacities). Provinces establish funding targets for a number of reasons. One is to ensure that a provincial policy is carried out as intended. For example, if it has established a priority on early intervention with students at risk of failing in reading, the province might set aside funds that may be spent only for that purpose.

Another reason that provinces establish funding targets is in response to pressure from particular groups. Advocates for students with special needs, for example, have sought funding targets to guarantee that those children receive services and schooling that will ensure their success. Some advocates believe establishing funding targets is the only way they can hold local school boards accountable. The number of students with special needs is relatively small compared with other interests, and advocates say that school boards faced with fiscal pressures and demands from competing interests will not attend to the students with special needs if the funds are not targeted for that purpose. School boards will simply use the money intended (but not targeted) for special-needs students in other areas.

Funding caps are limits placed on the amount of money a school board is allowed to spend in a particular area. Some provinces are concerned about school board spending on administration and trustee stipends. They want to limit expenditures in these areas to ensure that scarce resources are devoted primarily to classroom instruction. As a consequence, they have established funding caps for the amount of money spent on administration and for trustee compensation.

Provinces require school boards to comply with the regulations their ministries have established for the use of the funds provided. They have relatively detailed accounting manuals to provide guidance for reporting expenditures for preparing annual budgets. In addition, some provinces conduct compliance audits, which are designed to determine whether the money provided by the province for particular programs for a designated group of students has been spent as intended.

School boards do not like their discretion limited by provincial regulation. They argue that they were democratically elected by local citizens to reflect their preferences concerning the programs offered and to oversee the schools in their jurisdiction. As anticipated by Ryerson, there has been persistent tension between school boards and provincial governments concerning funding and administration of public schools.

In British Columbia, conflict erupted between one of the province's largest school boards and the Ministry of Education when the ministry conducted an audit of targeted programs. The audit team examined the district's list of students supposedly receiving additional assistance for English as a second language. The team found students on the list who did not require and were not receiving the assistance. The ministry reduced the next payment to the district by an amount equal to the number of ineligible students.

Although it may create a political hot potato, a minister of education may dismiss school boards that submit budgets that would result in a deficit. That's exactly what happened in Vancouver in 1985. The Vancouver School Board defied the government by approving a budget that exceeded limits imposed by the minister of education. The government appointed a team to scrutinize the financial situation. In its report to the minister, the team indicated that the Vancouver School Board's budget could be reduced. On the same day, government appointed one of the budget review team members as an official trustee, and the members of the Vancouver School Board were informed that they had ceased to hold office.

Five of the dismissed trustees filed a petition in the Supreme Court of British Columbia. They sought an order from the court declaring the Order-in-Council appointing the official trustee without force or effect. And they sought another declaring that the elected trustees had not ceased to hold office.

The court dismissed the petitioner's arguments, saying, "Even if the petitioners had a constitutionally protected liberty to be school trustees," they "lost it by their own unlawful acts when they failed to comply with a constitutionally valid statutory requirement."

Provincial governments may wish to abolish school boards as a way of controlling expenditures and reducing organization complexity. Many of the regulations about which local jurisdictions complain arose from attempts by provincial governments to control deviant school boards. For example, in British Columbia, a major school district was planning to keep their school libraries open during lunch and then count the lunch period as instructional time as a way of meeting a commitment it had made with the local teachers' association. As a consequence, the provincial government created a regulation to prohibit the school board's action.

Provincial governments use compliance audits to respond to deviant behaviour on the part of school boards. Including students on the list of ESL students who did not require or who were not receiving additional instruction is an example of such a violation. Rather than dismissing a school board for violating government policy and thereby stirring political sensitivities, governments have used the audit process to "recover" money from school boards that have disregarded provincial government regulations.

Governments looking to increase professional autonomy and accountability might be attracted to eliminating school boards and establishing direct links with individual schools. As superficially tempting as this might appear, however, such a move would probably create more problems than it solved.

There are a number of values at play when considering school budgets. It is often the different emphasis placed on each value that leads to conflict about public school funding. *Universality* is concerned with ensuring that all children of school age are able to attend and benefit from public schooling. Universality obliges public schools to accommodate children whose physical, emotional, or intellectual characteristics might preclude their attendance or their achievement of the benefits of schooling. To achieve universality children whose physical conditions require ramps and wheelchairs to negotiate entrances and hallways should have these needs accommodated. Public schools should provide material in Braille for seeing-impaired children and teachers who can sign for students who are hearing-impaired. *Productive efficiency* is concerned with producing the maximum benefits possible for the given expenditure of public monies. *Equity* is concerned that expenditures are made to reduce educational gaps between identifiable groups of students (boys and girls, native-born and immigrant, aboriginal and non-aboriginal, rich and poor). *Accountability* is concerned with reporting to the public about how resources it provided have been used to achieve the goals of public schooling. *Flexibility* is concerned with permitting the widest possible latitude in decisions about the expenditure of funds. Although people might prize all of these values, all five cannot be fully realized simultaneously. No matter what approach lies behind the allocation of funds, by far the largest portion of the money is spent on salaries.

## TEACHER BARGAINING AND EDUCATION FUNDING

DURING THE LAST TWENTY-FIVE YEARS, provinces have assumed more responsibility for bargaining with teachers. Today, Newfoundland, Prince Edward Island, and New Brunswick bargain all matters at the provincial level. Nova Scotia, Quebec, Saskatchewan, and British Columbia have two-tiered systems where salaries and benefits are bargained at the provincial level and other provisions are bargained at the local level. Only in Alberta, Manitoba, and Ontario does bargaining still occur at the local school board level.

Centralized financial and regulatory control and episodic rounds of school district amalgamation portend a future where all bargaining occurs at the provincial level. It makes little sense for teachers' unions to attempt to bargain with local school boards when the boards cannot determine levels of funding.

It also seems that provincial governments are increasingly willing to impose contract terms on teachers. This is done directly through legislation or indirectly by reducing the capacity of unions to strike by passing essential-service legislation. British Columbia recently adopted both courses of action, introducing essential-service legislation while provincial bargaining was underway, and then imposing a legislated settlement on the parties. Shortly after B.C. took these steps, Alberta did the same, arguing that despite a system of local bargaining, the money available for salary increases was limited. Alberta's attempt to curtail teacher job action was overturned by the courts.

Provinces are becoming more fiscally conservative. They have increasingly assumed responsibility for funding and reducing the number of school districts to achieve administrative and financial efficiencies. In announcing the appointment of an Ontario School Board Reduction Task Force in 1995, Education and Training Minister David Cooke said, "The economic reality today, and for the foreseeable future, is that education budgets are not going to grow. By cutting administration costs these initiatives will result in fewer, more efficient school boards that will more effectively serve the needs of Ontario's students."

The centre-left New Democratic government in which Cooke was minister was subsequently defeated and replaced by a centre-right Conservative government. In August 1996, just prior to the start of the school year, Ontario's new minister of education, John Snobelen, issued two reports. The first one was devoted to a study of education costs and the other concerned school board taxes. The press release about the reports compared the salaries paid Ontario teachers and teachers in other provinces with data about the number of school boards (one hundred) that had increased property tax rates. The release quoted the minister as saying, "These reports show that the system is not responsive to the needs of students or taxpayers."

The next day, the government issued a press release announcing plans to review what it referred to as outdated school board/teacher bargaining rules. That press release pointed out that teachers' unions in Ontario negotiated salaries and benefits with their local school boards every year. The press release said, "This adds up to 166 school boards negotiating almost 300 collective agreements. That's a lot of duplication, and a huge expenditure of time and energy. It's bound to affect the quality of our education system, because it means less time, energy and money is available for the students in Ontario's classrooms."

The Ontario government did not eliminate local bargaining, but the following year it passed legislation changing the terms of teacher collective bargaining, removing principals and vice-principals from teachers' unions, and reducing the number of school districts in Ontario from 172 to 116. Similar measures have been introduced in other provinces. Recent reductions in the number of school districts in Canada include: British Columbia, from 75 to 60; Alberta, from 181 to 64; Quebec, from 158 to 72; Nova Scotia, from 22 to 7; Prince Edward Island, from 5 to 3; and Newfoundland, from 27 to 11. There has been a corresponding decrease in the number of school trustees.

## SCHOOL BOARD GOVERNANCE

SCHOOL TRUSTEES, the public's elected representatives to school boards, are almost completely consumed with financial matters. The changes to public school funding in the past century do not seem to have made a difference to this preoccupation. Whether the funds come primarily from local or provincial sources, school trustees spend most of their time focused on finance.

Even in the period of rapidly rising expenditures during the 1960s and early 1970s, when finances were less of a concern, school trustees seemed unable to devote much attention to any other topic. Decisions regarding building tenders, the choice between day labour and contract labour for construction, the consideration of the quality of supplies and materials, and the remuneration of teachers and other staff members appeared to be made primarily on the basis of "whatever is least costly yet within regulations."

While not insignificant topics for public school trustees to consider, financial issues seem to crowd out consideration of other matters – especially educational ones. When an educational issue comes to the attention of trustees, they invariably turn it over to senior staff.

One way to help school boards focus on educational issues, as opposed to finances, is to free them from managing and operating schools and the administrative responsibilities that go along with those tasks. Provincial governments could create special operating agencies (SOAs) or Crown corporations that would handle school maintenance, plant operations, transportation, payroll, accounts payable and receivable systems, and the like. Schools would become "turnkey" operations. This would free local school boards to focus exclusively on education.

Canadian school boards have failed to implement efficiencies that would enable them to devote a larger proportion of their resources to the classroom. Virtually every school board in Canada operates independently, with little sharing of resources or services. There are few common payroll systems, little pooling of purchasing power, and not much co-operation to achieve efficiencies to redirect scarce resources from board offices to classrooms.

The general public doesn't have much sympathy for the one card that school boards play over and over again. School boards argue that they are uniquely suited to serving the local community because they know the community and what it needs. But few people can name their local school trustees. If a trustee has name recognition, it is often because he or she has voted to close a neighbourhood school.

In some provinces local trustees have led "counterattacks" against provincial governments that have cut or frozen funding for education. But while the counteroffensives have helped the trustees to get re-elected, they do not often turn the tide as far as funding is concerned.

People don't know what value school boards add to the educational equation. Deborah Land of Johns Hopkins University recently reviewed the literature of the past twenty years on the role and effectiveness of local school boards, especially with respect to their influence on students' achievement. She found no evidence linking school board governance to positive academic outcomes.

## INTERNATIONAL CHALLENGES TO
## CANADIAN AUTONOMY IN EDUCATION

PROVINCIAL GOVERNMENTS and school boards may not continue to be the jurisdictions that govern the content and provision of public schooling. Decisions about public schooling might eventually fall under the ambit of the World Trade Organization (WTO).

The WTO was designed to smooth the flow of trade, eliminating restrictions and unpredictability. Since the end of the Second World War, the General Agreement on Tariffs and Trade (GATT) has been the international mechanism for the regulation of trade in *goods*. In January 1995, however, the General Agreement on Trade in Services (GATS) came into force, which established legally enforceable rights about trade in *services*. The GATS agreement includes 160 service sectors, and schooling is definitely a service.

The problem seen by some is that the WTO seems to have greater legislative and judicial authority than its 135 member nations concerning trade in goods and services. And while it is too soon to determine the impact of the WTO on the governance of public schooling, there is good reason for Canadians to be concerned and vigilant.

A number of school boards throughout Canada provide education to international students in exchange for tuition payment. British Columbia and Ontario operate schools offshore that offer students the opportunity to study the provincial curriculum and earn diplomas issued by the sponsor province.

Thus far, WTO member nations have made few commitments about educational services. Canada has not made any commitments in education, and so far says it will not make any agreements affecting educational services from kindergarten to grade twelve.

Nonetheless, many people are concerned to protect education in general, and public schooling in particular, from competition from schools from other nations. It is feared that, if public schooling falls under the ambit of GATS, it may mean the end of provincially determined curricula and with it the means of communicating unique dimensions of Canadian society.

Some people worry about the ambiguity of a key provision of GATS. The provision is contained in subsections 3(a) and 3(b). Subsection 3(a) indicates that services "includes any service in any sector except services supplied *in the exercise of governmental authority* [my italics]." Subsection 3(b) says, "a service supplied in the exercise of governmental authority" means "any service which is supplied neither on a commercial basis, nor in competition with one or more service suppliers."

Do these clauses provide protection for public schooling? Part of the problem is whether subsections 3(a) and (b) protect educational services provided by the many school boards engaged in the private marketplace.

Canadian provinces appear to be in agreement that public schooling should not be included as a service under the provisions of GATS. They have expressed their concern about the issue to the Government of Canada. The federal government says that it has not placed education or health care on the GATS table and that it will not do so. What concerns some people is that Canada has also said that it wants to create opportunities for Canadian health and education providers in other countries. Under the provisions of GATS, it is possible to open education and health for export purposes and protect them for domestic purposes. But what is worrisome to some is the intense pressure to make domestic concessions in one sector for increased export access.

Only time will tell whether public schooling in Canada will eventually fall under the ambit of the WTO. If it does, the legislative and judicial provisions of GATS or other agreements may take precedence over provincial laws and the decisions of local school boards. Under those circumstances, it will be much more difficult for Canadian public schools to retain their distinctively Canadian character.

chapter eleven
••••••••••••••••••••••••••••••••••••••••••

# THE FAILURE OF LEADERSHIP

C anadians, like their counterparts in most post-industrial countries, have less confidence than they used to in governmental and non-governmental institutions and defer less to the people who lead such institutions. In their examination of Canadians' confidence in public institutions, UBC's Neil Guppy and McMaster's Scott Davies make it clear that education has fared better in this respect than many other domains. The decline in confidence in education, they say, is due to a gap between rapidly growing (and perhaps unrealistic) expectations people have for their schools and the capacity of the schools to fulfil those expectations.

I agree. Expectations have grown rapidly. Many of the public's expectations are especially unrealistic given the resources governments are willing to devote to education and the impractical timelines governments set for the implementation of new initiatives. But the gap between the goals we have set and the schools' capacity to achieve them is also due to a failure of leadership.

## THE FOUNDATIONS OF LEADERSHIP

DURING THE TIME I SERVED as deputy minister of education, only one or two of the deputy ministers of education from other jurisdictions across Canada had a formal background in education.

Knowledge of education and an understanding of public schooling, I found, were indispensable in carrying out my responsibilities. They enabled me to speak authoritatively to my colleagues across the country and to the politicians I served.

Like many organizations, governments at various levels have departed from hiring leaders with expertise in the area for which they are responsible. Whether in the private or public sector, in place of persons with particular expertise, businesses and governments have hired people who are expert in management or administration. As a consequence, the leadership provided does not have the same basis in knowledge of the field.

If we want people who can provide leadership in education, we do not have to choose between hiring people with expert knowledge in the field and people with management and administrative expertise. The key word in the last sentence is "if." I am assuming that leadership is a desirable set of attributes that will benefit public schooling. If we want people to devote all of their time to administering and managing, then the present practice of hiring generic managers may be adequate. But I doubt it. Even effective management and administration requires an understanding of the domain.

Effective leadership in public schooling depends upon a foundation of knowledge of the nature and conduct of education. While those who do not possess such knowledge may be able to manage and administer, they will find it difficult to provide leadership without significant dependence upon those who possess such expert knowledge. This is true at all levels.

## SCHOOL-BASED LEADERSHIP

PRINCIPALS ARE TOO EASILY distracted from the central work of public schooling. It is easy for them to become preoccupied by the press of events. The presence of an intruder at the school, episodic violence, and accidents can distract attention from the very difficult, but important, work they must do: providing leadership.

The safety and well-being of students and staff are important and should not be ignored. Obviously, anything that affects them must be addressed, as it could have significant consequence for those directly involved and result in distress throughout the school and community, district, or province. Too often, however, such concerns preoccupy administrators and turn them from leaders into managers.

Leadership and authority are confused and contentious concepts in contemporary public education. Once part of a unified educational community, school administrators now distinguish themselves and are distinguished by others from teachers. School boards expect principals to manage schools on behalf of boards, and this often involves administering the provisions of complex contracts with teachers and other staff.

The exclusion of administrators from teachers' unions in Ontario and British Columbia has made the relationship less collegial and sometimes more adversarial. In the past, membership in teachers' unions tempered the principals' exercise of "management rights." Decisions were more apt to be made after extensive consultation and often in concert with teachers. The removal of principals from teachers' unions has eliminated those tempering influences.

Today's teachers do not accept the paternalistic style of leadership typical until the 1960s, thanks, in part, to the consciousness-raising of the women's movement. But the collegial leadership of the 1960s to 1980s has given way to confrontation. Collegiality between teachers and administrators seems unlikely to return. Governments across Canada seek to assert greater control over teachers. They see school administrators as their representatives in carrying out government policy.

There is comparatively little in their professional preparation that equips public school administrators to administer collective agreements and ensure compliance with provincial statutes and regulations. They are not well equipped to provide instructional leadership and support. They often do not know how to respond to growing demands from parents for involvement in the education of their children and in the affairs of the school.

I do not want to give the wrong impression; there are examples of leadership in Canadian public schools. One in particular illustrates how leaders make a difference. The example is one of many that came to my attention when I was deputy minister.

A grade eight student arrived at a new school in mid-November. The school counsellor met with mother and son to organize the boy's class schedule. Because the student had attended two other schools since the beginning of September, the counsellor was worried about him. She wondered how he would settle in and cope with his third school in as many months.

So the boy – I'll call him Mike – started school the next day, following the schedule the counsellor had arranged. He arrived in the morning, but by noon he had gone home, telling his mother he would not return. He said the other students had given him a rough time, calling him "loser" and a variety of other names. He'd had enough. He couldn't face it again. Mike simply refused to return to school.

His mother phoned the school in tears. The vice-principal took the call. Hearing the story, she became very upset. The school was in the third year of a focus on improving the school's climate. Everyone had made a commitment to the initiative, including a significant attempt to prevent bullying.

Over the previous two years, there had been much school-wide talk about respectful types of behaviours and school expectations. The school had planned, and was implementing, a multi-level approach. There were assemblies, classroom-based initiatives, and actions directed at particular students. Teachers had made an effort to be present in the hallways when students changed classes to catch students being "good." A bullying video was shown and discussed by all classes. Teachers and administrators began each school year discussing the kind of environment they thought should prevail and eliciting suggestions from their students.

Immediately following the telephone call from Mike's mother, the vice-principal, the counsellor, and the principal met to discuss the situation. They decided they had to share what had happened that morning with the whole school. They wanted to see if they could get some help from the students.

They wrote a brief statement to be read to every class in the school and over the public address system asked each teacher to send a runner to the office for an "important message to be shared immediately."

It began with the request: "All teachers please read this to your class and read it with all the passion you can muster." The statement explained what had happened, leaving out the name of the student. The message was clear and pointed. It even included one sentence that the authors had agonized about but eventually included. It read, "Shame on our students who did this." The message ended by asking if any students were willing to help out with this situation and, if they were, telling them to please show up at the office at the break between afternoon classes.

When the break between afternoon classes came, the office began to fill with young people. Within a few minutes it was crowded with at least eighty students, including former "victims" and "bullies." A quick discussion led to some students volunteering to make a giant card for the new student welcoming him to the school.

At the end of the day another PA announcement was made saying that there was a card in the counselling office and that anyone wanting to sign it should show up there after school. As soon as classes ended, a steady stream of students lined up to sign the card. The principal, vice-principal, and counsellor were amazed. With the card completed, the counsellor went to the Mike's home and talked with him about coming back to school.

The next morning he showed up with his mother. The vice-principal was called to the office to meet them. When she saw the mother, baseball cap pulled low over her eyes, standing in the office with the giant welcoming card rolled up in her fist and looking very serious, she began to wonder if maybe the mother was upset with the way they'd handled things. But the mother was there to say how grateful she was. She said her son had had difficulties with bullying before and no one had ever done anything about it. It was a good meeting, a thank-you meeting.

An interesting ripple continued in the school for some time. Mike stayed in the school and did well. The whole school learned who he was. He continued to carry an invisible mantle of protection throughout that year and the years following. Parents learned about the incident and told the principal and vice-principal that the incident had made an enormous impact on their sons and daughters. Several of them said they've never had their children talk so much about school.

## DEFERENCE AND LEADERSHIP

AS I MENTIONED BEFORE, formality and deference once characterized the relations among those involved in public schooling and between education professionals and the public. In the postwar period – and especially during the 1960s and 1970s – that began to change. The formality imposed by British legal and constitutional traditions, the austerity of the Depression, and the discipline imposed in wartime began to disappear. Provincial departments of education and local school boards began to exercise their jurisdictional responsibilities with less formality.

The increasing demand for teachers and the improvement in their preparation played a part in changing the relations among those working in and for public schools. People who believed that school should change society went into teaching. Policies calling for greater consultation among the various interests involved in public schooling were implemented at local and provincial levels. Formal authority relations changed in some jurisdictions.

Today's parents are, as I've said before, better educated than the parents in previous generations. And because they are better educated and have greater access to media, parents are generally more broadly informed than in previous generations. The educational gap between parents and teachers that existed in the past has reduced dramatically. Parents are less likely to accept what teachers and other professional say without adequate justification.

The local schoolmaster in Upper Canada was much less well educated or prepared than the typical Canadian teacher today. Today's teachers, having received more than twelve years of schooling, four years of university education, and at least one year of professional preparation, possess knowledge and expertise unimagined by the nineteenth-century schoolmaster. In addition, the schoolmaster of Upper Canada had no union to look after his interest.

In all Canadian provinces, unions represent public school teachers, and they have grown significantly in membership and influence in the last fifty years. They are devoted primarily to teacher welfare, negotiating salaries and working conditions, defending teachers accused of professional misconduct, and advocating on their members' behalf.

In the past, teachers' unions bargained successfully for better salaries. They were also persuasive in negotiating collective agreements that improved the conditions under which teachers work and students learn. Better working conditions were often linked to improvements in the conditions affecting student learning. Teachers in many local and provincial jurisdictions secured contractual provisions concerning preparation time, provision of professional development, limits to the numbers of students in their classes, specifications for the assessment and placement policies affecting students with special needs, and the like.

Teachers have different interests than those of provincial and local governments. Teachers believe they possess the professional and moral authority to speak about education and the interests of the students they teach. Teachers' unions have become independent, well-organized, and articulate advocates for their members and their interests. However, as events of the past ten years have shown, teachers possess less influence than they once did.

Teachers have lost some of their moral and professional authority because a better educated public has become less deferential. They have also lost authority because the organizations that represent them have resisted regulation in the public interest, opposed heightened accountability, and refused to accept greater parental and public involvement in schooling.

More knowledgeable parents are demanding the same privilege of consultation as teachers and other educational professionals, although they are less well organized and possess fewer resources. As a consequence of these changes, members of the public generally, and parents in particular, are much less likely to defer to the judgment of education professionals.

Formal parental involvement typically involves providing advice to school staff members, the principal, or school board, and acting as a liaison between the wider parent community and the professional staff of the school. Since 1972, Quebec has required that school councils be established in every school. Alberta, Newfoundland, New Brunswick, and Ontario also set out in legislation the requirements for school councils and the matters on which they may provide advice. Nova Scotia's legislation is permissive, allowing parents to advise the board, principal, and staff respecting matters related to schooling. The department of education in Prince Edward Island outlines the role that such councils may play.

British Columbia recently established School Planning Councils. The school's principal sits on the council along with a teacher elected by the staff of teachers. The council also includes three parents elected by the other parents whose children are enrolled in the school. The councils are expected to examine how well students are performing and develop an annual plan that includes goals for improvement.

By the end of the 1990s, there were also many advocacy, ethno-cultural, business, labour, national, provincial, and community groups with strong interests in public schooling and the expertise and organization to advance those interests. These groups often compete with one another for scarce education dollars. There are, for example, more than fifty advocacy groups for students with special needs in British Columbia. Most of those groups are concerned about students who have some form of disability. A few are advocates for students who are gifted or talented.

Parents have a direct and relatively short-term interest in education. They are concerned primarily with the well-being of their children. With rare exception, their interest lasts only as long as their children are enrolled in school. Teachers complain about the narrow perspective that most parents bring to discussions of school issues, and say that they take an interest in school issues only so far as they affect their own children. Teachers say that parents are not sympathetic to their need to take all students into account when they make a decision.

Parental myopia is understandable in discussions with the classroom teacher, but when the same perspective is brought to school-level or district-level discussions, it creates significant frustration for teachers, administrators, and even for other parents.

Over the past twenty-five years, as parental organizations gathered influence and legitimacy within the education arena, those who served as parent representatives sought, or were sought as candidates for, the office of school trustee. School board elections are often testing grounds for those seeking political office. More than a few municipal and provincial politicians were first elected as school trustees.

Many of those seeking election as school trustees are often single-issue advocates. Whether it is daily physical education, a more inclusive school environment for gay and lesbian youth, or fine arts education, single-issue advocates are rarely disposed to fashion a coherent educational agenda with their fellow trustees. Making the transition from advocacy to trusteeship is a process made doubly difficult by the failure of leadership among directors and superintendents of education.

## PASSING THE BUCK

PROVINCIAL POLITICIANS seem to possess only a passing acquaintance with educational issues. Issues such as the education of aboriginal students, immigrant students, and students with special educational needs, the fragmentation of the educational experience of high school students, and the difficulty of developing a common citizenship among students of diverse backgrounds are largely ignored in favour of procedural matters such as accountability, autonomy, and flexibility. Rather than articulate a coherent vision of education, provincial politicians attempt to appease citizens making diverse educational demands with concepts such as choice, accountability, and local autonomy.

The audience for the actions of politicians is the electorate. Voters remember the commitments made by politicians or their parties during election campaigns and their responses to pressing events during their tenure in office. The timing and rhythm of political life affects the issues to which politicians respond.

It is a rare politician who appreciates that improving teaching and learning are lasting objectives of public schooling. They are not "problems" to be fixed and, once fixed, forgotten. They need constant attention. Each year brings a new combination of student characteristics, experiences, and challenges that require the exercise of judgment and imagination. Having successfully encountered a particular set of challenges in a given year provides a foundation for meeting similar challenges, but the challenges are never identical.

Provincial politicians avoid having to take a position on pivotal issues facing public schooling by delegating decisions to local trustees. It absolves them from having to take responsibility. In the contested and confusing arena of public schools, attention is diverted from the provincial level of government to the local level. While it may prove to be a successful strategy for provincial politicians, it is not a good way to address issues of public policy.

Ever mindful of the electoral horizon, provincial and local politicians pursue educational agendas designed to give them visibility and produce few, if any, issues to be managed. The rhythm of electoral politics is not in synch with the need for sustained, systematic improvement and capacity building in education. This mismatch results in complicated education issues being ignored in favour of high-profile initiatives designed to attract immediate attention. The temporal framework of some politicians hardly extends beyond the daily six o'clock news.

A related problem at the provincial level is centralization of political control in the office of provincial premiers. Centralization makes cabinet government difficult, if not impossible. Too much control by the premier undermines both the interest and the capacity of the government's ministers to address important issues. It seems a common practice to make frequent cabinet shuffles and changes, which guarantees that ministers do not develop the interest, knowledge, or capacity to have significant influence on their portfolios. The problem is compounded when deputy ministers are also moved frequently from portfolio to portfolio.

School district superintendents and directors of education are beholden to the trustees who employ them. But many superintendents and directors of education are ill-disposed to bring coherence to the disparate personal agendas of school trustees. Forging a common agenda has at least two risks for the superintendent. That agenda might not include the issues favoured by powerful trustees upon whom the superintendent might depend for support. And many directors and superintendents use infighting among trustees to preserve and enhance their own power.

## IMPATIENCE WITH THE STATUS QUO

EDUCATIONAL IMPROVEMENT – whether for a student, a school, or an entire school system – requires continuous attention rather than the sporadic and episodic attention it typically receives. With an eye always on the next election, most governments are abysmal at implementing real improvements, because they are unwilling to commit the effort and resources that change requires without immediate and visible progress.

Relations between provincial governments and teachers' unions are becoming increasingly poisonous. The consequences are bad for everyone involved and for the public's view of the education system. Parents and students feel they are the victims of the conflict. Many students and parents recognize that teachers have limited means of making their displeasure felt by governments. But they are growing impatient with teachers who withdraw from extracurricular activities and refuse to perform certain work.

Parents and the general public are becoming upset with governments that say they value education but are unwilling to provide public schools with the financial resources and support they need to do a good job. Their abrupt changes in educational policy and funding prior to elections reveals a cynical view of the electorate.

Most members of the public are fed up with governments that behave that way. That's one reason why there have been some dramatic shifts in support for Canadian political parties in the past dozen years. Annoyed with governments that view and treat voters cynically, the Canadian electorate is becoming more volatile and unpredictable.

## WHAT CAN BE DONE?

PUBLIC EXPENDITURES for elementary and secondary schooling account for a sizeable portion of provincial government budgets. Thus, it isn't surprising that, while the timing and details may differ from one jurisdiction to another, disputes over funding for public schooling have been a recurring theme in most Canadian jurisdictions. Educational funding and governance are controversial and highly intertwined issues.

People react strongly to changes, however major or minor they may be. Public opinion forced New Brunswick to reverse its recent decision to eliminate school boards and replace them with school councils. Protracted public conflict about educational governance and finance has occupied the attention of Ontarians and British Columbians for several years.

School boards need to put their houses in order. They need to seek efficiencies and become more firmly engaged in the educational issue affecting their communities. If they fail to do so, they will continue to be reduced in number or eliminated altogether.

Provincial governments can help steer school boards the right way by appointing the director of education (or superintendent of schools) in each local jurisdiction. Direct appointment will reduce the directors' (or superintendents') dependence on local school trustees. This would make it easier for them to provide policy advice to local trustees from their knowledge base as educators.

Provincial governments should also ensure that large and geographically dispersed districts are organized on a ward or community basis. Trustees would be elected from specific areas in the district. The purpose would be to create a closer connection between the elected trustees and the residents of the community or ward. This should help encourage trustees to learn more about the educational needs of the students in the community or ward they serve and bring those concerns to their planning of educational programs. At the same time, public accountability would be served by the appointed director. Such an appointment would ensure greater compliance with provincial regulations and a closer link between provincial and local policies.

The appointment of directors of education (or superintendents of schools) would also help make the educational system more responsive and better prepared for change. My belief is that direct appointment would make governments pursuing new initiatives realize their obligations to build capacity in the system for the changes they wished to implement. Direct appointment would increase the success of changes in policy and practice. As employees of the province, directors of education would have to make sure their ministries understood what human and material resources were required for successful implementation.

Canadians should stop pretending that education is not and should not be political. It is and it should be. Education is about realizing a society's vision. Different people prize different things and will seek to influence education to achieve their vision. By pretending that education isn't political, we diminish the importance of values in our vision for society. As someone said recently, democracies don't contract to management consultants the important public decisions that must be made. As messy and contentious as those decisions may prove to be, they are part and parcel of living in a democratic society. School trustees must be strong and vocal advocates for sound policies, adequate funding, realistic and focused expectations, and, above all, universally accessible, equitable, and free public schooling.

School boards need to consider how they make decisions about education and about managing the scarce resources they are given to do society's most important work. There is much that they might do to manage their resources more efficiently. School boards need to share services with other boards. For example, there shouldn't be separate payroll systems for each school board in a province.

School boards should consolidate purchasing to achieve economies. They should consider establishing Internet-based purchasing systems containing information about goods and services of potential interest to boards, including pricing and volume discounts. Only suppliers willing to offer volume discounts for consolidated purchases should be able to list their goods or services on such a site.

Educators have traditionally been appointed to the highest positions of responsibility in schools and school boards in Canada. Principals and directors of education (or superintendents of schools) typically have teaching backgrounds and have earned advanced degrees in education. But too often the direction they provide to the districts or schools ignores the considerable knowledge base that has developed for education over the past hundred years. While not as well developed as in the field of medicine, educational research provides evidence to give directions to educational policy and teaching practice.

When they ignore educational research, directors of education and school principals forfeit their claim that the positions they occupy should be filled by people with educational credentials. In the United States, school boards have hired people from diverse backgrounds to provide leadership. The ranks of school superintendents there have included corporate managers, lawyers, accountants, and retired military personnel.

There is a story about one large urban district in the United States that hired a retired army general to provide leadership. The district had suffered very poor student performance, labour strife, an exodus of families seeking better schools, and a number of other serious problems. After several years of unsuccessful attempts to address the district's problems, the retired general quit, saying, "This is one war I cannot win." I don't think Canadian school jurisdictions should go in this direction. But if leaders continue to make decisions without regard to accumulated evidence and knowledge, it is an inevitable direction for Canadian education.

Everyone involved in public schooling must avoid the temptation to substitute ideology for logic and evidence. Principals have a particular responsibility to exert their leadership in using evidence. We know from the research, for example, what factors work to increase student success. In places where schools are improving, principals devote more time and attention to: encouraging a clear curricular focus; establishing a positive school and disciplinary climate; setting high standards for student achievement; monitoring student performance in light of those standards; building a sense of team among the school's staff; fostering parental involvement; and focusing professional development in areas where improvement is needed.

We need a much higher level of skill in using assessment data. Let's not be afraid of it. There will be both bad news and good news. We have to look at the bad news not as a criticism but as an opportunity to improve. A single approach won't work. The data will tell different stories from one district to another, districts will need to devise their own solutions to address local problems. Central solutions will become increasingly rare.

We also need a much lower reliance on additional money to solve problems. We will have to use our existing resources more effectively and efficiently. Further, whatever money is spent will be increasingly tied to results. Until now, the system has been structured to focus on equal inputs, such as funding. Shifting our focus to achieving desired outcomes may require us to consider using unequal inputs in order to obtain equitable results.

Leadership – the determination to make a difference – should not be remarkable, but, because of its scarcity, it is. We are too apt to confuse dramatic pronouncements with leadership. To the extent that we do, we encourage politicians to attempt snowy, short-term changes. Such changes are unlikely to work, but they will reinforce cynicism among those who work in schools every day. The "been there, done that" syndrome is all too familiar to education professionals, who simply wait things out until there is (a) a new minister of education, (b) a new government, or (c) both. Lack of leadership, highly publicized but meaningless or ill-conceived short-lived changes, and cynicism will not improve public schooling.

chapter twelve
·······································

# ACCOUNTABILITY

anadian public schools work well for the majority of youngsters. In comparison to most other countries, Canada can take pride in the quality of its public schools and the education they provide. But there is room for improvement. I have made some suggestions elsewhere about what needs to change and why – and even how to make the changes. In this chapter I want to tackle the issues of school accountability and improvement.

## AUDITS

PROVINCES MAY PURSUE educational accountability from different perspectives. The audit concept is based on the notion that something has been stated and must be proven (attestation audit), or that something has been delegated to a person, group, or body and we want to see if they have complied with procedures (compliance audit) or achieved a goal (outcomes audit). What and how one audits depends on what one values. The audit process is one of examining sufficient evidence to determine whether something is true.

Financial accountability is usually pursued with attestation audits, which review financial statements to determine their reliability. *Were the funds that the statement says were expended for the purchase of particular supplies and services actually spent on those items?*

Attestation auditors often issue a report about the reliability of a school board's financial reports.

School boards, public schools, and those who work in public schools are governed by established policies, regulations, and procedures. Provinces sometimes choose to audit the practices of school boards or public schools to determine whether they are complying. Compliance audits might look at whether the school board is adhering to the time allocations specified for a particular curricular area or whether the topics required have actually been taught, if such matters have been specified in policy.

Suppose that a province believed it was important that particular learning concepts were taught. The province might audit school programs to determine whether the educational program included the concepts and whether they were being addressed in a satisfactory manner. It would need to define "satisfactory" and determine relevant criteria that could be used in such an audit. It would be important for the province to engage teachers and curriculum specialists in the process. They would help identify what would constitute proper and effective coverage of the concepts for the particular grade level. They would need to specify what auditors could use as evidence of how well each teacher was meeting the specified criteria.

The problem with this approach is that it places emphasis on specific content or instructional processes. It would be wrong to make inferences about the quality of a school board or a particular school from the presence or absence of the specified content or process. For example, you can't judge the quality of a social studies program from the inclusion or omission of the Industrial Revolution. Such an approach is too prescriptive. A system that prescribes in detail what students must be taught shackles teachers. Such prescription diminishes the importance of the professional judgments teachers should make.

If what a province *desires* is that students are able to read, but what it *prescribes* is a highly controlled language arts curriculum, then whether or not that curriculum produces readers can be considered the ministry's problem. Such highly specified account-ability mechanisms place the responsibility on the province to determine correctly how instruction should occur. If the audit finds that practices are as specified but that students are not learn-ing, it is the province's responsibility to rectify the situation.

An alternative type of audit looks at whether school boards or individual schools are successfully achieving particular outcomes. During my tenure as British Columbia's deputy minister of edu-cation, for example, the province introduced annual assessments of reading, writing, and numeracy at grades four, seven, and ten. The assessment was designed to determine whether students at those grade levels had achieved particular desired outcomes. The outcomes measured (or audited) were broad-based competencies, such as the ability to comprehend the literal meaning of a passage.

Suppose the evidence indicates that 120 of the 150 grade three students in a school can meet the reading standards appropriate for that grade level. A province will be pleased to know about the 120 successful students, but it should be concerned about those who were not successful. The province would certainly want a further audit of the "management and educational processes" at work to try to determine how 30 students were unsuccessful. But these types of audits should occur among the members of the school staff rather than at the school district or provincial level. They are appropriate at the school level, because school and class-room policies and practices account for most of the differences in student achievement. In fact, the differences are greater within a particular school than they are between neighbouring schools.

If 30 of the 150 students are unable to read, there is probably something that educators would agree should be happening that isn't. If the problem persists over time, school boards might want to make use of a "performance management" audit. This audit would identify, in consultation with educators, the elements of effective school and classroom practices. These effective practices would then be compared to what is happening in the school with the consistently poor student performance.

## THE POLITICS OF ACCOUNTABILITY

WHETHER SEARCHING FOR A QUICK FIX for perceived school problems or simply to boost their own political longevity, politicians have flocked to testing, standards, accountability contracts, school councils, and other "accountability mechanisms" like flies to honey. You can't really blame them. Politics has its own logic that requires politicians to do *something* – even if it is the wrong thing.

As I have said before, one of the problems of living as close as we do to the United States is the rhetorical spillover from those Americans who say "our schools are failing." Sputnik helped fuel the demand for more mathematics and science graduates to help Americans compete with the Soviet Union in what was called the "space race," code words for the Cold War. Like the Cold War, Hollywood, McDonald's, and countless other things American, the rhetoric of a nation at risk because of school failure overflowed into Canada.

It would be dangerous for politicians to question the applicability to Canadian schools of such a claim. After all, there is always room for "educational improvement," by "raising the achievement bar," and "promoting school success." A politician who argues, "Our schools are doing just fine, thank you" is begging for negative attention by the media and heading for electoral trouble.

The problem with a phrase such as "lack of educational accountability" is that it evokes an image of a system in which people act without regard to consequence. Accountability is a vague and easily misunderstood concept capable of arousing strong passions. Once aroused, these passions are not easily satisfied. It is important to probe beyond surface impressions about schooling and ask: To whom and for what should schools be responsible? What evidence should be used to judge the performance of public schools? Who should gather and interpret that evidence? With what frequency should the evidence be gathered and interpreted? What consequences should befall public schools that do not fulfill their responsibilities? What mechanisms can be used to improve educational outcomes?

Canada's strong, centralized provincial ministries of education have evolved along the lines envisioned by Egerton Ryerson, who believed that "if it is the duty of Government to legislate on the subject of Public Instruction, it must be its duty to see its laws executed." The practices employed today to ensure that the public's interest in education is realized can be traced to the practices of the first departments of education.

Then and now, the number and responsibilities of school boards, the methods and extent of education funding, the curriculum and examinations, and the criteria for teacher certification are all matters centrally controlled by the provinces on behalf of the citizenry. Provincial jurisdictions require schools to report regularly about student educational progress to parents and guardians. They conduct periodic and regular assessments of student achievement, and they participate in national and international assessments. Many people's opinion of schools is based on the results of those assessments.

### SETTING THE STANDARDS

MOST JURISDICTIONS PROVIDE CURRICULUM guidelines for teachers. The guidelines often specify the goals that the jurisdiction thinks are essential to achieve. In addition, with varying degrees of prescription, some jurisdictions specify or recommend materials, instructional strategies, and methods of assessment, but, appropriately, most leave these matters in the hands of classroom teachers.

To save money, jurisdictions are sometimes tempted to import curricula from elsewhere or to purchase them from commercial suppliers. This poses a number of challenges. First, there is the issue of credibility. Will teachers in jurisdiction A find curricula from jurisdiction B as credible as those developed by trusted peers? Second is the issue of validity. Will curricula from the other region reflect what is valued in the local jurisdiction and what students have the background to achieve?

Jurisdictions that involve teachers in the curriculum design or revision process often encounter less resistance to the material because it represents the thinking of respected peers. The process is time-consuming and expensive, but it is worth it. The experiences that classroom teachers have had teaching the curriculum, and their knowledge of the student population for whom the curriculum is intended, will help guarantee that the criteria developed are reasonable. In addition to the added credibility that comes from teacher involvement, the process is a useful form of professional development for the participants.

In setting the curriculum for the province's schools, the ministries of education ensure that a school's program of studies harmonizes with that of other schools. Students moving from one school to another should have continuity in their education. In most jurisdictions, the province sets the goals that must be achieved. It permits teachers to exercise professional discretion about organizing their classes in order to accomplish the goals. Inspectors, who once travelled from school to school, visiting classrooms and offering advice to the teachers and school principal, have given way to performance standards and periodic assessments.

Performance standards are criteria that educators use to determine whether a student has met, exceeded, or fallen short of an established level of performance in a particular area. The most useful performance standards include comprehensive examples of student work (exemplars).

When I was deputy minister in B.C., the ministry published a set of performance standards for reading, writing, numeracy, and citizenship and social responsibility. Performance standards were designed to help teachers improve their in-class assessment of student work. Two features distinguished the B.C. approach from the approach taken in other jurisdictions. First, and perhaps most important, was the involvement of grade level teachers in the process. Second was that the standards were derived from student work that exemplified particular attributes the teachers thought important in light of their understanding of the curriculum's goals.

Some jurisdictions, by not including teachers in the process of establishing standards, are missing a crucial reality check on the definition and setting of those standards. And some jurisdictions do not provide exemplars from student work. This leaves to the individual teacher's judgment whether a particular work meets, exceeds, or falls short of the standard. Without broad experience with students across regions, teachers' judgments are likely to prove inaccurate.

Not long ago, I was talking with teachers from California, a state that recently embarked upon a "standards-based" approach to education. According to these teachers, the group who articulated the standards took the opportunity to "raise the bar" by incorporating at earlier grade levels goals and objectives that had previously been associated with more advanced levels. Although they were not certain, the teachers did not believe that any representative of grade level teachers had been involved in the process.

The material they showed me provided no examples of student work that satisfied or failed to satisfy the standard. The impression I drew was that as sympathetic as teachers might be to a "standards-based" approach – and the teachers with whom I talked were sympathetic – the initiative was likely to have a more difficult time reaching its objectives in the absence of teacher involvement and examples of students' work.

## PROMISES, PROMISES

POLITICIANS OFTEN HAVE UNREALISTIC EXPECTATIONS. Part of the problem comes from their need to be seen to be decisive, results-oriented people. Part of the problem is the time frame in which politicians are forced to work. The electoral process means promises made during the heat of a political campaign must be seen to be fulfilled well before the next election. Initiatives mounted during a politician's term must also begin to show results before the next election. Failure to keep promises or to show results for initiatives originating from one's office is a sign of lack of concern, weakness, or insincerity.

School councils – attempts to have parents and professionals work collaboratively for the betterment of local schools – illustrate the problem of unrealistic political expectations. With rare exception, school councils have, in the last twenty-five years, persistently failed. And despite their failure, the idea regularly recurs, only to run into the same problems. British Columbia's introduction of school planning councils is a textbook illustration of problems created when politicians do not appreciate the complexity of the initiatives they want or set unrealistic timelines for their achievement.

The government of British Columbia amended the School Act in 2002 to provide for a school planning council in every public school in the province. The councils will examine how well students are performing. The legislation requires school planning councils to develop annual plans that include goals and outcomes for improvement. Boards of school trustees will have to consult with school planning councils about educational services and programs offered in the school, the allocation of resources, and matters contained in the board's accountability contract with the ministry. The plans developed by individual schools will be used as the basis for developing the annual accountability contracts that the ministry requires of school boards.

What the minister fails to appreciate are the many conditions that must be fulfilled for effective planning to improve student success. At a minimum, such conditions include:

- establishing broad agreement about which school outcomes are essential for all students;
- ensuring these areas are clearly articulated in the curriculum and are supported with appropriate time and instructional material;
- articulating high, but reasonable, expectations of student success;
- holding students, parents, and teachers accountable for those outcomes;
- assessing student progress in the areas of importance at different times over their school careers;
- employing practices and policies that increase learning outcomes for all students; and
- examining rates of student progress as well as gradients in student progress associated with such background factors as socio-economic standing, gender, and ethnicity.

However, meeting these conditions will not achieve the desired results if the public school curriculum remains overcrowded and the priority among outcomes remains unclear.

The members of the planning councils will need preparation for talking about school policies and practices in non-threatening and productive ways. Principals will need to learn how to support and lead such discussions. All of the participants on the school councils will need practice interpreting information for the purposes of improving student achievement, developing plans that are achievable, monitoring progress, adjusting policies and practices when necessary, and engendering commitment on the part of those not directly involved on the planning councils.

Council members will have their work cut out for them. The one teacher representative will have to figure out how to communicate with a sometimes large and usually varied staff of teachers. The principal will have to juggle his or her present work with the additional tasks of preparing for school planning councils, working with the councils, and following up on the agendas that the councils will set for the school. If school planning councils take principals away from the limited time they spend providing leadership for instructional improvement, they will not have been worth the trade-off.

The challenge for the three parents who will sit on school planning councils is formidable as well. Participating on a school planning council that takes improving student success seriously will require significant amounts of time. None of the participants on school councils is likely to be adept at interpreting information for the purposes of improvement, but parents are probably the least well-prepared for the task.

Parents on school planning councils will have a steep learning curve. In addition to discussing school policies and practices in non-threatening and productive ways, they will need to learn about student assessment, interpretation of assessment and other data, and about the range of policies and practices that affect student achievement. They will also need support for communicating with the broader parent community about the issues under discussion, obtaining advice from the broader community of parents, and seeking their commitment to the plans that are adopted.

By virtue of their preparation and responsibilities, teachers and administrators are accustomed to having a broad perspective on schooling and considering the general welfare of students. Parents tend naturally to view schooling largely in terms of the welfare of their own children. A significant challenge for parents will be to balance their concern for the welfare of their own children with the general welfare of all students.

There is a danger that school councils will become a power-base for those who already possess influence rather than a means of ensuring greater participation and involvement among those whose voices have not been heard. The narrow range of parents currently active in school matters will dominate the councils. Outreach is needed to the wider community to ensure that its citizens recognize how they are affected by what happens at school.

The composition of the councils may also pose problems. Limiting them to a single teacher, three parents, and the school principal is likely to mean that, if there is significant turnover from year to year, valuable time will be spent reviewing previous discussions and decisions. Expanding the councils to include more teachers would help. Extending participation on the councils to include community members who do not have children in school would anchor planning councils more firmly in the community and perhaps give councils more credibility. It would also make community members who do not have children aware of the contribution that schools make to the large community.

School planning councils are unfamiliar structures in British Columbia with no records of accomplishment. They were introduced in B.C. in 2002 at the same time as school district budgets were frozen. Much of the time that school board members might have devoted to considering ways of improving student performance on a system-wide basis was spent managing resources. Furthermore, school boards do not have the capacity or the time to make productive use of the information that school planning councils are intended to provide.

As school planning councils were introduced in B.C., teachers were facing the spectre of larger classes and less support from specialist teachers. The changes government introduced caused tensions between principals and teachers. Those tensions reduced the chance that principals and teachers will be able to engage in the kind of productive discussions that will need to occur if school councils are going to deliver on their promise.

A number of people have questioned the capacity of parents to make a meaningful contribution to school planning councils. They ask why administrators and teachers should spend valuable time educating parents about what took them years to learn. Physicians do not do the same for patients, lawyers for their clients, or architects for home buyers.

The B.C. government's intention to improve student achievement is laudable. Given that lack of attention to crucial details and timing, however, school planning councils are almost certain to have the same fate as their predecessors in Quebec, Ontario, and elsewhere.

## IN LOVE WITH BOX SCORES

POLITICIANS OF WIDELY DIVERGENT political orientations think testing students will improve learning. Testing has increased dramatically in the past ten years, and if it worked in the simplistic way that some politicians seem to think, kids today would be the most learned students ever.

"Increased" is the operative word, since testing has always been a prominent assessment tool. Teachers use tests to assess student learning and the success of their teaching. Tests are also used to motivate students to learn prescribed material and to make sure that all of the students in a school or district at a particular grade level have achieved common outcomes considered important.

Some provinces use tests at the senior secondary level to ensure common outcomes and determine eligibility for provincial scholarships. Sometimes the scores on these tests are factored into the student's final grade by weighting the provincial examination score and the score assigned by the teacher based on the teacher's classroom assessments. In British Columbia, for example, provincial examination scores count for 40 per cent and the scores awarded by a teacher count for 60 per cent of the student's overall mark in grade twelve examinable subjects.

Provinces also use examinations to assess whether the curriculum in a particular subject area is achieving the outcomes intended. Such tests can help to determine whether subjects are being over- or under-emphasized, or whether the sequential relationship among the topics is appropriate. Such tests are administered infrequently or to just a sample of all the students in the province. The following table summarizes the assessment practices of Canada's provinces. The numbers in parentheses indicate the grade levels at which the tests are administered.

In 1993, the Council of Ministers of Education Canada embarked upon a national testing program known as the Student Achievement Indicators Program (SAIP). Under SAIP, tests are administered to students from thirteen to sixteen years of age in mathematics, reading and writing, and science. The third cycle of SAIP began in 2001.

The variation among curricula from one provincial or territorial jurisdiction to another makes comparisons difficult. Nonetheless, SAIP tries to assess and compare what students have learned in common areas in order to determine if students in different regions are achieving similar levels of performance at roughly the same age.

Canada also takes part in a variety of international assessments of student achievement. The Programme for International Student Assessment (PISA) is an initiative of the Organization for Economic Co-operation and Development. The program assesses the performance of fifteen-year-old students in reading, mathematics, and science literacies using common tests. Thirty thousand Canadian students participated in the most recent PISA.

By itself, testing cannot improve learning. The popular saying these days is, "You can't fatten the pig by weighing it." Testing is only one factor in a complex set of factors that are necessary for improving achievement. But despite their utility for (a) determining whether students are meeting the standards set for their achievement, and (b) for providing information for improving student achievement, large-scale assessments (as the tests are called in the education community) are not typically used well.

The differences between norm-referenced and criterion-referenced tests confuse many people, including some educators. *Norm-referenced assessments* are primarily aimed at determining how well students perform in relation to one another. *Criterion-referenced assessments* are primarily used to test an individual student's knowledge. They try to determine which students have achieved mastery of a body of knowledge deemed appropriate for the students taking the test. They are occasionally used to make comparisons among students.

A successful testing program requires a match between the test and the curriculum. The test must address material that students are expected to have mastered by the time the test is administered. The effective use of results from large-scale tests depends upon clearly articulated curricula, specific learning outcomes, and widely accepted curricular exemplars. The curricula should specify clearly the knowledge that students are expected to learn and when they are expected to have learned it. Curriculum exemplars of acceptable student work, student work that exceeds expectations, and work that falls short of the desired standard are necessary for the construction of good tests. The exemplars are also helpful to teachers and parents in understanding the relationship between student performances and the standard.

The involvement of classroom teachers is an important part of successful testing programs. Teacher involvement helps create a match between the assessment and curriculum. The participation of teachers at all stages of the assessment process (that is, development, field-testing, administration, marking, standard-setting, interpretation) is critical to gaining trust and grassroots support for the testing program. Such support will be necessary later when teachers are encouraged to adjust their instructional

## Provincial Assessment Practices
(numbers in parentheses represent grade levels)

| Assessments / Tests | Credentialing Examinations |
|---|---|
| **Alberta** | |
| Mathematics Language Arts (3, 6, 9) French Language Arts, Science & Social Studies (6, 9) | Various subjects (12) |
| **British Columbia** | |
| Reading, Writing & Numeracy (4, 7, 10) Other areas (as determined) | Various subjects (12) |
| **Manitoba** | |
| English Program Reading & Numeracy (3) | English Language Arts, English Language Arts Immersion & Anglais Standards (6) |
| French Program Lecture & Notations de calcul (3) | Francais Langue Premier & French Langue Seconde Immersion Standards Test (6) |
| French Immersion Program Reading & Notations de calcul (3) Lecture (4) | Mathematics (S1) |
| | English Language Arts Standards Test (S4) |
| | Immersion Standards Test (S4) |
| | Mathematics/Mathematique Standards Test (S4) |
| **New Brunswick** | |
| Language Arts, Mathematics & Science (3) | Mathematics (11) |
| Language Arts, Mathematics, Science & Writing (5) | English (11) |
| French Immersion Language Arts (6) | |
| Mathematics & Language Arts (8) | |

## Newfoundland

Mathematics, Science, Core French
& Writing (3, 6, 9)

Atlantic Provinces
Educational Foundation
Chemistry (12)

Canadian Test of Basic Skills
Language Arts, Mathematics,
Work Study Skills, Science (4, 7, 10, 12)

All Subjects (12)

## Nova Scotia

Mathematics (5, 8)

English, Science &
Mathematics (12)

Language Arts (6, 9)

## Ontario

Reading, Writing & Mathematics (3, 6)
Mathematics (9)
Literacy (6, 9, 12)

Reading & Writing (10)

## Prince Edward Island

Teacher discretion

Teacher discretion

## Quebec

French, Language of Instruction
(6 Sec III)

Elementary Level [French,
English Language Arts,
Mathematics] (3, 6)

Language of Instruction,
Second Language, History of
Quebec & Canada, Physical Sciences
(Sec IV & V)

Secondary Level [French,
Language of Instruction,
Mathematics]

## Saskatchewan

Mathematics, Language Arts (5, 8, 11)
Technical Literacy, Critical &
Creative Thinking (5, 8, 11)

All Subjects (12)

---

*Source: Alan R. Taylor and Teresita-Salve Tubianosa, "Student Assessment in Canada: Improving the Learning Environment through Effective Evaluation," Raven Research Associates, 2001.*

programs to improve student success. While many Canadian jurisdictions involve classroom teachers, many American departments of education hire companies to develop, mark, and interpret the results of their tests.

Involvement of local teachers in all aspects of the process is beneficial for everyone. Teachers benefit professionally by learning about assessment practices and from their collaboration with other teachers from elsewhere in the jurisdiction. Ministries of education benefit from the development of valid and better respected testing instruments.

Centralized testing regimes can produce unintended and undesirable consequences. Teachers faced with centralized testing regimes feel they must ensure that students have mastered the knowledge that will be assessed. Based on prior tests, they may start "teaching to the test," sacrificing other important aspects of the subject being assessed, or "borrowing" time from curricular areas that are not assessed. Thus, it is important that the required learning outcomes that will be formally tested are clearly indicated, are achievable in the time allocated for instruction, and can be achieved without sacrificing other important learning outcomes.

The success of testing regimes depends upon teachers having sufficient and appropriate instructional material. It is important that the instructional material available be closely linked to the curriculum. If knowledge is important enough to be tested, it is essential that the knowledge be addressed well in the instructional support material.

Testing standards must be widely accepted for test results to be credible. Determination of standards of mastery must be made prior to the construction of the test. The process should involve parents, teachers, administrators, and representatives of the broader public. Policy-makers should be prepared for the increased time required for standard-setting and preparation of the assessment. They must also expect the conflict that will likely ensue when expectations of constituencies differ.

Business people, university educators, teachers, and parents will hold different perspectives about standards. While it is possible and desirable to obtain agreement about standards with the involvement of a wider constituency, it takes work. It is easier, but not wiser, to involve grade-level teachers or subject specialists. Jurisdictions that do not involve a range of educational partners in the standard-setting process run the risk that the standards will not be respected by everyone. Community support for the tests and follow-up process is essential to the successful use of the information for improving student learning.

The teachers from California to whom I referred earlier told me that in the last five years statewide tests have changed dramatically from year to year. In fact, California, putting the cart before the horse, developed the first phase of its testing regime *before* the standard-setting process began. I'm not surprised that, following the standard-setting process, they found it necessary to make substantial revisions to the tests. Such an apparently ill-conceived process is likely to undermine credibility and consequently reduce its effectiveness in the long run. People – especially the teachers upon whom the success of the process depends – will feel that too much is in flux for them to make systematic adjustments in their instructional programs.

With large-scale testing regimes, it is important to ensure the standards remain consistent from one year to the next across successive administrations. Jurisdictions that want to use different tests to assess growth over time will need to employ proper test-equating procedures. Otherwise it is difficult to compare the results of different tests in different years.

Use of these types of test-equating procedures will also help address problems if different standard-setting panels create inconsistent standards. Test equating also eliminates the need for annual standard-setting activities because the same standards could be applied across a number of years of assessments. Periodic reviews every four or five years would ensure the standards reflect current expectations. If the assessment addresses broadly accepted and important dimensions of learning, the standards should not change dramatically over time.

In California, teachers whose students showed dramatic year-over-year improvement received salary bonuses. I have my doubts about the effectiveness and propriety of such incentives. Those doubts aside, I do know that the teachers who were rewarded (and others implicitly punished) were treated unfairly; the changes that had been made to the tests from one year to the next almost certainly compromised the comparability of one year's results with another's. In addition, relatively small changes in school populations from one year to the next can create conditions that make year-to-year comparisons unwise. Before major adjustments are warranted, one needs to have several years' data from tests with items that can be equated.

As I cautioned earlier, policy-makers should be aware that centralized testing regimes may have a deleterious impact on teaching and learning. The promotion of students from one grade to the next, teacher and administrator reassignment, and school closures are examples of "high stakes" consequences of assessment. The prospect of such consequences have produced a variety of undesirable behaviours, including coaching students while the test is being conducted or inappropriately excluding students whose performance is likely to negatively influence the class and school results.

Even when the stakes of assessments are seemingly non-existent, there are unintended consequences that must be taken into account. Knowing that the results do not "count," students may not put much effort into their responses. Policy-makers should avoid either extreme. Making the test a small part of the final grade students receive in the subject assessed should guarantee that students take the test seriously.

## FACTORS AFFECTING STUDENT ACHIEVEMENT

MANY FACTORS AFFECT an individual student's achievement. It is influenced by the student's interest in the subject being tested and the attitudes that the student has toward the subject. Is the student interested? Despite her level of interest, does she have a positive attitude toward the subject and feel that she can be successful even though there are other subjects in which she is more interested? Does she have the vocabulary necessary for understanding the questions posed about the subject? Has she had prior experience with the subject matter in other classes or outside of school? Can she, in the face of distractions and difficulty, focus on the tasks at hand?

The student's peer group affects her performance. Does the peer group show an interest in the subject? Is it cool to show one's interest or is it necessary to pretend disinterest? Has the peer group prior experiences they can bring to bear on the subject? Have they visited places relevant to the subject and can they bring that experience to bear in the class, influencing the student's understanding and interest in the subject?

We are accustomed to thinking of the classroom in which the student learns as the primary influence on student achievement. The way that the teacher has structured the lesson and the methods that a teacher uses to present the material to the students has an obvious influence on a student's achievement. Less obvious is the relationship between the teacher and the student, but it, too, influences the student's achievement. All other things being equal, students who like and respect their teachers perform better than students who do not. Teachers who are enthusiastic about the subject promote greater student achievement than those who appear indifferent.

The disciplinary climate of the classroom and the size of the class affect a student's achievement. Students in smaller classes tend to perform better and behave better than students in larger classes. In a recent article in the *Quarterly Journal of Economics,* Edward Lazear argues that misbehaviour by some students is suffered by the entire class. He points out if each student misbehaves just 1 per cent of the time the disruptions reduce the effectiveness of teaching in a class of twenty-five students to 78 per cent. In a class with forty students, the effectiveness drops to 67 per cent, according to Lazear. That's why both class size and the disciplinary climate of the classroom influence student achievement. If students misbehave 2 per cent of the time, the effectiveness figures for classes of twenty-five students and forty students drop to 60 per cent and 45 per cent.

The student's family influences his or her achievement. Do family members read to the student, express support for the school, provide opportunities to go to museums, and provide good models for the use of language? Is the parenting style punitive or kindly? Is there sufficient food or does the student go hungry from time to time? Does the student have a quiet place to study and do homework? Do parents value education and encourage their child to achieve?

School factors are also important influences. Do the staff and students in the school express an interest in learning? Do the students feel safe in the school? Are students grouped or rigidly streamed? Is the atmosphere friendly or forbidding? Do the students and staff manifest school spirit? These and other home- and school-related considerations affect the individual student's achievement.

It is crucial for provinces to investigate relationships among variables, such as those mentioned above, over which the system exercises control or is capable of exercising control. The utility of a testing regime for improving student achievement depends upon it. The effective use of the information that testing provides is directly related to the ability to use advanced statistical techniques to investigate relationships. Provincial ministries of education should be able to integrate data from academic tests with other relevant information and provide the analysis and interpretation necessary to isolate factors over which schools have control. The ability to identify classroom and school attributes and relate them to results is essential to making full use of such tests.

Those who wish to use tests for school improvement must disentangle the influence of non-school variables on the achievements of students. Doug Willms at the University of New Brunswick argues persuasively that it is necessary to take into account the school's "contextual" effects. This means distinguishing between such factors as the socio-economic profile of the school community, school policies and practices (such as educational leadership, academic expectations, curricular focus, disciplinary climate, and parental involvement), and the effects specifically attributable to teaching (for example, the use of strategies that maximize the achievement of all students). From an educational standpoint, it is the effects that are attributable to teaching and school policies and that are of greatest interest. As difficult as it may be, in order to identify the effects of teaching and school policies and practices, it is necessary to isolate them from effects of student background (socio-economic status, gender, ethnic group membership, and so on) and aptitude (for example, prior ability and attitude toward school).

Tracking the performance of specific students over time and computing the school's impact on their growth in learning achieve the maximum benefits of a testing regime. Studies comparing one year's results with another for different groups of students are of more limited use in determining student improvement than studies that track and measure the performance of the same students at various stages in their school careers.

## THE USE AND MISUSE OF TESTING

THE POTENTIAL FOR MISUSING the results of testing is great. While intended primarily for professional use and for informing parents about the progress of their children, others – including education professionals, local and provincial politicians, and the media – may unintentionally or wilfully misuse the results of the assessments. In the latter case, teachers may see tests as weapons to be used against them.

Teachers are not likely to embrace the use of provincial testing as an aid to instructional decision-making if the environment is punishment-centred. Comparisons among classrooms, schools, or districts, without proper regard for and control of situational or other differences between them, are likely to increase teacher opposition to the use of such information.

Administrators, school trustees, parents, and politicians who misuse the results as a measure of teacher performance or productivity are likely to lose teacher confidence in the process. Invidious comparisons of classrooms, schools, and districts abound in the popular media. Politicians and educators who should know better make inappropriate comparisons. Jurisdictions using testing regimes as a part of their educational improvement initiatives must, therefore, plan carefully for the dissemination of results. They should prepare professionals, journalists, and politicians for their appropriate use, and deliberately counter misuse of the data.

Effective use of test results depends upon a school environment that fosters a sense of collective responsibility for the educational success of students. Much of the variation in student achievement that is amenable to intervention occurs at the classroom level. Instruction is the principal, but not sole, mediating link between assessment and student achievement. As I mentioned earlier, other variables include the disciplinary climate of the school and the school's emphasis on academic achievement.

School principals and teachers have to be able to make productive use of the information conveyed by the tests. This is the only way that student achievement will truly improve. But the interpretation of results should not rest on the shoulders of individual teachers. The effort must be collective, involving all of the teachers at and below the grade level of the test. The test makers must provide an interpretation book that indicates what each of the items or group of items on the test measures, what errors students made on the items, and the implications of the mistakes for the instructional process. Teachers must enjoy the support and cooperation of the school's administration in making changes in their approach to instruction as well as to the school's policies and practices.

Testing makes little sense if there are organizational obstacles to learning. These obstacles include inadequate hours of instruction and inappropriate timetabling of subjects. Nor can testing assist in improving student learning if the teachers do not have sufficient time to review the assessment data collaboratively. They must have time to consider what, if any, modifications should be made to their instructional plans, to the methodology they employ in the classroom, or to school policies and practices.

Unfortunately, few if any of the necessary conditions I have described have been met. In fact, the trend toward larger class size, more difficult working conditions, and inadequate funding means Canadian public schools are moving further away from the ideal.

Inadequate preparation of teachers is another obstacle to the effective use of testing regimes. Faculties of education should make sure that those preparing to teach know how to use assessment information correctly for instructional planning and implementation. Generalized measurement courses do not typically develop the knowledge one needs to use information from such tests in the context of instructional planning and implementation. Such knowledge should be developed in curriculum and instruction courses. Learning how to use provincial and district-wide test results should complement the instruction about teacher–designed assessments already included in those courses.

Continuing professional education should be provided for experienced teachers in the use of assessment information for instructional planning and implementation. Responsibility for providing such continuing education falls to the jurisdiction responsible for the assessment. In Canada, provinces typically promulgate testing regimes of the sort I have described. They must also provide for the professional education that practitioners require.

As my earlier comments suggest, the absence of school-based leadership can be an obstacle to the use of the information provided by large-scale testing. The importance of school leadership has been well established, though less well developed in practice. Insufficient attention has been given to instructional leadership ability in the recruitment, selection, and preparation of school-based administrators. As a consequence, school and district administrators are often ill-disposed and ill-equipped to lead the staff in carefully considering the results of tests. They may not understand the implications of the results for school policies and practices and for instruction.

If improving student success is to remain a central goal of education, administrators must be steeped in the intricacies of using information from testing productively. Such expertise must become a prerequisite for holding an administrative position. Responsibility for providing continuing professional education for currently employed administrators falls to the jurisdiction responsible for the tests in question.

There is no place in the process for the mistaken attribution of success or blame as apparently occurred in the example from California described earlier. Nor is there room for the kind of behaviour described to me by staff members in a school whose pupils performed poorly. The principal called the staff together and waved a sheaf of papers in his hand. "These results stink," he said with derision. Pointing at the teachers seated in the staff room, he continued, "It's your job to fix them." Then he turned, walked out the door, and returned to his office. This is not what I would call educational leadership.

There is much work to be done to help teachers reduce the achievement gap among students in general and between identifiable groups of students in particular. The agencies responsible for certification of teachers and administrators must work closely with faculties of education and the other agencies that provide for professional education. Provincial departments and ministries of education need to work with school boards, senior administrators, teacher organizations, and parent groups to facilitate understanding of and support for the appropriate use of assessments involving large-scale testing. School boards must monitor the information provided by large-scale tests and take it into account in their performance plans. Ensuring school success for all students requires jurisdictions to distribute resources to foster equality of outcomes, especially for those students for whom learning is more challenging because of poverty and discrimination.

Large-scale testing schemes do not by themselves improve the performance of students. Without making sure that a large number of other factors are present, it would be unrealistic and unsound to embark upon such assessment. The use of large-scale assessments to inform changes at the school and classroom level must address the aforementioned obstacles and challenges.

The *National Post* recently carried an encouraging story about Ontario teachers who have made good use of information from the results of large-scale student assessments. According to the article, teachers skeptical about testing had become advocates after spending a year focusing their instruction on weaknesses the tests revealed. Teachers would analyze the results of the tests to identify areas that would benefit from additional instructional effort. Although year-over-year comparisons are often misleading, the results reported in the *Post* article were impressive.

As I hope I have made clear, improving student success rates will depend as much upon other factors as it does on the assessment system itself. Improving the capacity of teachers to employ teaching strategies that increase the performance of all students, developing the capacity of principals to provide instructional leadership, helping district administrators to acquire the capacity to interpret and use the information provided by large-scale student assessments will require thoughtful and focused professional preparation and continuing education. Educating school district or provincial politicians about the impact of their comments about the results of such assessments, and countering erroneous or wilfully misleading representations of the results of such assessments by the media or others, will be challenging and will require significant attention.

Despite the challenges and obstacles to their effective use, if the data from large-scale tests are subjected to rigorous statistical analysis and interpretation, they can be very useful in improving the conditions influencing student achievement. Unless ministries of education are willing to analyze and interpret the data with care and rigour, I fear that large-scale student assessments will be used to bludgeon schools and teachers rather than help them consider the changes that might be made to improve student success.

Too many people – including ones who should know better – invest too much importance in the results of assessments and too little in the analysis and interpretation of the results. These people are anxious about the future of the next generation. Policy-makers would do well to consider the differences between blunt and ideologically motivated analyses of data, such as the Fraser Institute's annual reports on secondary schooling, and more finely honed and useful analyses.

The analyses and interpretations of the data from large-scale measures of student achievement are best used on small-scale initiatives to improve student achievement. Consider how Canada uses periodic reports on the fluctuations in its economy. It invests little importance in short-term fluctuations, reacting only to patterns that develop over time. It seldom responds to the data by making system-wide economic changes. Instead, it intervenes in specific areas of the economy.

The problem with the large-scale assessment programs I have seen is that the data prompts the call for radical reform of the system. What is really needed is thoughtful consideration of classroom and school practices. Policy-makers need to get beyond viewing large-scale student assessments as "accountability" measures and embrace them as one – and only one – source of information that can be used to improve student success in school.

We are becoming more sophisticated about the strengths and limitations of large-scale student testing. And we are beginning to see that we must be clear about the importance of what we measure. Otherwise we will encourage teachers to teach things that are unimportant. We are also beginning to appreciate that the curriculum must be oriented to a relatively small number of important objectives that are supported with appropriate resources.

Regrettably, we are less aware of some of the other crucial elements in achieving the results we seek. I fear that we fail to see that improving learning for students is an enduring goal, not one quickly or easily achieved. I also fear that we undervalue the central part teachers play in achieving the outcomes we want from our schools.

I am encouraged by those who realize the complexity of improving public schooling. I am heartened when I hear people speak about the interplay among community, school, class, and individual factors affecting what and how students learn. Schools try to reduce the challenges to learning posed by the differences that students bring to school. Those who support policies to strengthen families and communities are helping to make the task of public schools more reasonable and more likely to succeed.

We have yet to develop a sufficiently sophisticated system for monitoring the performance of youngsters in ways that are helpful to the teachers and principals. We know how to test, but we are just learning how to create useful tests and how to interpret their results in an educationally sound and helpful manner.

We have a long way to go in helping educators use evidence to improve performance. More focused professional development is needed for everyone in the system. The responsibility rests with provincial jurisdictions that have not as yet devoted sufficient resources to the task of improving people's knowledge of assessment and its relation to instruction.

Until sufficient resources are provided and capacities more fully developed, Canada would be wise to avoid putting undue emphasis on large-scale student testing as a vehicle for improving public schooling. That means that people – especially provincial and local politicians and representatives of the media – should avoid making strong pronouncements about the successes or failures of public schooling on the strength of short-term improvement or decline. Such pronouncements might make for colourful politics and a wider audience, but they do little to affect what happens in public schools except to harm the morale of teachers and students.

chapter thirteen

# HOW TO CHANGE PUBLIC SCHOOLS

n comparison to the dynamic nature of many aspects of our
society, schools appear static and resistant to change. One
school day is much like another to the untrained observer.
Most of the changes students exhibit occur so slowly and are so
minute they exceed the ability of many to observe them.

Educational changes may seem slow and insignificant, but
change is complex, takes effort, and requires adequate time and
resources. This is often a source of frustration to politicians
and others who wish to see rapid results, usually for their own
reasons. But if they were to stop to think about it, significant and
enduring changes rarely occur rapidly.

Automobile manufacturers know how difficult it is to redesign
a vehicle and retool the processes for its assembly. Employees
involved in manufacturing may have mastered a considerable
body of knowledge about the techniques of their trade, but they
do not exercise much critical judgment in the application of their
knowledge. They are primarily involved in repetitive assembly-
line tasks. By the time the lengthy redesign process has been
completed and the new cars start rolling off the line, the bugs
have usually been worked out by the designers, engineers, and
management over many years.

Teaching is different. Every class is unique. In adapting their
instructional programs, teachers expect to use their considerable

knowledge of the craft of teaching, their knowledge of curriculum, and their knowledge of the students in front of them. Teachers must be motivated to change. They need to understand the reasons for the changes sought. They need time to practise new techniques or study the new knowledge they are expected to use. They need support in making the changes.

Teaching is more subtle, unpredictable, and complex than manufacturing. Most of the "bugs" affecting the process are the intricacies of teaching, requiring considerable professional knowledge and practical experience. The process is time-consuming. If, however, teachers understand the proposed changes, want to make them, and possess the knowledge and experience needed to implement them, they can be incorporated easily.

## RESISTANCE TO CHANGE

THERE WAS CONSIDERABLE CONTROVERSY in the late 1980s and early 1990s about the educational changes proposed by the government in British Columbia in an initiative called Year 2000 affecting all public schools. But teachers in elementary schools responded positively to those changes in the primary program that were designed to make instruction more "child-centred." They were willing to adopt these changes since they were extensions of practices already being used by many of the primary teacher leaders in the province. Because the changes were built upon a familiar foundation and were seen as desirable by the majority of primary teachers, they produced little negative reaction.

If proposed changes are not properly understood, or are opposed by those who must implement them, their successful implementation is unlikely. This is true even when the changes appear to be well motivated. One of the proposed changes to the British Columbia primary program involved "dual entry" to kindergarten. Children were to have entered kindergarten at one of two points in the year, depending upon their birthdates. The change was intended to ensure that students entering kindergarten were sufficiently mature to benefit from the experience. The change would have altered the traditional start date in September. Youngsters who had reached their fifth birthday by June would enter kindergarten in September. Youngsters born in the fall would have entered in January.

The idea made educational sense. Less mature children would not have to learn routines and concepts at the same time as their more mature counterparts. Dual entry would have been especially beneficial for boys born later in the year. Typically less mature than girls, boys born late in the year are doubly disadvantaged by entering school in September. The later starting date would enable them to begin with children of similar maturity. The younger children would learn from their older classmates.

Both parents and teachers opposed the idea. Parents who, for a variety of reasons, were anticipating that their children would begin school at the customary time were not in favour of waiting four months. From the parents' point of view, the change would have meant that some children's entry to schooling would be "delayed" from September until January. They felt their child would be missing out on what was taught during those four months.

Kindergarten teachers – even those teachers who favoured a child-centred educational program – were opposed. From their point of view, they would have to plan two kindergarten programs. One program would be designed for students starting kindergarten in September. The other program, designed for students beginning in January, would also have to take into account the students who had begun four months earlier. The plan might have made educational sense, but it created complex logistical problems for teachers. In the face of objections by both parents and teachers, government withdrew the proposal.

The introduction of Career and Personal Planning (CAPP) to elementary and secondary schools in British Columbia shows what happens when politicians attempt to impose changes on a system without an appreciation of the impact of those changes. CAPP was designed to prepare students for the decisions they would face as they progressed through school. The goal was that students would acquire the knowledge, attitudes, and skills needed to lead healthy and productive lives. Under the heading Personal Development, students were to study "Healthy Living, Family Life Education, Child Abuse Prevention, Substance Abuse Prevention, and Safety and Injury Prevention." The topics under the heading Career Development included "Career Skills, Career Exploration, and Career Preparation." Career and Personal Planning also included thirty hours of work experience, for which students received credit.

The Ministry of Education made an effort to prepare teachers for CAPP. It created a curriculum that included suggested activities, assessment strategies, and resources. It organized regional meetings for school district representatives to learn about the curriculum and to discuss strategies for its implementation. Regional coordinators were available to provide help for CAPP as well as for other ministry initiatives.

CAPP had no natural constituency among teachers. Few teachers had an affinity for the extremely broad range of topics included in the curriculum. The home economics teachers, who also taught courses in childcare, were comfortable with some of the family life topics. Teachers who had responsibility for teaching "consumer education" adapted to similar aspects of the CAPP curriculum. Business education teachers were able to use their knowledge and connections with employers to help give direction to the work-experience part of the curriculum. But most teachers assigned to teach CAPP had little experience or education that was directly connected with the program. In addition, finding thirty hours of meaningful work experience for every student proved difficult, time-consuming, and costly.

The introduction of CAPP met with overt compliance and covert resistance. Teachers in elective subjects were hostile toward CAPP, since it would replace one of the slots available for electives. Most students felt the same. They were not keen to replace art or music with CAPP. Some schools ignored the requirement that students enrol in the program, allowing them to continue with preferred electives. Some secondary schools made it a part of the daily homeroom period. Among the teachers who took to CAPP, the program was implemented as well as could be expected given the lack of formal preparation. But, for the most part, CAPP was implemented poorly. Not long after its introduction, students began to insert the letter R after the C in CAPP.

What happened in British Columbia with CAPP has parallels across the country. Changes seen as a threat to the customs, traditions, and values of the group will be resisted. Integrated studies of the sort favoured by the progressives of the 1930s have never had widespread acceptance among secondary teachers. They likely never will for a number of reasons.

Schools are designed to pass on to the next generation the ideas and values a society deems important for them to know. Schools conserve the past as much as they prepare students for the future. Society selects as its teachers those who appreciate the "conservative" nature of schooling.

Teachers are not disposed to change. Those who are drawn to teaching are attracted by prevailing norms and practices. Their preparation for the profession is conducted by more experienced teachers who are the main carriers of the prevailing culture.

Secondary teachers resist change because most of their preparation for teaching has been subject-centred. Certification as a secondary teacher typically requires that the person has studied one or two subjects in depth at the university level. While a few of them might find integrated or interdisciplinary studies attractive, most are so closely identified with their disciplines that they are unlikely to be willing to change.

Most parents see secondary schooling as preparation for university study. Although the world is not divided into disciplines, universities are. Study of discrete disciplines is the core of university and scholarly life and have been since the middle ages. Integrated programs or departments of interdisciplinary studies are typically marginal in most universities. Parents are unlikely to favour changes in secondary education that appear mismatched with university requirements.

High school teachers have traditionally derived much of their status from their disciplinary focus. There is prestige in the part that the high school plays in preparing (selecting) those who will go on to further study. There is also a discernable status hierarchy among high school disciplines. When I attended school, Latin was the most prestigious course. It distinguished those worthy of going to university from those who were not. Today, advanced mathematics has the most prestige. At the bottom of the high school hierarchy are the courses that have no apparent connection with an identifiable discipline, such as Career and Personal Planning, Media Studies, Consumer Education.

Teachers in elementary schools resist changes to their preferred practices. For example, classes that combine students from two grade levels in the same room are disliked by most teachers – even by many who profess to be "child-centred." The additional work required to teach students working at different grade levels is considerable.

One element in the implementation strategy adopted by some school districts is to reassign innovative teachers to the district level in the hope that these "insiders" can facilitate system-wide changes. Once reassigned, however, these "insiders" become "outsiders" from the perspective of the teachers with whom they had previously worked. A similar pattern can be discerned when respected, innovative teachers are assigned to positions of special responsibility such as department heads and coordinators within their own schools.

There will always be changes that are resisted by teachers and, for that matter, by parents, regardless of their obvious benefit. "Year-round schooling" is not likely to find widespread acceptance among parents or teachers. Advocates of year-round schooling argue that, during the two-month summer break, students forget what they have learned.

Proponents of year-round schooling favour dividing the whole year into shorter periods of study with four-week long breaks instead of one long summer holiday (as well as Christmas and spring break). In addition to the educational advantages claimed for year-round schooling, some school trustees like the idea because it allows them to make better use of capital facilities. Through staggered scheduling, the year-round arrangement allows them to accommodate a larger number of students in the same size facility. Despite these advantages, I doubt that year-round schooling will universally replace the traditional pattern because that pattern is predictable and too well integrated into other aspects of our lives. Change will require significant planning for those affected.

Year-round schooling is more likely to be adopted when a new school facility is contemplated. Parents might be offered the opportunity to choose the new arrangement for their children. Teachers could be given the same choice. With sufficient time to contemplate and plan for year-round schooling, a segment of the population might adapt to the arrangement. If it is imposed upon parents and teachers "from above," it will meet with resistance. The political costs of implementing the arrangement might be far greater than its educational or economic benefits.

There are other important reasons teachers appear to resist change. Changes are seldom supported by adequate resources and are often managed by people removed from the practice of teaching. Teachers are more often directed to change rather than engaged in the change process.

## MEANINGFUL CHANGES

CHANGES ARE MORE LIKELY to occur in periods of crisis than in periods of stability and calm. During the period beginning with the launch of Sputnik and ending with the withdrawal of troops from Vietnam, a variety of educational changes took place in the United States, including "open-education," "humanistic education," "anti-racist education," and "anti-sexist education." These changes spilled over into Canada.

During the years that followed, relatively fewer changes were introduced, and the changes that were introduced were more conservatively oriented. The period saw a clamour for increased competition and a return to "the basics." In other words, following periods of rapid change, institutions often seek to achieve stability by adapting to the changes that have occurred or by attempting to make the changes compatible with traditional values of the institution.

Changes that occur within an institution are least likely to come from those who occupy the most powerful positions. In fact, most changes come from persons who are regarded as deviant or marginal, people who embody countercultural values. The alternative schools movement of the 1960s and 1970s typically drew its leadership from teachers who were younger, relatively more advantaged, and more cosmopolitan than their peers.

Today, the calls for changes in public schooling often come from parents and politicians. They think public schools are broken and look for solutions. But most proposed solutions to school "problems" increase the workload of teachers who are already working flat out. Rather than increasing a teacher's workload, we should be seeking solutions that *reduce* the demands upon them and allow them to concentrate on teaching the things we value.

In comparison to other occupations, teacher working conditions are poor. They rarely have proper work areas; they cannot go to the washroom except at scheduled times; they have to compete with one another for the use of telephones and computers to contact parents or gather information.

Deciding on what we value is a necessary, but difficult, undertaking. Our initial tendency is to outline in vague terms those things that we value. Getting beneath the surface of generalities creates conflicts. We discover that, as we specify them more precisely, some of the things we value are incompatible.

Eventually we will need to distill what we value to something that can be taught within the limited time available. We have to consider what schools can do well and what should be left to other institutions. Elsewhere, I have suggested that my preferences are for a curriculum that would provide students with a strong foundation in reading, writing, science, and mathematics, and equip them with knowledge of human civilization and an understanding of where Canada fits.

Our curricula should be modified in accordance with the social and historical changes that have occurred in Canada, as they do not adequately reflect the multicultural and plural nature of Canadian society. The contribution of Canada's indigenous peoples to our development as a nation, the influence of immigrants and immigration, and the perspective provided by the music, art, and literature of Canada's cultural groups are relatively absent from the formal school curriculum. The consequence of this is that students are deprived of perspectives that differ from their own that may shed new light on enduring issues.

The curriculum and the conditions affecting student learning should dispose students to treat others with respect and to work co-operatively with others. It should engender curiosity and develop their love of learning. It should require students to develop a critical intelligence that is adaptable to circumstances unforeseen.

If time permits, it should provide opportunities for students to explore their interests through elective studies and extracurricular activities. Public schooling should be fun and make students optimistic about the future.

We cannot simply decide what it is we value and not think about the issue again. It should come up regularly. The problem is, we do not have structures that enable such discussions to occur. School councils hold promise for promoting discussions of educational issues at the school level, but they have not proven to be very workable institutions for reasons I have mentioned elsewhere. Nonetheless, if their deficiencies can be addressed, participation more broadly defined, and parochialism avoided, school councils might be made to work. To do so will require conscious and continuing effort and leadership.

School boards are another level at which this might occur on a regular basis. At present, such discussions are typically perfunctory exercises that few – even among those involved – take seriously. They rarely engage the broader parental and professional community, much less society as a whole. To work effectively as vehicles for determining the broad goals of education, school boards need to confront some of the same structural and procedural defects as school councils. Communities need to take their local school boards more seriously. They need to elect neighbours capable of seeing beyond a single issue to the more general welfare of all students.

National and provincial leadership is essential to a refocusing of public schooling in the interest of Canada. Federal and provincial politicians must recognize that public schooling is an important instrument of social policy. Recognition itself is a necessary, but insufficient, condition. Understanding, too, is required. For too long, the changes that have been introduced in public schools have been driven by ideology, fad, and fashion.

## FEDERAL LEADERSHIP IN EDUCATION

CONFEDERATION WAS A POLITICAL compromise that deeply influenced the character and development of Canada. The British North America Act, 1867 – now the Constitution Act, 1867 – was the expression of a set of compromises. The fathers of Confederation carefully set out the responsibilities of each provincial legislature in section 93 of the act, stating that in each province, "the Legislature may exclusively make Laws in relation to Education."

Limitations were placed upon the jurisdiction of the provinces to prevent the prejudicial treatment of denominational schools or the diminution of the powers and privileges of the Protestant or Roman Catholic separate schools. The fathers of Confederation gave special attention to education in section 93, because it was necessary to protect the education rights of religious minorities.

Although the provinces were granted exclusive jurisdiction to make laws in relation to education, there is nothing in the Constitution Act that prevents the Canadian government from using its leadership role and spending powers to influence public schooling in Canada. Whenever the government has wanted to influence public schooling, it hasn't been discouraged from doing so. In fact, the government has supported or undertaken a number of initiatives in the realm of public schooling.

The School Achievement Indicators Program (SAIP) is a program to assess the achievement of Canadian students in mathematics, reading and writing, and science that has been conducted periodically by the Council of Ministers of Education Canada (CMEC) since 1993. The annual cost of preparing and administering SAIP is approximately $3 million. Human Resources Development Canada, a federal department, provides approximately 50 per cent of the resources for the program as a financial grant to CMEC. The other half of the required resources is provided in the form of human and material contributions from Canada's provinces and territories.

The Pan-Canadian Education Indicators Program (PCEIP) is an initiative designed to provide policy-makers and the public with information about education systems in Canada. It, too, is jointly sponsored by CMEC and an agency of the federal government, Statistics Canada. CMEC and Statistics Canada consult with provincial and territorial ministries and departments of education across Canada. They seek to determine comparative information about the costs, processes, and results of provincial and territorial education systems.

The Summer Language Bursary Program is another initiative funded by the federal government (the Department of Canadian Heritage) and administered by CMEC in co-operation with the provincial and territorial departments responsible for post-secondary education. Bursaries are provided to Canadian students to facilitate their participation in a five-week immersion course in English or French at accredited institutions.

The Department of Canadian Heritage is deeply involved in education. Its Multiculturalism Program objectives include improving the ability of public institutions (boards of education, colleges and universities, banks, hospitals, and the media) to respond to ethnic, religious, and cultural diversity. The program provides assistance in identifying and removing barriers to, and equitable access and participation in, public decision-making.

The Interchange on Canadian Studies is a national organization that receives substantial support from the Department of Canadian Heritage for its work with school-age Canadians. The organization attempts to foster participation of young Canadians in the political, economic, social, and cultural life of Canada. It tries to promote their understanding and tolerance toward others as well as an appreciation for Canada's diverse heritage. The organization provides the opportunity for young Canadians to meet and listen to prominent Canadians, and to share ideas and experiences significant to Canada. It has been held in a different province or territory each year since 1972. Each province and territory is entitled to send ten high school students. Provincial and territorial governments, corporations, school boards, and student registration fees fund the Interchange on Canadian Studies. The Department of Canadian Heritage through its Exchanges Canada program provides travel to the conference.

The Society for Educational Visits and Exchanges in Canada (SEVEC) is a reciprocal home-stay exchange program for groups of young Canadians between the ages of eleven and eighteen. SEVEC receives substantial support from the Department of Canadian Heritages. The exchange students are typically members of school groups or community youth groups. The federal government, through SEVEC Youth Exchanges Canada, provides transportation costs for participants.

The above are all examples of federal government involvement in education. But I think it should go further. We need a federal department of education.

There is no constitutional impediment to the federal government establishing a department of education so long as it does not attempt to make laws regarding education. Even if it did, I doubt that most Canadians would care. If public schools require federal leadership to ensure they work well, I am certain Canadians wouldn't object.

Canada must use its leadership position and its spending power to ensure that Canadian public schools remain the strong institutions they are. A department of education should provide leadership and funding to public elementary and secondary schooling in areas central to the interest of all Canadians, and to coordinate the work of the various federal departments and agencies that are engaged with public schools.

The federal department of education would: sponsor research about the efficacy of various approaches to education; develop policy papers to stimulate public debate about the directions that

public schooling might take; coordinate the collection and interpretation of data pertinent to such issues and decisions; and
report periodically to the Canadian people about their public
schools. With a federal department helping guide national standards and practices, moving from a school in Calgary to one in
Fredericton could be done more smoothly.

Canadians are hungry for information about the quality of
their public schools and do not want the requirements and standards applied in one jurisdiction to constitute a barrier if they
choose to move to another province or territory. The federal government should convene representatives of the provinces and
territories to establish pan-Canadian standards for student performance. It should also lead the provinces and territories in
determining how the School Achievement Indicators Program
might be modified to provide information about how well students are meeting pan-Canadian standards.

There are several specific areas that I think demand the attention of the government of Canada. First and most important is
the education of aboriginal learners. Significant achievement
gaps between identifiable groups detract from the promise of
Canadian public schooling. The promise is that the outcomes
of schooling should not be impeded by one's background. The
significant gaps between aboriginal and non-aboriginal students
is a national disgrace requiring immediate coordinated attention
for which the federal government should provide leadership.

For the same reason, it is important for the federal government
to provide coordination in the identification of educational
achievement gaps between other groups. It should also provide
leadership in identifying strategies to overcome the differences. For
example, policy, programs, and support for students with special
needs across Canada are uneven. For a brief period, there was a
modest attempt to address this important area under the auspices
of the Council of Ministers of Education Canada. But it did not

last. The issue has not received attention in recent years largely as a consequence of changes in the composition of the council. Given the traditional reluctance on the part of federal politicians to become overtly involved in education, they will be timid about tackling the recommendations I have made. Putting public schooling on the Canadian agenda requires a champion of great stature who can explain its importance to Canada and Canadians.

## ERASING INEQUALITIES

A FOUNDATION FOR LIFELONG LEARNING is established during a child's early years in the home and the community. Many of the challenges that public schools confront arise because of inequalities among families and communities, and addressing them is costly and imperfect. It makes sense both educationally and economically to get children off to a good start. Part of that good start is universally available childcare. Canada needs a national childcare policy. The federal government should look at the strengths and limitations of the policy developed in Quebec over the past decade where inexpensive childcare is available.

The government of Canada has promised leadership and financial support for childcare on a number of occasions, but it has not delivered. A national childcare policy will have demonstrable benefits for young and old alike. But the burgeoning population of articulate and active seniors may be unwilling to have their taxes spent on such a program. That would be short-sighted. Canada needs to prepare a healthy, well-educated workforce to pay for the services that Canadians have come to enjoy.

The provision of support for English- and French-language education for immigrants has been a point of contention between the provinces and the federal government. This has been largely, though not exclusively, a matter of concern for provinces with significant immigration. The federal government has used the argument that education is a responsibility of the provinces to avoid providing the resources for language programs for immigrant students or students whose parents were immigrants.

Part of making immigrants feel welcome in Canada is providing support for their language of birth or that of their parents. Support for heritage-language programs is consistent with the values that distinguish Canada from other nations. Most Canadians value the principle that people should be able to retain their heritage languages and cultural identities so long as they do not lead to inequalities. In addition to their value in helping to maintain culture, heritage languages are an asset to Canada's economic and diplomatic relations.

Support for the study of Canadian public issues is another area in which the Canadian government should provide leadership. For reasons I have explained elsewhere, Canadian students should be able to locate themselves in time and place in relation to other nations. They should be able to appraise the strengths and limitations of the approaches that Canada has taken to the problems of human kind: social cohesion, poverty, international relations, environmental sustainability, and the like. Students need to know what makes Canada unique. The government of Canada is well situated to provide support for the development of material and approaches to the study of Canadian public issues. It is in the interest of all Canadians that it does so.

Provincial capacity for sustaining and improving public schooling is uneven. The government of Canada can use its leadership position and resources to foster policies and practices that provinces cannot create on their own. When it was developed, the Councils of Ministers of Education Canada held promise that it would play a central part in such a process. But that promise has not been fulfilled. Some jurisdictions – most notably Quebec, Alberta, and Ontario in recent years – seem to view participation in the CMEC as a means of fending off what are imagined to be incursions of the federal government into the field of education. This is similar to the adversarial stance that provincial premiers usually take with regard to the federal government. As a consequence, many initiatives of potential value across Canada have failed to get off the ground.

## RESPONSIBILITY VERSUS ACCOUNTABILITY

WE HAVE TRADITIONALLY CONSIDERED the issue of educational quality and its achievement from the perspective of command and control. Our logic has been interesting. We think that by monitoring achievement and reporting the results, we can cajole, coax, or coerce teachers – take your pick – to improve student learning or, at the very least, improve the results students achieve on the tests (which may or may not be the same thing).

I think there is merit in monitoring performance and providing the information to the professionals for interpretation and action. However, I think we need to think about the process in a different way. The difference is subtle but important.

We should create an ethic of responsibility for the welfare of all students that includes two related sentiments: (1) that the success of the individual is the success of the entire class or school; and (2) that if one student fails, we have all failed. By imbedding these sentiments firmly, each school or classroom celebrates individual achievement and takes responsibility to ensure the success of every student.

We still must monitor the progress of children in school. Such monitoring will make certain that students receive the resources that will prevent school failure.

All children enter school with the expectation that they will learn. We fail those children – and we fail the larger society – when we do not ensure their success. Given the link between school failure and poor economic performance, dependence on social support, poor health, and even deviance, it is prudent to foster student success as early as possible.

There are important differences between encouraging responsibility versus holding people accountable. One difference is

how we regard people. There is a threat implicit in the accountability model. Punishment – whether in the form of shame or
sanctions – is implied in the narrow view of accountability
that currently prevails. The accountability approach absolves
everyone except the teacher, and perhaps the principal, of any
responsibility in the process.

I think student success is better served by imbedding responsibility in public schools and classrooms and beyond. Teachers and
administrators are clearly responsible for student learning. But so,
too, are students and parents, both individually and collectively.
I think the notion that "we can do this together" is preferable to
a "make them (or me) learn" mentality.

The approach I am recommending makes student success a
responsibility of the entire community. It cannot succeed without
leadership from principals and teachers. They must assume
responsibility for addressing the challenges they find. They must
commit themselves to using their professional resources so that
students derive the maximum benefit from their schooling. They
must monitor the situation and observe improvement. And principals and teachers must inform relevant audiences about what
has been achieved and what additionally might be achieved with
their support.

### EVIDENCE-BASED DECISION-MAKING

LET ME BE BLUNT. In too many cases we have lost sight of what
should be the enduring goals of public schooling: fostering
student success and reducing inequalities among students in terms
of what they achieve from their schooling. It may have been
acceptable for schools to see themselves primarily as gatekeepers
or sorting mechanisms when Canada had less need for well-
educated citizens. But, that time has long past. Canada cannot
afford to waste its human resources.

Perhaps the most significant obstacle to overcome is the uncertainty surrounding the goals of education. For most of this

century, schooling has been directed toward the achievement of four broad aims: intellectual preparation, vocational preparation, personal development, and social development. There has been little agreement on the meaning of those aims, the relative priorities placed upon them, and, most important, the particular goals they suggest. Indeed, if one were to select a single word to characterize our attitude to the goals of education, it would be "uncertainty." Organizations that are uncertain about their goals are not capable of making fundamental changes.

We have been conducting educational research for more than one hundred years. As early as 1896, the University of Chicago opened a "laboratory school" under the direction of education theorist John Dewey. Dewey began to experiment with the "activity" or "project method" of teaching. About a year later, J. M. Rice published the first modern educational research report, "The Futility of the Spelling Grind" in *Forum* magazine.

Educational research was becoming an established discipline. In 1924, Franklin Bobbitt published a book in which he showed how to apply scientific procedures to curriculum building, *How to Make a Curriculum*. The same year, J. H. Putman, senior inspector of schools, Ottawa, and G. M. Weir, professor of education, UBC, conducted one of the first system-wide studies of Canadian education, surveying the British Columbia school system. Two years later, educational philosopher William H. Kilpatrick produced one of the first works to suggest that social and economic changes require educational changes, *Education for a Changing Civilization*. In 1926, psychologist Jean Piaget published one of the most influential books ever written about child development, *The Language and Thought of the Child*.

By the 1930s, research had begun to focus on policy issues. The Progressive Education Association began the "Eight Year Study" in 1935 to assess the effects of progressive practices in thirty high schools. In 1942, W. M. Aiken, the director of the study, reported the generally favourable results in *The Story of the Eight Year*

*Study*. In that same year, Ralph W. Tyler proposed that educators define clear objectives and gather the information needed to determine whether the objectives were achieved.

Over the last hundred years, the volume and quality of educational research has increased dramatically. Today, research forms a base of knowledge about educational policy and practice. We can improve student success and reduce inequalities in achievement among students by making decisions based on that research and evidence. But while there is much talk about making evidence-based decisions, decisions are seldom made that way.

To the extent that evidence is used to make choices, it is too often employed in the service of ideology. From politicians to classroom teachers, people use evidence not to evaluate claims dispassionately, but to prove they are right. The tendency so permeates the field of education that changing the established pattern will require significant effort.

Drug abuse education is an illustration of just one of a large number of areas where decisions are made in ignorance of the evidence. DARE (Drug Abuse Resistance Education) is a program widely used in Canadian schools to educate youngsters about drug abuse. Originally developed in the United States, the initiative involves a seventeen-week program often sponsored and delivered by police departments. The program is more than ten years old and the subject of a number of studies. Follow-up studies show that DARE does not have a lasting impact upon drug use or attitudes toward drug use. It doesn't work, but it continues to be offered.

Schools also spend considerable effort, time, and other scarce resources to reduce the risks of smoking among children and youth. Recent evidence suggests that the benefits of such interventions are not uniform across student populations. Professor Roy Cameron headed a group of researchers at the University of Waterloo that looked at the impact of an anti-smoking program in one hundred schools. The researchers classified schools according to a school risk score. High-risk schools were ones in which there was a high rate of smoking among older students.

The results of the study were interesting. The intervention did reduce smoking rates, but not uniformly. Grade eight smoking rates in high-risk schools declined, but not in low-risk schools. The investigators suggest that intensive intervention may only be effective in high-risk schools, which have high smoking rates among older students. The study deserves replication. If similar results are obtained with further study, it will confirm that the same population level impact can be achieved for a fraction of the time and cost by directing such interventions only to high-risk schools.

Teachers and administrators should possess knowledge of research methods sufficient to evaluate claims about practice. My colleagues in faculties of education have a unique responsibility to ensure that teachers and administrators acquire such knowledge. They also have an obligation to use research and evidence in ethically honest ways rather than in the service of ideology.

Research and the intelligent use of evidence will not completely eliminate the philosophical conflicts described earlier, but they can help address the claims made by proponents of different philosophical positions. Research and evidence can contribute to the growing knowledge base for education and inform professional practice and public discussion of educational issues more than it does presently.

Research has a number of contributions to make in the educational policy processes. First, it can help to determine the universe of alternatives available in pursuit of particular values. It can also help to decide among the alternatives. In the policy process, research must attend to the relationship of means to ends and to the relative costs of various means-ends relationships.

Research can provide information to help select the most effective policy. Suppose, for example, we want to increase student achievement. Research can help define the alternatives to realize this outcome. Consideration might be given to early identification of and intervention with students at risk of failing, the provision of learning assistance, a reduction in class sizes to enable teachers to focus more on each student, or the use of incentives such as scholarships. Research can provide an indication of the effectiveness of each approach and the magnitude of the return on investment for each of the alternatives considered.

We need more and better research to improve student achievement. In particular, we need to address the following questions. How can we ensure that beginning students develop a foundation for and a love of learning that will last the rest of their lives? How can we diminish the failures that accompany transitions from grade to grade or school to school? How can we ensure that students with special education needs develop the knowledge and dispositions they will need for adult citizenship? How can we eliminate the predictive power of economics, gender, and ethnicity on educational outcomes?

## LIFELONG LEARNING

PUBLIC SCHOOLING through grade twelve was once regarded as a luxury for all but a few students who went on to study for professional careers. The time for thinking that way is long past. Today, a grade twelve education (and beyond) is a necessity. Public schooling is now regarded as an essential foundation for workplace training, post-secondary education, the preservation of democratic institutions, and the informal learning that enriches our lives.

There are at least three conditions necessary for lifelong learning. One is public support for formal education. The second is equality among citizens in their attainment of learning outcomes. And the third is free or inexpensive opportunities for lifelong learning.

Canada provides most of the basic resources needed for making lifelong learning a possibility for all. Despite variations among jurisdictions, Canada provides financial support for the provision of education from kindergarten to grade twelve, allowing most young Canadians to acquire the skills and inclination to continue learning for the rest of their lives.

If citizens have not succeeded in acquiring the foundations for lifelong learning from their years in public schools, they will not be able to take advantages of the opportunities for further education that are available. Poverty is the most common problem. Children living in poverty typically do not achieve the same levels of proficiency in foundational areas as their more advantaged peers. As a consequence, after they leave school they are often employed in work where learning is not valued. Their pay is often so low they cannot afford to take part in the learning opportunities available to others such as night school and post-secondary study.

Lifelong learning for all citizens also depends on the availability of inexpensive learning opportunities. Such resources are more plentiful today than a century ago, but there is room for improvement. Libraries are widely available in most communities. Newspapers, books, and magazines are affordable for most of us. Internet access is becoming less expensive and more widespread. Radio, television, and films provide inexpensive and readily available resources to the person sufficiently well educated to take advantage of the best of what they have to offer.

The opportunities for lifelong learning are growing. Retirees are beginning to use learning opportunities to enrich their retirement. People who had little success in formal schooling are seeking learning opportunities to improve their career prospects. Employees are signing up for educational programs to improve their work skills. Educational programs once unavailable are being offered as recreational activities to people who have developed a thirst for learning.

Eliminating early school failures would alter the nature of students' subsequent ability to participate in these opportunities for lifelong learning. With increased public school success, lifelong learning programs would not be needed to remediate the failure to acquire basic skills. Resources would be freed to address more advanced personal and career development programs. Investment in public schooling saves government's money in the long run. Improving foundational knowledge and graduation rates reduces public expenditures in income support, health care, and criminal justice. The better educated citizen generates more wealth, and their positive attitudes toward schooling (plus their taxes) can bolster support for public education.

Improving quality is slow, hard work. The greatest improvement is likely to be achieved by focusing effort and resources in two places: on the 2 to 3 per cent of students who are at the bottom on any important measure of performance; and on students in their first years of schooling. Improving the situation for such students is effective and necessary, but not something that will happen overnight.

Large-scale, high-stakes testing increases the visibility of results but does not necessarily raise performance. If it is used, it must be combined with focused effort to improve policies and practices at the school and classroom level. Government must be willing to support intervention strategies if goals and standards are to have any meaning and success achieved.

One of the main purposes of public schools is to provide for cultural and social stability. Schools are naturally conservative institutions. They pass on the accumulated knowledge of who we are and what we have achieved. They are more oriented to the past than the present or the future. They were established to resist dramatic change. So we shouldn't be surprised that they don't change more rapidly.

In addition to the natural inertia built into the system, there are other obstacles to rapid and dramatic changes. One is the failure to appreciate that structural changes will never improve what students learn as much as good teaching can. Changing requirements, timetables, establishing new school calendars or school councils, and annual testing are unlikely to make big differences in what students learn and how well or quickly they learn it. We must be more attentive to attracting to teaching well-educated and prepared individuals and should expect them to use their professional knowledge rather than dogma or fashion as a guide to their professional practice.

That local and provincial jurisdictions control educational policy and administration has been an impediment to changes that would improve public schooling. The inter-jurisdictional battles between local school boards and provincial governments do not serve public schools well. Despite the constitutional limitations on the role of the federal government, it is time it played a larger part in public schooling. I have outlined a number of ways in which it can make a significant contribution without running afoul of the Constitution. The other day, I noted with modest optimism that the prime minister had mentioned education as a priority of the government of Canada. We will see what that might mean for public schooling by the time you read this book.

Our public schools have served us well, but they can benefit from meaningful changes. We need to be clear about the goals we want our public schools to achieve. We need to be realistic about the ability of our public schools to achieve those goals given the resources at our disposal and our willingness to devote them to our public schools. I have said that we will not decide these issues for all time. They require regular attention. We must revisit them continually and make adjustments rather than wait for a crisis.

I have argued throughout this book that our public schools are not just another institution to be managed. They are simply too important for us to take them for granted. We need provincial and federal politicians whose vision of Canada is linked to their understanding of and support for the indispensable contribution that public schooling makes to the welfare of all Canadians and to Canada as a nation.

# CONCLUSION

One day, early in the 1999 school year, I was reading the *Globe and Mail*. Normally I don't pay much attention to the advertisements, but one of them caught my eye. It was advertising the *Globe*'s series of reports celebrating Canadian developments during the twentieth century and looking ahead to the next hundred years.

This particular announcement proclaimed "A CENTURY OF CANADIAN EDUCATION." It read:

> Since the early days, the Canadian education system has grown and evolved into one of the best in the world, an achievement that was not without growing pains. The school system continues to evolve, trying to keep ahead of changing demand, technology, student demographics, continuing education, and much more. The future is bright for Canadian children, thanks in no small part to the firm foundation they receive in Canadian schools.

I agree. Although newspapers rarely mention it, the accomplishments of public schooling are rather remarkable. In approximately 130 years, we have developed a system of universal public schooling in Canada that ensures nearly universal literacy and preparation for the responsibilities of adult citizenship.

Few institutions can match the accomplishments of the Canadian public school. High levels of literacy and a demand for post-secondary education that outstrips the supply are just two of its achievements. To a great extent Canada's success at integrating people with differing backgrounds, interests, and capacities into the social and cultural fabric of the nation is testimony to the success of its public schools. The values that bind Canadians to one another and distinguish them in subtle but important ways from the citizens of other countries were acquired primarily in public schools.

Growing inequalities threaten Canada's social cohesion, however, and erode the institutional supports upon which Canadians have depended in the post–Second World War period. Much of the pressure to introduce market mechanisms in education and to diminish government's role in education, health, and social services comes from the most advantaged Canadians. Their affluence shields them from the need for social services. They are able to buy their way to the head of health-care queues and purchase educational services for their children from private providers. They do not want to see their tax dollars go to support the public services upon which most of us depend.

An increasing number of advantaged parents are removing their children from the public system. Some seek to shield their children from contact with peers who must contend with learning disabilities, poverty, and the need to learn English or French by taking refuge in specialized, boutique public school programs. Those students left behind in mainstream public schools are deprived of the positive peer influence of students who do not struggle to overcome adverse circumstances.

The segregation of advantaged students from their less-advantaged peers intensifies differences and diminishes the social sensitivity upon which a compassionate and democratic nation depends. When the segregation of differences along economic lines coincides with religious or cultural differences, or differences in skin colour, such segregation has the potential to create divisions that will tear apart Canada's social fabric.

I have argued that under the best conditions, Canada is a fragile nation. It lacks strongly evocative unifying symbols and is beset by regional differences that are often easily exploited by provincial politicians for their own short-term advantage. This is made easier because of the timidity of our national leaders. Inequalities in income and education add to Canada's fragility, threatening its social cohesiveness.

Public schooling reduces educational and income inequalities, though it cannot completely eliminate them without complementary social policies. What is equally important is that public schooling is the principal vehicle for the acquisition of the values that distinguish Canada from other nations and Canadians as socially responsible, democratically inclined citizens. It does this because – as my good friend Kit Krieger says – "public schools are society's last meeting place." What he means is that there is no other place in Canadian society where people from diverse backgrounds regularly come together for significant periods of time during which they must learn to work together, respecting the differences among them. That is why I say, if we care about Canada, we must care about our public schools.

Our public schools cannot continue their successful trajectory if they are starved for resources, overburdened by demands too numerous to be achieved in the time allotted, pulled in different directions because of competing expectations, destabilized by changes arising from fads, fashion, and ideologies, and staffed by people who are routinely ridiculed, only modestly paid, and work under adverse conditions. Unfortunately, these are becoming the dominant trends in Canadian public schooling.

Public schools require support from complementary social policies designed to support families and communities. Such policies include decent minimum wages, generous parenting policies, universal daycare and early-childhood education, fair employment standards, and health care. People's lives are not divided up into departments like governments or universities. Although public schools are the obvious places to integrate the delivery of many services, they should not be responsible for addressing issues beyond their capacity.

We must allow public school teachers to put their publicly funded education to its intended use. In other words, we must let them teach. We must recruit the most intellectually capable and compassionate people to public school teaching, pay them well, and create the conditions most likely to favour their successful achievement of the goals we set for public education. Teachers need more time to plan for instruction and to work collaboratively in support of the enduring tasks of improving student learning and reducing the inequalities among students in terms of the outcomes of schooling.

Teaching is complex work. It is more intellectually challenging and emotionally demanding than most people appreciate. Over the past twenty years, teaching has become more difficult as a consequence of the integration of students with special needs, the provision of English- and French-language programs for immigrant students or the children of immigrants, the proliferation of specialized programs, and increasing pressure to ensure that students perform well on provincial, national, and international assessments. Schools cannot continue indefinitely to perform as remarkably well as they have without changing the conditions under which teachers teach and students learn.

Ensuring appropriate conditions for successful teaching and learning will require additional resources. If applied thoughtfully, the resources will more than return their initial investment in terms of improved student success, less need for costly remediation, fewer school dropouts, and more and better-educated graduates. If the society is able to provide meaningful work and appropriate opportunities for lifelong education, there will be fewer demands on social service, criminal justice, and health systems. By diminishing gender, ethno-cultural, and socio-economic inequalities and by placing greater emphasis on shared values, public schooling will enhance its already significant contribution to social cohesion.

My point throughout this book has been that our choices matter. I think most Canadians want this country to be a socially cohesive society. They want people to have a sense of who they are as Canadians based upon shared values. They want a society where the similarities among us outweigh the differences, but one in which the differences are respected.

My argument has been that public schooling is directly connected to the maintenance of a socially cohesive society and the quality of Canadian life. A recent editorial in the *Globe and Mail* put it well: "Public schools are the place where children from diverse backgrounds learn to live together as Canadians." The writer's description of a Toronto schoolyard might just as well have been a description of a schoolyard in Montreal or Vancouver. "Walk into any schoolyard . . . and you will encounter children from scores of different national, religious and ethnic backgrounds: Vietnamese and Jamaican, Hindu and Muslim, Slav and Tamil, all mingling together as if it were the most natural thing in the world." In public schools children learn to respect one another "by playing and learning side by side."

The lesson for the *Globe and Mail* writer was clear: "A society that accepts as many immigrants as ours – and Canada takes more immigrants per capita than any other country – has to have a way to weave the newcomers into the broad fabric of society. That fabric may have many threads and many colours, but it must hold together. That is just one reason why a province such as Ontario should be shoring up its public schools."

I am worried about the crisis I see coming to our local public schools and so to Canadian society. Our public schools are changing and being changed in profound ways with shifts in the wider society that alter the meaning and conduct of schooling. The problem is we are not discussing and debating the changes, and, in many instances, do not even recognize that they have occurred. In doing so, we may be guilty of allowing our public schools to change in ways we will later regret.

If we look carefully, we will see some disturbing trends. We will see a tendency to redefine schooling from a public responsibility to a private responsibility – from a public good to a private privilege. A closer look will also reveal a system stressed by competing expectations and demands that cannot be easily fulfilled. If we spend some time in our public schools, we will see an experience for enriching and developing our society turned into a commodity to be consumed.

I do not think we want learners turned into consumers. Nor do we want activity for its own sake without regard to the purpose that the activity serves. I think most Canadians want their sons and daughters to be challenged by their studies and make meaningful connections between their studies and the lives they are living and will live.

Canada will need to experience a dramatic change in its orientation toward its public schools to realize their full promise. Such a change will not occur in the absence of strong leadership – especially from federal and provincial politicians – and co-operation among the organizations and interests most centrally involved in public schooling, including parents, teachers, administrators, and school trustees. Chief among the conditions that will need to prevail is the ability to see beyond the horizon of individual and organizational self-interest to the common good upon which Canada's future depends. If we continue failing our kids, in the long run we will fail Canada.

# INDEX